Winning at Risk

WILEY FINANCE SERIES

Founded in 1807, John Wiley & Sons is the oldest independent publishing company in the United States. With offices in North America, Europe, Australia, and Asia, Wiley is globally committed to developing and marketing print and electronic products and services for our customers' professional and personal knowledge and understanding.

The Wiley Finance series contains books written specifically for finance and investment professionals as well as sophisticated individual investors and their financial advisors. Book topics range from portfolio management to e-commerce, risk management, financial engineering, valuation, and financial instrument analysis, as well as much more.

For a list of available titles, please visit our Web site at www.WileyFinance.com.

Winning at Risk

Strategies to Go Beyond Basel

ANNETTA CORTEZ

WILEY

John Wiley & Sons, Inc.

Published by John Wiley & Sons, Inc., Hoboken, New Jersey.
Published simultaneously in Canada.

For general information on our other products and services or for technical support, please contact our Customer Care Department within the United States at (800) 762-2974, outside the United States at (317) 572-3993 or fax (317) 572-4002.

Wiley also publishes its books in a variety of electronic formats. Some content that appears in print may not be available in electronic books. For more information about Wiley products, visit our web site at www.wiley.com.

Library of Congress Cataloging-in-Publication Data
Cortez, Annetta.
  Winning at risk: strategies to go beyond Basel/Annetta Cortez.
     p. cm. -- (Wiley finance series)
Includes index.
  ISBN 978-0-470-92466-2 (hardback);
  ISBN 978-1-118-07826-6 (ebk);
  ISBN 978-1-118-07827-3 (ebk);
  ISBN 978-1-118-07828-0 (ebk)
  1. Risk management. 2. Portfolio management. 3. Financial services industry. I. Title.
  HD61.C675 2011
  332.1068'1—dc22
                                                          2011002027

Printed in the United States of America

10 9 8 7 6 5 4 3 2 1

To my loving, patient, and ever supportive family.

Contents

Foreword

Every ten years or so, after another financial crisis, we relearn the importance of risk management. The recent global financial crisis made us sit up once again and take notice. Moreover, it required us to concede that we were not very well prepared.

In hindsight, it seems clear that we had relied far too much on models, simple assumptions about liquidity, and processes. But our models, our assumptions, and our processes were clearly not up to the task.

Following the crisis, we learned a great deal. We learned that we need to understand the role of governance, incentive structures, information technology, and internal controls. I would add these to this list of crucial lessons we learned from the crisis:

1. Get the right people from across the firm to the table to discuss risk and establish a common language around risk.
2. Maintain a healthy skepticism regarding models.
3. Understand the value of stress testing.
4. Develop a culture that supports the fundamentals and eyes return with an expectation of the appropriate level of risk.

One of the key lessons we have learned is that the basics of risk management have not essentially changed. While it might seem that the world has changed dramatically and that the traditional risk management approaches no longer apply, we discover through each crisis and failure that the basics still do apply. We need to be skeptical when we see outsized returns against risk. It is easy to get excited about high growth, but we need to be cautious—anything growing too fast is likely to be a weed!

Winning at Risk presents the basics of risk management in a frank, clear fashion that allows senior management and boards to understand and act on core factors that lead to success. Annetta Cortez goes beyond measurement to present a holistic framework for risk management. She explores the difficulties and benefits of a robust ERM program. She clearly points out a path for ensuring that risk management is more than a department or function but a culture, an integrated strategy for running a business—especially when the business is a financial institution. She also shows how risk management can help organizations generate real value, without falling into the traps that lead us to crisis.

This comprehensive book provides an excellent foundation for senior executives who are rebuilding their businesses and preparing for the next rounds of global competition. Reading this book will help them understand the regulatory frameworks and generate better returns over the long term. Ideally, it also will help them avoid some of the mistakes of the recent past.

Ken Phelan
May, 2011

Preface

We learn in Finance 101 that profits rise in proportion to risk. To make any reasonable money, we need to take risks. That goes for any business but is particularly true of financial institutions. Banks and other financial institutions effectively put money in the hands of others and hope it comes back with excess returns.

This is the ultimate in risk-taking. Banks are betting that the individuals and companies to whom they lend capital will earn enough money to pay back their loans. Insurers are betting that certain events won't happen. Put in those terms, the financial services industry seems hardly better than a trip to Las Vegas.

But if you're planning a trip to a casino—and are planning not to lose your shirt—you might want to prepare by finding out which games provide the best chances to win and learning how to play them. You might even buy an instructional book or DVD. You wouldn't just show up at the casino unprepared and hope for the best. Or would you?

Over the years, we have seen successive changes in regulation and sweeping improvements in risk management capabilities across most institutions in most countries. Nevertheless, we still manage to have crises and individual catastrophic events. Every time this happens, the market cries that the risk models must have been wrong.

In reality, this is rarely the case and certainly not the crux of the story. If the risk is being modeled at all properly, most models will be sufficiently predictive to warn that a real problem is brewing. Most will even be able to pinpoint the sector or instrument that will be the root cause. But no model can predict timing—if they did, all of those Ph.D. modelers would be sitting on a beach sipping rum drinks. That's where vigilance, discipline, and governance take over.

The stark reality is that financial institutions too often get lax. They believe they've made an adequate investment in risk management and that, somehow, "everything will be fine." What happens next? Governance relaxes, investment in risk management declines, and overall institutional interest in the topic dries up.

The irony of the regulatory push is exactly this: It forces many institutions to make large initial investments then lulls them into a false sense of security. What's worse, many recent regulations, such as Basel II, were devised as trade-offs between improved practices and lower capital levels. So what happens when the institutional rigor over those practices wanes?

If you're reading this book, chances are that you're concerned enough to care. Maybe you've had a run-in with the local regulator, maybe your team is planning for the next big implementation, or maybe you're one of the lucky ones who think everything is under control because your risk managers have convinced you that everything is OK.

Or maybe you have some of those same Ph.D. modelers who can boast that they predicted the last crash or big event (unlikely, or they wouldn't still need to be working.) If you're in this latter camp, then you have all the more reason to be truly scared.

In any event, this book will help to sift through the noise and cut to the chase. You will find out what's important, what's not, and learn how to deal with the key risk management issues facing financial institutions in a globalized economy.

A key thing to remember when reading this book is that risk management is the offspring of two parents: basic management principles and statistical science. None of the core concepts of risk management are complex.

That being said, many people will try to convince you that you need a Ph.D. to understand risk management. That is simply not true. Yes, there are advanced risk management applications requiring sophisticated quantitative skills. But understanding the basics of risk management requires no more than knowledge of multiplication and division. Anyone with a high school education will do just fine with this book. Don't let the math scare you off. I wrote this book because I want to demystify risk management, and I promise not to intentionally confuse you with a lot of arcane or irrelevant details.

Most of the concepts discussed in this book can even be applied as provided. Some types of risk models, particularly those used to determine exact pricing formulas and capital measurement, will require levels of rigor and sophistication beyond the scope of this book. In general, however, the broad approaches outlined here will improve your overall understanding of risk and should help you make better business decisions.

Not infrequently, too much complexity can be a bad thing. Broadly speaking, the 80/20 rule applies to risk management in the same way it applies to practically everything else in business. It's important to remember this fundamental fact of life, especially as organizations grow more complex. There will be times when you will need to pare back some of the complexity and resort to simpler frameworks or analyses to achieve sufficient transparency. That's OK. Most of the time, the gain in trust and clarity outweighs the loss of accuracy.

Here's a story from my own experience that illustrates my point:

I was working with a client firm on pricing strategy, and I needed a high-level estimate of economic capital for each product segment. The firm had not yet developed measures of its own, so I used a simple Excel-based model to generate a quick approximation. The whole exercise took slightly more than a week; I spent most of the time gathering data. What I did not know, however, was that the firm's finance team was in the process of implementing their own capability—due to be implemented that very week. They had already invested a significant amount of time and money building a more robust model. Their model generated roughly the same results as mine. The situation was embarrassing, to say the least.

I'm not advocating the use of "quick and dirty" models; the model I built would never have been suitable for day-to-day use, but the moral of this story is that you don't always have to spend huge sums of money building fancy and complex risk models when a simpler version may suffice. The 80/20 rule does apply and something closer to that point may be the best place to start. The reason you build models is to identify risks so they can be managed before bad things start happening.

Putting it bluntly, it's more important to have a simple working model that will set off alarms than it is to build a highly complex prototype that just sits there. In many cases, identifying a risk is more important than measuring it. If you know the risk is out there, you can take steps to manage it. If you need to measure it down to the hundredth decimal place, you can do that later.

Generally speaking, companies are brought down by the risks they do not see. A truly robust risk management strategy focuses as much on monitoring as on measuring.

Acknowledgments

I'd like to thank all of the people who helped me pull this book together: Ed, for bringing the gang together; Mike, for injecting humor, wit, and his great experience and skill; Tim Burgard; Stacey Rivera; Natasha Andrews-Noel; and all the folks at Wiley who kindly and patiently pulled this project through to the end.

Introduction

SEARCHING FOR A SOLUTION

Holistic. Comprehensive. Multi-disciplinary. Science-based.

If these terms aren't part of your risk and capital management strategy, you and your organization might be heading for trouble.

Navigating the waters of risk and capital management in today's environment can be intensely challenging. If you are a senior manager or executive with risk management responsibilities, but you have not been formally trained as a risk management professional, beware. Risk management doesn't lend itself to "do-it-yourself" approaches. You can't pick up the essentials by watching an instructional video on the ride from the airport to your next meeting. You can't delegate it to your assistant. You really need to understand it.

More and more we are seeing regulators, legislators, and the press turning to senior executives and board members and expecting surprising levels of depth and articulation regarding risk management in general and the details of how it plays out in their own firms. What's worse is that this level of depth is expected at a time when regulations are more complex than ever, and growing in both size and complexity every day, while as global markets display the highest level of sustained volatility ever experienced in history, while as shareholders are crying for relief and a source of earnings growth, and as the press is putting intense scrutiny on the response to every action and continues to heat up the fervor around all that is wrong.

Sadly, amidst all of this, it is surprisingly difficult to find a single reliable source of information that provides the answers and advice you need, when you need them. Internal risk management teams are notoriously siloed and specialized. Many risk management professionals have strong skills and capabilities, but relatively few have the perspective and business experience required to see the "big picture" as it plays out across the incredibly complex landscape of risk management. Consider the variables: regulation, internal measurement, policy, organization, business strategy, and multiple risk classes. Only a handful of risk managers have the abilities and experience necessary to discern the materiality and relative weights of these issues. What is an executive to do?

I wrote this book to help you, the busy executive, sort through the complexities and eliminate some of the noise. I've tried to bring a practical perspective to understanding what is important, where to place focus, and how to use the best of risk and capital capabilities to the institution's advantage.

As a risk and capital management expert, I've seen what makes companies succeed and what makes them fail. I've served as an executive within large corporations and worked as a consultant. I've helped the best and the worst, picked up after crashed economies and collapsed institutions, and have also made a lot of money for my clients. I have literally worked literally all over the world with financial institutions, central banks, and regulators on every continent except Antarctica—at the board level and shoulder to shoulder with analysts and across every major risk class. I know what goes on, where the skeletons are hidden, and where the opportunities lie. The purpose of this book is sharing my knowledge with you, so you can avoid some of the mistakes that have been made in the past.

When it comes to understanding what makes winners and losers, the answers are remarkably simple. Most business failures are less about what institutions did and more about what they didn't do—what they didn't measure, what they didn't monitor, and what they didn't resolve . . . until it was too late.

Winning strategies are about taking the resources and information at hand and leveraging them into smarter, better, faster business decisions that keep you ahead of the competition.

Whether you want to invest in building leveraged capabilities or you are just worried about managing your downside, it's about proactive management and continuous improvement. Your risk and capital management strategy is an essential component of your overall business strategy. It's never a good idea to ignore risk. In today's turbulent global economy, ignoring or downplaying the impact of risk is a recipe for disaster.

WHY MANAGE RISK?

Considering all the pressures, demands, and challenges of the global economy, is it reasonable to expect companies to invest additional resources in risk management strategies? Does it make sense to do more than the absolute minimum? Is risk management a commodity? Can it be outsourced? Why does risk need to be actively managed? Is managing risk as pointless as trying to manage the weather?

Many institutions struggle with these questions, in one form or another. There is little doubt that many organizations question the value of investing in risk management processes beyond the minimum regulatory requirements.

Although the regulatory burden is certainly increasing, the mandates still fall short of those we would expect to find within a well-run and well-optimized institution. In other words, the official minimums are inadequate, and merely meeting them will not safeguard your organization against a catastrophe. The bar is simply too low to be genuinely meaningful.

Take a moment to digest this thought:

Imagine you own a building, and you've done everything to meet the city's fire codes. And now you're hearing that meeting the code isn't enough and that if a fire breaks out in your building, it will burn to the ground.

Now imagine you are an owner or stakeholder of a financial institution. Doing the minimum won't save you from a disaster; in fact, it might even hasten your ruin because you will be making decisions with a false sense of security. You will believe that everything will be OK because you've met the minimum standards. You might even see those minimum standards as an impenetrable wall standing between you and misfortune. Instead you will discover they are just what they are—minimums.

Would you buy a car equipped with minimally efficient brakes or minimally effective airbags? Would you buy a bicycle helmet for your child that was minimally protective? Of course not!

And there are plenty of good reasons beyond plain common sense to set your standards higher than the regulatory minimums. Good risk management can provide a competitive advantage. It can improve your firm's ability to manage and reduce earnings volatility, support successful growth strategies, and help the firm manage and increase its overall shareholder value. For many institutions, particularly in today's ultra-competitive markets, *the ability to do a better job managing risk than your competitors* can yield numerous strategic benefits.

Think about how many companies and institutions have collapsed in just the past five years. A brief list of reasons for these failures would probably include:

- Strategic inability to compete
- Merger or takeover
- Fraud
- Loss of a key supplier
- Loss of a key customer
- Force majeure

But the simple truth is that most companies are brought to ruin by financial failure, the inability to manage cash flow. There can be any number of underlying and interrelated causes, but the main reason companies go belly up is that they run out of cash.

As an experienced risk management consultant, I perceive a strong connection between financial failure and lack of appropriate risk management processes. When I look at companies that have failed, here's what I tend to see:

- Over-concentration in a risky asset or over-reliance on a risky activity
- Inability or unwillingness to identify and parameterize certain key risks
- Unwillingness or inability to respond to warning signals

When you look at your firm's risk management strategy, what do *you* see?

EXAMPLE

Banker's Trust was famous for inventing new ways of thinking about risk management. The bank was also known for its risk management blunders. One such blunder involved Russian bonds. It was one of the last straws that brought down the bank.

After the bank's collapse, I had the opportunity to meet its chief market risk executive (he was looking for a job). When I asked what happened, he told me that the models didn't fail. The bank knew it was overexposed in Russian bonds but was making so much money on them that senior management couldn't resist holding the position. As time went on, the concentration of risk grew and he continued to escalate the issue to more and more senior levels. They finally told him to stop or they would usher him to the door. In the aftermath, many blamed the collapse on inadequate risk models. But it wasn't that, nor was it a lack of reporting. It was the bank's organizational culture and its unwillingness to respond to real warning signals.

I ask my clients to look at risk management from two simple perspectives: downside and upside. No matter which perspective you look from, you can see benefits.

For example, when you look at managing downside risks, the benefits include:

- **Fighting fewer fires (figuratively).** Consider how frequently we stay late at work, work over the weekend, and divert valuable resources and management attention to address the latest problem. These little emergencies can not only create strain and fatigue on the organization but also can put at risk the company's reputation with customers, regulators, and shareholders.
- **Reducing management surprises.** How often do we think things are ticking along just fine, and then discover a major loss, a missed performance target, a market crash, or other serious problem? No matter the cause, it can derail an otherwise well-planned board meeting.
- **Reducing business interruptions.** Many other types of risks can creep up in day-to-day operations. They need not constitute a "fire" or a surprise worthy of senior-executive or board-level attention, but they do create interruptions. A good acid test is to think about what systems or processes concern you the most—what is in the most need of an upgrade. Chances are that these are causing smaller, annoying disruptions from the day-to-day flow and may be frustrating your customers or other external stakeholders as well. They may end up becoming one of those "fires" to put out.
- **Reducing budget blowouts.** Budget blowouts don't always stem from poor management of day-to-day expenses. They are often generated from the "surprises" and "fire fighting" we discussed earlier, or they may be associated with a major project—or several—that go haywire. In any case, they disrupt management time, attention, and efficiencies—and they contribute to earnings volatility.
- **Reducing earnings volatility.** If earnings volatility is viewed as risk, then the ability to forecast, manage, and potentially reduce it, is a key outcome. Earnings volatility is also uniquely tied to market returns. So general return performance on par or ahead of expectations may not be adequate if volatility has been sufficiently marring or if underlying businesses are generating surprises.
- **Protecting assets.** Some things about risk are basic. In financial services, we often discuss the protection of financial assets. This is critical, but it's important not to forget another big piece of risk management that is fairly straightforward: It's also about protecting equipment, facilities, and personnel.
- **Reducing litigation.** Litigation from any number of sources likely would be diminished. With improved relations with consumers, counterparties, shareholders, and the like—all stemming from a more

discrete and informed management of comprehensive risks—the firm would be less likely to take on expensive and unplanned litigation.

- **Reducing consequences of missed financial obligations.** Since much of financial risk management focuses on ensuring that the institution meets its financial obligations, the improvement in this ability yields a direct effect. More specifically, consider that a downgrade in credit rating or depressed share price may have longer term implications that would be costly, or in a more extreme case, impossible, to overcome.
- **Reducing insurance costs.** With fewer surprises and mishaps and with better management of transactions, processes, and equipment, there are likely to be fewer insurance claims and a better overall track record of events. All of those result in lower insurance premiums.
- **Reducing fines and compliance costs.** The ability to adequately manage risk can support management of compliance requirements, but it also tends to engender confidence in employees, regulators, and the public. The institution is less likely to attract detailed regulatory scrutiny and more likely to remediate a breach efficiently.

When you look at the upside of risk management, you will see benefits so meaningful that they can be leveraged to form core strategies that generate real business value. The upside benefits include:

- **Improved competitiveness.** Risk management can give the best institutions a competitive advantage. Those that are able to analyze new markets, introduce new products, and price more efficiently and more accurately can outperform their competitors. Also, in the world of changing regulation, it is advantageous for banks to have knowledgeable senior people to face off with regulators and influence the shape of new policies and how they are implemented locally.
- **Improved returns relative to risk.** With the capabilities we just mentioned, organizations can also ensure that returns are not only more consistent but better overall. There are fewer incidents of default, missed trades, and other miscues, plus overall improvements in strategies and tactics, such as pricing.
- **Improved efficiencies and quality.** Typically, organizations that adopt risk management capabilities also can improve processes and adopt a risk culture that supports improved outputs in all their dealings.
- **Improved communication.** Organizations that adopt a language to describe and articulate risk tend to excel at other aspects of business management. It further aids greater efficiencies, problem resolution, and strategic management.

■ **Increased employee confidence.** Companies that adopt solid risk management practices also engender employee confidence, improved retention, and greater dedication. Employee empowerment is likely to thrive as a result of clear direction and strong risk/return philosophy with clearly articulated limits and goals.

■ **More efficient issues resolution.** With methodologies supporting how we think about, talk about, measure, and analyze risks when issues do arise, we can get to the underlying cause and develop mitigation much more efficiently than in their absence.

In my experience, smart companies view risk management as a "two-for-the price-of-one" deal: It protects you from harm and it improves your ability to make money—the ultimate goal of any business.

WHY IS RISK MANAGEMENT DIFFICULT TO IMPLEMENT?

Implementing a robust risk management strategy, or even making substantive improvements in existing risk management processes, is a long journey. There are no short cuts, no magic bullets. Even when an organization perceives the value of risk management and is willing to invest in a strategy, it can take years—and even a few negative events—before the organization achieves a high level of confidence in its risk management capabilities. So it's fair to ask: "Why is it so difficult to implement a practical risk management strategy?"

The simple answer is that it's difficult to implement *any* new strategy in a corporate environment. The larger the corporation, the more difficult it is to implement company-wide transformation. But risk management takes on special challenges; the disasters prevented are often hard to quantify or even identify and the ability to realize upside potential can often become a multiyear strategy. So, investment in risk management can sometimes feel like a matter of faith.

Like many things, most of the specific actions and capabilities associated with adoption of a solid risk management strategy are fairly straightforward. Developing an integrated, enterprise-wide strategy, as opposed to implementing a series of small-scale models at the departmental level, however, is a formidable task. It will likely require the involvement and cooperation of hundreds—possibly thousands or even millions—of individual persons in various locations across the enterprise and its extended ecosystem of suppliers, business partners, stakeholders, and customers.

And where people are concerned, there are always complications of culture, biases, and personal preferences.

Some of the greatest difficulties implementing risk management plans involve the people factor. Here's a brief list of typical challenges:

- **Resistance to change.** "Why change if things are going well?" Many organizations fall into the trap of thinking they are impervious to serious disaster, particularly if they have survived a major downturn. They may be convinced that everything they need already is in place. This mantra alone can be one of the most widely used excuses. It even can fool some regulators, particularly when they have more important issues to address. It's easy for an organization to rest on its laurels. But it's important to continually assess organizational approaches, culture, and capabilities. It's easy for approaches that worked today to become aged.

  Believe it or not, many organizations just get "lucky" when it comes to survival. More than a few were unable to follow their peers into disaster—not because of smart management or prescience but because they were unable to execute efficiently. Not exactly the most sound basis for risk management leadership.

  One sadly amusing anecdote on this involves a client that I worked with after the peso crisis. It was a fairly large bank that had significant Mexican holdings and, to its credit, was taking on a sweeping implementation of risk management capabilities. However, its market risk area was a challenge. The bank was convinced it was already quite good, the reason being that it had far fewer losses than its local peers. Unfortunately, the reason behind this was not good management, monitoring, or smart hedging strategies. It was because its dealing room had been too inept to get the deals off rapidly enough while the market was moving at breakneck pace. When the crash happened, it happened fast and they were simply out of the market. Unfortunately, the myth perpetuates that they were "smart" and truly sound risk management practices were challenging to implement going forward.

- **Not invented here.** This issue is sometimes one of the hardest to overcome, particularly when risk capabilities already exist in house. It is important to consistently look for methods of improvement and routinely review capabilities, coverage of risks, measurement approaches, and other techniques. Consider who your thought leaders are and ensure they have sufficient budget and organizational support to progress; conversely, ensure they are not blocking new innovation. Size and complexity need to be reevaluated—what worked before may no longer be appropriate. But it's also true that greater sophistication is not always warranted, particularly for smaller or simpler institutions.

- **Transparency.** Risk management enhances transparency and can often expose weaknesses and under performers. Needless to say, this can threaten sometimes powerful stakeholders. This issue is one of the key reasons why support from the board and senior management is critical to the process.
- **Do we *have* to do it?** This is the "we're too busy" phenomenon. Often this excuse can be much of a chicken-or-egg problem. Businesses complain that they don't have time or resources to support risk management improvements. This, however, often is due to many issues bogging down the organization—issues that may be reduced through sound risk management. Implementing risk management is an ongoing commitment, not a one-time or occasional activity.
- **Finding and manipulating the right data.** This is a common problem voiced in risk management circles and sounds convincing. It may be true that the right amount and quality of information are not currently available or in a form that is readily manipulated to produce ideal models and tools—or even adequate models and tools. However, if we don't embark on the journey, we will never develop the right data. It's always better to start with whatever is available, no matter how little or patchy, and simultaneously put in place mechanisms to collect the right data. This creates the foundation. It is equally important to create a conscious, funded plan to revisit capabilities and upgrade those tools reliant on that early foundation. This is not only important for the evolution and quality of models and tools but also critical to ensuring that organizational dissention does not set in due to the inherent inadequacies begat through incorrect data. It is a conscious step with knowledge of the downsides but enormous upsides.
- **How do we know that it's right?** Here again, this is a common argument against change. Many organizations become embroiled questioning whether they are taking the right steps or whether the specific measures are correct. There is no doubt that these can be valid questions, but they can also bog things down and even frustrate to the point of abandonment. It's important to consider a practical path forward. Often the specific way forward is less relevant to the overall outcome. It's important to choose a path that feels right for the organization. Likewise, if the numbers don't feel right, then it's likely that they aren't, particularly if they seem too low. The prudent approach may be to take a conservative route in the early days in order to ensure safety and soundness. Later on, when capabilities are more developed, the organization can sharpen its pencil and refine approaches.

■ **Achieving a balance.** It's important to find a level of implementation that supports the size and complexity of the organization as well as the sophistication of its risk culture. This is not just a regulatory dictate but a practical consideration. It's important to focus on the more material risks and issues first, and then move on to more detailed and finely tuned considerations. Many organizations over-reach in their initial stab at risk management approaches. As a result, they may become disillusioned when they come up short or may fail entirely. Conversely, under-investment can be equally debilitating, particularly if key risks or key management capabilities are left unaddressed.

■ **Senior management/executive support.** As we've seen through all of these issues, board and executive-level support is critical to set the tone, drive momentum, ensure resources are in place, and to navigate through potential challenges of competing priorities. Moreover, regulators today are closely scrutinizing the knowledge, involvement, and degree of responsibility taken by boards and senior management. Many even require documentation of their knowledge and assurance of their continued oversight.

CHAPTER 1

What is Risk?

EXECUTIVE SUMMARY

In this chapter we come face-to-face with the core concepts of risk management strategy. Once we get a handle on these fundamental ideas, we can begin looking at risk management from a high-level business perspective. Executives in the financial services industry are already familiar with these concepts, but they tend to regard them mostly as processes for managing downside risk. In this chapter, we look at risk management as an enterprise strategy for making better business decisions, minimizing losses, avoiding catastrophe, improving profitability, and growing your business in a turbulent global economy.

THE BUSINESS OF RISK

Here's a simple fact of which we often lose sight, particularly in the fray of day-to-day business: Banks and other financial institutions are in the business of risk.

Since risk plays an absolutely crucial role in a financial institution's very existence, you would expect it would know virtually everything about risk. You would expect all of the institution's executives, managers, and employees to possess a strong understanding of risk, and you would expect the institution to have specialists in every aspect of measuring and managing risk. You would also expect the institution to have developed a common language for discussing and evaluating risk with maximum clarity and transparency.

Chances are good, however, that reality would not live up to your expectations. Not because your expectations are unreasonable; in fact, they are quite reasonable.

Consider a firm that manufactures widgets. We would reasonably expect the firm to understand every aspect of the widgets it produces—it would perform measurements of quality and numerous attributes of the widgets at every step of the process. It would monitor the widgets closely in simulated and actual performance over time. We might even expect the firm to use Six Sigma or some other formal process to ensure continuous improvement of the widgets and the processes required to manufacture them.

Why are we suddenly talking about widgets? Because risk is to a financial institution what a widget is to its manufacturer. Each transaction or contract represents a risk "widget."

This basic truth is inescapable. You can't really understand finance unless you understand risk. You can't just *skip over* the risk component of finance. That would be like taking an advanced class in molecular biology without first understanding basic chemistry. It ain't gonna happen—or if it does, watch out.

And that's why risk management must be a core competency and primary capability of every financial institution.

Instead, risk management is often considered a burden, something that controls and restricts legitimate business activities without adding any real value. Risk management is seen as something that holds back the business and restrains creativity. Risk management is also viewed as a "back office" function, something that takes place in dark basement rooms or far-off cubicles. In many companies, it's considered a cost of doing business.

Some companies have moved beyond these parochial notions and have embraced risk management as a strategy for growth and profitability. They have taken their risk management capabilities and turned them into assets. Using their understanding of risk management, they create better products and services, boost efficiency, reduce costs, and improve margins. I've worked with companies whose risk management strategies have resulted in better reviews from industry analysts. The people at these companies think of risk management as a strategic platform rather than as an annoying burden placed on their shoulders by regulators.

That's why it's critical to develop a practical framework and a common language for describing, measuring, and managing risk across all of its many levels.

DEFINING RISK: LOSS, UNCERTAINTY, AND HORIZON

If you're in the risk business, there's no excuse for not spending the time necessary to understand it thoroughly. The first step in this process is defining what we really mean when we use the word "risk." Since so many finance professionals don't give risk a second thought, most of them can't define or explain the various pieces of the risk puzzle. Specific definitions of risk are frequently disregarded or misunderstood.

But these definitions and explanations are important, because risk needs to be discussed and measured in highly specific terms. Just like our hypothetical widget manufacturer, we really need to understand everything about our product, down to the smallest detail.

As we dig into the process of defining loss and its inherent behaviors, we discover that risk is a multi-faceted concept in and of itself. Its properties and manifestations drive the ways we measure, manage, and mitigate. In this book, we mainly address methods associated with financial risks, although we will discuss strategic and operational risks as well and their implications to measurement, management, and regulation.

Possibility of Loss: Expected Loss

Most lay people and many definitions describe risk as the possibility of injury, damage, or loss. Risk is often perceived as the negative downside of an action, enterprise, or financial transaction. Risk professionals usually refer to this aspect of risk as *expected loss*. That is the loss we consider most likely to realize over a defined time horizon—usually one year—and is therefore "expected." We think about expected loss as the product of the probability of loss, the exposure to loss, and the severity of loss. Here's the formula we use to calculate expected loss:

$$\text{Expected Loss} = \text{Probability of Loss} \times \text{Exposure} \times \text{Severity}$$

As you've probably noticed, the formula is fairly simple. Don't worry— we'll revisit it when we discuss risk measures later in the book. If you are particularly sharp, you might also have noticed that this equation is also used to calculate *mean loss*.

I point this out because it illustrates a problem in the risk management field: Risk management professionals love to rename even the simplest of concepts so they can employ their own special jargon. Keep this in the back of your mind, and try not to worry too much about terminology. I will be throwing lots of new terms at you, but I promise that I won't try to confuse you. The good news is that all of this is not nearly as mysterious as it may initially seem.

Uncertain Outcomes: Volatility

Although expected loss is a widely used concept and integral to the measurement of risk, risk professionals generally define risk as *volatility*. The formal definition of risk that most economists and actuaries use is *volatility of returns,* also called *earnings volatility.* Although this is a more encompassing and more accurate assessment of risk, we more often substitute *volatility of losses* as a proxy for that definition, because it is more readily modeled and managed.

As a warning to the uninitiated, you will discover that many risk professionals often use other terms, such as *value at risk,* to describe volatility—and rarely use the word volatility itself. Why they do this is a mystery that shall remain unsolved for the time being.

At any rate, we think of volatility as the true measure of risk for the simple reason that it is the "unexpected" aspect of loss that is of real concern. If we were certain that the mean or expected loss would occur each and every time, then it would be fully predictable and we would bake it into our expectations. This is why we call it "expected" loss. Conversely, volatility is more likely to morph and change. We can parameterize its likelihood, but there is always an aspect that remains "unexpected." For this reason it is often called *unexpected loss.*

So, we now have two terms that refer to each of the core concepts: expected loss (equivalent to mean loss) and unexpected loss (equivalent to volatility). The terms are often used together, making it easier to define the basis of a loss distribution. In addition, expected loss is traditionally linked to *reserves,* our buffer against loss we "expect to incur," and unexpected loss is linked to *economic capital,* our backstop in the event of more than expected losses. We will discuss these concepts later on as well.

MORE WAYS TO THINK ABOUT RISK

We often characterize risk by the way it materializes within a portfolio or by its sources and behaviors within an organization. In particular, we like to consider how these risks behave during times of stress. This line of thinking leads us to different ways of naming types of risk, their individual measurement, and management techniques. Associated with this are several conventions to get familiar with:

- **Idiosyncratic risk.** A risk that is unique. It often also is referred to as *specific risk.* Typically we think of it as specific to a transaction. It may also be the unique risk associated with a project or operation. Idiosyncratic risk is generally at least partially diversifiable.
- **Systemic risk.** Risk that is not unique. It is associated with market movements and may be present regardless of the specific nature of the transaction, project, or operation. It is generally not diversifiable and for this reason it is often called residual or *undiversifiable risk.*

- **Concentration.** Risk associated with developing too many risks of similar profile such that the risk becomes large or significant. The larger the concentration, the more difficult or expensive it is to diversify and thus reduce the risk.
- **Contagion.** Risks that are linked to each other and therefore may trigger an effect in which one risk can set off another—much like a domino or snowball effect.
- **Extreme or "long tail" events.** Risks that are rare or infrequent but can become significant during times of stress. These are referred to as "long tail" events because they exist at the tail end of the loss distribution. Their probability is very low.

TAXONOMY OF RISKS

In addition to the ways of describing risk behaviors, we also name the types of risks by way of their sources. This approach is particularly common in financial services and is important to understand, as risk management measures and approaches and regulation are developed on this basis.

In general, the conventions for naming risks are constructed in most organizations such that they are *mutually exclusive and collectively exhaustive* (MECE). We like to ensure that we can count up each of the risks by class and sub-class to reach a consolidated whole. That is, we account for all of the risks in the organization through this method. Unfortunately, even with more and more advances in risk metrics as well as discrete regulation—which has crystallized certain conventions—there still are some classes of risk that may vary among companies (and among regulators from various countries) by definition, emphasis, and management and measurement techniques. We will mention these as they come up throughout this book and in our definitions of risk classes outlined below.

Risks tend to fall into three very broad categories:

1. Financial risk
2. Operational risk
3. Strategic/business risk

In financial services, we typically further break down financial risks into the major categories of *credit risk, market risk,* and *insurance risk.*

Financial Risk

In financial services firms, these risks tend to be our key focus. They are the risks most in mind and with which we should have the greatest familiarity.

These risks will be the most discussed in this book. They break down into several subcategories:

- **Credit risk.** The potential for economic loss due to the failure of a borrower or counterparty to fulfill its contractual obligations in a timely manner. This usually happens because of an inability or unwillingness to pay. Examples of credit risk may be found in most areas of banking, including settlement risk in the trading operation as well as the more obvious risks associated with lending obligations.
- **Market risk.** The exposure to potential loss resulting from changes in market prices or rates. Market risk further breaks down into traded market risk and non-traded market risk.

  Traded market risk is most notably associated with those risks that affect the trading desks: foreign exchange (FX), commodities, equities, fixed income, and others. Traded market risk generally has shorter term effects associated with daily and weekly movements of the markets.

  Non-traded market risk is associated with the risk evident in the structure of the business. It traditionally breaks down into interest rate risk and liquidity risk. These are often referred to as "balance sheet risks" because they are structurally inherent in the nature of the balance sheet and the way that a financial institution conducts business against its balance sheet through its funding and leveraging approaches. They are often referred to as "mis-match risks" or "asset/liability risks" as they are associated with the ways in which assets and liabilities match—or do not match.

  Interest rate risk also breaks down further and is frequently discussed in terms of *repricing risk, basis risk, yield curve risk,* and *optionality risk*. Each of these describes separate aspects of how interest rates on the liability side of the balance sheet can fall out of line with interest rates on the asset side of the balance sheet:
- **Repricing risk.** The risk associated with liabilities and assets having different maturity characteristics and, thus, repricing at different times at different rates.
- **Basis risk.** The possibility that a hedge with two different rate bases will have the rates move out of perfect sync with each other, thus creating a loss.
- **Yield curve risk.** When the yield curve changes from expectations, resulting in a market rate change on fixed income instruments.
- **Optionality risk.** Risks due to embedded options within the underlying liability or assets within the banking book that can dynamically change the structure of the book. These are typically associated with prepayment on loans, withdrawal of deposits draw down against lines or limits, or indeterminate maturity, such as found in credit cards.

Other key financial risks include *insurance risk*, associated with the possibility of unexpected claims on insurance policies or changes in insurance rates, renewals, or policy lapses. And there are a number of subcategories associated with this risk class, such as *pension risk*, which is the possibility that the institution will not be able to support its pension obligations when they are due.

Operational Risk

Operational risk is by far the most ubiquitous risk as it affects literally every aspect of our operations and every type of business. It includes both internal operational risks and those caused by external events, such as natural disasters and security breaches. It is formally defined as the risk of loss resulting from inadequate or failed internal processes, people, and systems or from external events. This includes fraud and security issues, plus outside occurrences such as natural disaster, political upheaval, and other causes of business disruption such as widespread power outages.

Because of its far-reaching nature, definitions of operational risk may vary, and a number of subcategories may be included. The Basel Committee includes legal risk but excludes strategic and reputational risk. Nevertheless, some institutions do include these or may address these as separate risk categories which are often referred to as "other risks" in the parlance of regulatory risk management.

Operational risk is frequently subcategorized into its sources in order to support identification, measurement, and management. These are as follows:

- **People/organizational risks.** Risk that results from human error, employment practices, staffing inadequacy, loss of key personnel (key man risk), employee errors, wrongful acts, and workplace safety. These typically also include internal and external fraud, although the Basel Committee breaks these out separately.
- **Business process management risk.** Risk resulting from disruptions of processes that cause losses. It includes the potential of loss due to service delivery (customer service, product and service delivery, poor response to customer complaints, and others); processes and controls (failed transaction processing, vendor and supplier miscommunication, process control failures, inadequate or failed internal documentation); and client, product, and business practices (documentation, disclosure advisory, product flaws or inadequate specifications, improper business or market practices). The Basel committee further separates these into two categories: (1) service delivery and (2) processes and controls.

- **Systems and equipment risk.** Risk resulting from business disruption and cost due to system failures or lengthy maintenance or replacement of equipment.
- **Legal and compliance risk.** Risk associated with compliance with legal requirements such as legislation, regulations, standards, codes of practice, and contractual terms. This also extends to compliance with contracts, customer requirements, ethical standards, the social environment, and internal management.
- **Security risk.** Risks to premises, assets, people, and information.
- **Project risk.** Risk of loss associated with failed delivery of projects, including overrun, failed or inadequate outcomes, and other causes. This may fall under business-process management risks we noted previously, but it is frequently separated out as it can account for enormous expenditures.
- **External event risks.** Risk associated with damage to physical assets from natural disasters or other events.

Because of its amorphous nature, operational risk can be one of the more difficult risk categories to address through measurement. We will discuss this later, but for now, consider the difficulty in attempting to predict the financial value of seemingly one-time events that may reach into the organization and create contagion—both operational and that which cuts across other risk categories. This is particularly complicated by the individuality of each institution's infrastructure and business mix. Therefore, no two operational-risk events are likely to play out precisely the same way.

Strategic/Business Risks

Strategic risk and business risk are often synonymous and involve concepts that are less well-defined than other risks. In this book, we'll consider them a class of risks that are synonymous.

These risks are broadly associated with changes in the business environment and how the company addresses or responds to those changes. They also encompass risks associated with how the company makes and implements strategic decisions.

Strategic/business risk is often defined as the current or prospective risk to earnings and capital arising from changes in the business environment and from adverse business decisions, improper implementation of decisions or lack of responsiveness to changes in the business environment.

It tends to include *commercial risk, stakeholder-management risk, technological/obsolescence risk,* and *reputation risk.*

It is often the hardest of the risk classes to define and to measure. Thus, we frequently see this risk or some of its subclasses reclassified with operational risk. On the whole, measurement and management techniques are still relatively crude, but they are worth discussing as an important component of the overall framework.

Overall, each of the deferent risk types presents different challenges in the approach and ability to measure and manage risk. Although the broad, underlying concepts are the same, notable differences define the issues, requirements, personnel, investment, and virtually all other aspects. Because of these differences, it is important that senior management and boards have among them at least a general, functional understanding of the differences and approaches.

RISK AND REWARD: MODERN PORTFOLIO THEORY

Part and parcel with risk is return, or reward. After all, the chance to make returns is why we take risks. The interplay of risk and return are fundamental to the way we think about risk, measure it, manage it, and ultimately utilize our knowledge of it to optimize our capabilities. We will frequently come back to the concepts around risk and return throughout this book as the foundation for our thinking.

Overview: Markowitz and MPT

Our thinking about the trade-offs between risk and return was crystallized with Markowitz and his Modern Portfolio Theory (MPT). MPT established the definition of risk as volatility, which we mentioned earlier. It further introduced the concept of diversification and its ability to reduce risk while yielding the same return.

Overall, MPT asserted that assets that have a higher volatility of return are riskier, so they must yield a higher overall average return to compensate for their higher risk.

MPT also asserted that all assets are not perfectly, positively correlated, and that we can reduce a portfolio's overall risk and maintain the same return by blending assets that are not positively correlated. The ideas behind *systemic risk* and *idiosyncratic risk* were introduced through these theories. In a perfectly diversified portfolio, all idiosyncratic risk would be diversified away and the only remaining risk would be systemic risk.

In a blended portfolio, we also can observe an *efficient frontier*. This is the line that describes the most efficient or best returning mix of portfolio assets relative to risk. It also demonstrates the overall efficiency of the

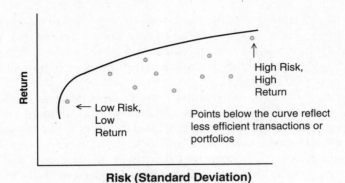

FIGURE 1.1   Efficient Frontier

portfolio relative to the risk-free rate, usually a U.S. Treasury or other high quality, AAA asset (see Figure 1.1).

Although today we realize not all of Markowitz's concepts hold perfectly true to reality, the broad ideas are supported, and they form the foundation for much of our thinking today about risk measurement, risk management, and return relative to risk. Even though portfolio theory was originally constructed for market portfolios, the concepts hold well for other types of assets and for the broad approaches to analyzing risk.

How Theory Has Evolved into Practice

Today, we can apply risk/reward concepts to every aspect of financial-services management. Linked to Markowitz's concepts of market returns, we find that an institution's underlying assets and the methods by which it manages risk are closely linked to the overall riskiness of its shares. Particularly in financial services, this process can be direct and relatively transparent.

This is a crucial point: Your ability to measure and manage risk is directly related to your ability to manage shareholder returns. In other words, the better you are at managing risk, the better you will be at managing returns.

Internal performance measures based in risk/return concepts provide a means to evaluate overall group performance, business-line performance, and asset, transaction, and customer-level performance. A well-linked framework for the measurement of risk-adjusted performance of every level of the institution ultimately will give senior management a clear means to steer the ship. It will help them provide direction for risk/return profile, asset and business line size and growth, plus supply the tools to communicate and manage expectations internally and externally. Linking this to compensation can ensure organizational attentiveness and the ultimate institutionalization of risk concepts and culture. These concepts also extend to pricing which can be constructed to support minimum rates that yield the required performance for the relative risk of each transaction. So, a fully integrated risk-adjusted performance framework includes all of these elements—from specific transactions all the way up to risk-adjusted returns at the group level. We will discuss the approaches and mechanisms for this in Chapter 7.

CHAPTER 2

Risk Management Principles

EXECUTIVE SUMMARY

In this chapter, we examine the key principles of risk management. Think of this chapter as a handy cookbook with lots of basic recipes and good advice for surviving in a volatile world. We look at which processes are critical for achieving long-term success, and we discuss the true relationship between risk and business strategy. We look beneath the surface to get a more nuanced "feel" for risk and to appreciate what risk really means to your business. If you only read one chapter in this book, this is the one to read.

WORDS TO LIVE BY

Companies that consistently demonstrate both the ability to survive *and* to excel strategically and economically over the long run share common characteristics. Although these characteristics tend to play out in different ways in different organizations, the "signs of success" are usually clear and fairly consistent. They typically include supporting innovation, investing in new technologies, anticipating and responding effectively to changing markets, adopting fact-based decision-making processes, and embracing workforce diversity. Over time, these characteristics grow into a philosophy or corporate culture that guides the organization, overtly and subtly.

I believe that the understanding, adoption, and enforcement of core risk management principles have joined the ranks of these critical indicators of success. Equally important is the continuing emergence of new global regulations that explicitly spell out the obligations of boards and senior management as key components in risk management frameworks. Key factors for success and those that have become increasingly adopted into new regulatory approaches to risk management include:

- Establishing risk measurement and management capabilities that are appropriate for the size and complexity of the institution
- Establishing an explicit and well understood risk profile
- Setting capital targets consistent with the overall risk profile
- Establishing consistent risk-based, capital-adequacy frameworks
- Ensuring transparency of activities that contribute to corporate risk
- Ensuring that systems and capabilities are put in place that identify, measure, mitigate, and monitor all types of risks

Overall, this means boards and senior management must take a deeper interest in risk management and the workings of risk-management teams like never before. They need to develop a working knowledge of the concepts and approaches—both generally and how they are being applied to the specific situation of their institutions.

The ability to deliver on these broad themes is supported by the following principles; think of them as "words for Boards to live by":

- Approve systems and processes, including approval of all material aspects of the rating and estimation processes.
- Develop a good understanding of the design and operation of rating systems and other risk-measurement models.
- Ensure the existence of independent risk units that are responsible for the design/selection, implementation, validation, and performance of the risk models. These units must be independent from the personnel and management functions responsible for originating exposures.
- Ensure the role of internal and external audit. This includes internal audit review of the institution's rating systems and operations on at least an annual basis and indicates that some regulators may also require external audit of the rating-assignment process and estimation-of-loss characteristics.

KNOW YOUR RISKS

That sounds fairly straightforward, particularly for a financial institution, yet missing key risks has been a consistent source of failure. Risk models are only as good as the risks they take into consideration and the assumptions they make. As we learned earlier, many risks are tough to model reliably.

So, although enticing, the answer is not just understanding what the models are telling us. It's usually more about understanding what the models are *not* telling us.

It's critical to *know* the key risks of the institution and to make sure these key risks are thoroughly understood, monitored, and managed. Where risk models are in place, it's imperative to understand the assumptions that are baked into those models—and those factors that may not have been considered, possibly intentionally. Understand where there may be deficiencies, particularly if the business environment and/or product profile has changed since the models were developed. Where risk models do not exist, consider if they may be necessary and, at a minimum, find ways to assess and monitor the situation through another method.

It's often useful to spend some time within the organization considering what's missing and looking at issues that are newly emerging. It's important to take some time to think about the risk categories that we discussed earlier to ensure that all categories are covered and that new and emerging risks are being consciously factored into the monitoring and management framework. The key here is to be proactive.

You want to be sure that concentrations are well understood, that all sectors of the institution's dealings are being covered—including those that may be unregulated, such as off-balance sheet activities or unregulated legal entities. Regulators are often reactive, and simply may not have addressed emerging risks. Although it may be tempting to ignore these risks, thus avoiding the costs of managing or remediating them, remember that these are the areas in which blowups often occur.

Openly discuss your options for dealing with emerging risks. Talk about how they may change portfolio makeup, generate new business sectors, deal types, or generally affect the risk profile. Consider applying scenario analysis or war-gaming as a method for evaluating the outcomes of strategies and the risks they may introduce. War-gaming is a competitive simulation of actions and counteractions, with the objective of determining one's own optimal strategy. It can also be used very effectively to evaluate how your tactics and strategies may be received by your customers and stakeholders, competitors, or the market at large—the response framework. This, in turn, can be put to use to identify new or emerging risks or shifts in the risk make-up.

All of this means that your risk organization should be involved in strategic planning at key stages in the process to support the development of analyses. Those may include "what-if" analysis or stress testing the current portfolio, as well as quantitative assessment of the impact of new risks. Strategies should clearly reflect this analysis and figure in the downside outcome into return estimates.

This type of thinking also should extend to the planning process. The capital planning process—and the broader financial planning process—should follow as a direct outcome of the strategic planning process. The strategic plan should include an outline of the institution's anticipated expense, provisioning, and capital needs—including anticipated capital expenditures, desirable capital levels, and external capital sources. The capital should be considered in light of future actions and related scenarios that include potential impact of risk.

EXAMPLE

Metallgesellschaft AG is a classic story illustrating this point. It was an old and famous German mining company that had become very large. As it grew, it also developed multiple trading arms. The New York office began trading heavily in commodities futures, which seemed like a smart idea since precious metals and other commodities were booming. However, the head office was unaware of the New York office's trading positions. There was no governance and no backstop. When oil prices suddenly dropped, the company was left paying prices that were far above market price, and it couldn't bear the load. The company ultimately lost $1.4 billion and went out of business—a sad end for an old and venerable firm.

There are numerous pitfalls that companies experience in this category. In the Metallgesellschaft case, we saw that one arm of the company didn't know what the other was doing. That is surprising but not unusual, particularly in large multinational companies. Other hazards include:

- Lack of a clear and comprehensive governance framework
- Lack of a routine and systematic assessment of risks
- Failure to set limits and boundaries

ARTICULATE YOUR RISK APPETITE

The *risk appetite statement* is increasingly becoming a standard inclusion in any reasonable risk capability set. For many organizations, the item is mandated or strongly encouraged by regulators.

This is both good news and bad news. On the positive side, it is forcing many institutions to at least put pen to paper. On the down side, a good number of these organizations are more interested in having something they can wave around than a document that has meaning and is useful.

So, what is the risk appetite really?

It defines the institution's willingness to take risk in clear terms the organization can follow to manage the profile of business conducted. The specific definition can be somewhat confusing—and varied among institutions. For some organizations, it is their risk strategy. It is incorporated into the strategic planning process. For other organizations, it can be a separate activity entirely, possibly more adjunct to the financial planning process. Either approach has merit, and in any case should be considered along with other activities within the institution.

The risk appetite defines the risk capacity and standard operating levels of the firm. It should consider how those standard operating levels may vary and to what extent and under what stress situations they could reach the firm's capacity. That is, it should define the buffer between the standard operating levels and the capacity of the institution. It should articulate the amount of capital the organization is willing to put at risk. It also should spell out the strategy for ensuring the maintenance of capital and reserves in light of forecasts and potential events, with an eye toward the ability to draw from external capital sources. The risk appetite establishes capital planning as a core part of strategic planning and coordinates risk teams with finance and strategy teams.

What results often is robust discussion about the comfort level of that buffer and potential actions if the buffer were to become uncomfortably thin. This also prompts development of triggers and limits around key risks and business-line risks. In turn, these parameters can be applied throughout the risk processes to inform models, limits, and approvals. The tolerances should ultimately be applied at every level and consider all evident material risks.

Risks that are hard to quantify should be considered, too. They may not have specific measures but could be addressed through process checks or established triggers.

For example, many organizations underestimate the impact of reputational risk. This one often is not directly baked into models—or if it is, not dynamically enough to support senior management. But this one can be high impact, rapid, and costly. It can linger on in share price adjustments that could be difficult to reverse, particularly under certain market conditions.

In addition to risk taking, the risk appetite should also take into consideration the outcome and expectations associated with return. What performance metrics will be used? How does the portfolio's risk-appetite directive affect return expectations? And what are the ranges that could result from such a strategy?

Overall, establishing an articulated risk appetite sets the tone, defines what acceptable day-to-day risk-taking is and what is not, and provides guidance on which signals and triggers should be monitored to avoid or miti-gate a more serious risk event. Generating the risk appetite statement is a process that allows the organization to communicate, strategize, and plan to not only meet the headline objectives but also support further development of a common language and foster the culture of transparent risk taking.

It wasn't long ago that almost no institution had a risk appetite state-ment in any explicit way. One of the useful aspects of a clear risk appetite statement is the understanding of what sorts of risk/return profiles are asso-ciated with each business. One institution I worked with had a problem I've seen repeatedly. It experienced a nasty surprise when we started to work through the risk/return profile of each of its business lines, and the growth and capital requirements that would be needed over the next few years. Al-though it had been starting to build risk adjusted performance metrics, it hadn't really given much thought to the actual capital implications. One business line had been progressively increasing its underlying risk position in order to generate increased growth. Although it was yielding strong re-turns, the risk adjusted returns did begin to drop. What was worse was that the institution was drawing down capital at such an alarming rate that it found its capital severely constrained. The good news was that because the institution had begun to work within a risk appetite framework, it was able to spot the problem early enough, make changes to manage the busi-ness line a bit differently while beginning to more aggressively plan and strategize around capital and capital generation.

A few of the things to pay attention to are:

- Setting tolerances or limits that are workable—that don't overly constrain the business but aren't so loose that monitoring becomes de minimis.
- An unwillingness to challenge risk appetite—many organizations sim-ply accept where they have been. This is a great opportunity to begin to understand the implication of decisions on strategies, funding, and other business management issues.

Consider risks beyond those that are easy to measure—how will reputa-tion and strategic risks be monitored? These are often those that create some of the biggest headaches in the normal operating environment.

DEVELOP A WELL-DEFINED RISK CULTURE

It's easy to drive an organization toward a focus on growth and return. Af-ter all, that's what shareholders want and what most individuals intuitively understand as the requirement for success. As a result, many, if not most, organizations develop a sales-driven culture. Consider those who manage the largest or most well known financial institutions—or any financial institution or any company for that matter. It is often those individuals who were the most successful at sales. But the real question underlying their success is "did they achieve the best quality of assets?" Were there any hiccups in the portfolios that they generated?

The idea is not to develop a culture that crushes sales but to develop one that is risk-aware and not driven purely by sales. It is a culture that is informed by risk information at every level and across all transactions. It considers risk in each of its processes, across all activities of the firm. It's a culture in which people identify, understand, discuss, and manage risk proactively.

Establishing the right risk culture is a balancing act. If the culture doesn't pay enough attention to risk, it is less likely to consider the consequences of risky behaviors. If it pays too much attention to risk, it can lose its competitive edge.

A strong risk culture is robust and pervasive. It is embedded in the way the firm operates and covers all areas and activities. It takes particular care not to limit risk management to specific business areas or restrict its mandate only to internal control.

Management should take an active interest in the quality of the risk culture as well. The risk culture should be actively tested and objectively challenged in a spirit of fostering greater resilience and encouraging continuous improvement, thus reflecting the organization's strategic aims. Culture is also important to maintaining risk capabilities. Cultures with strong risk awareness are more interested in maintaining and improving their risk measures, processes, and overall capabilities. They seek continuous improvement in line with the growth of portfolios and strategies.

The type of culture fostered also may streamline approaches and controls. A strong risk culture often can reduce the need for a highly monitored approach to limits and controls. In some cases, it may even suffice to use a simpler control framework and simpler measures. This juxtaposition is often where the power lies. A well-balanced risk culture can foster an interest in improvement. With less need to utilize risk processes and measures as a stick, it can be focused on areas where the firm can create the most value.

But we all know that changing a culture is easier said than done. This aspect of improving an institution's risk management can be the most challenging to establish or change.

Companies that are making the transition are:

- Changing compensation structure and policies to incorporate risk criteria

- Changing policies and procedures to introduce additional risk criteria to evaluation of decisions, including transaction-level decisions
- Emphasizing the role of risk as the common thread running through decision-making at all levels

In general it is the board and senior management's responsibility to create an organizational culture that places a high priority on effective risk management.

One bank I worked with finally changed its risk culture after an "event" (a trading loss) shook the organization to the point that it had to restructure its board. This dramatic change at the top resulted in a new approach to risk management throughout the bank.

USE A COMMON LANGUAGE

Establishing a common language within your organization for discussing risk is absolutely essential. In setting and articulating a risk appetite, and in forming a risk-aware culture, a clear and supporting step is developing a common language. It's not only about initiating dialogues about risk. It must include the language of risk in everyday discussions and ensure that everyone in the organization understands risk at a basic level and is aware of the consequences of ignoring risks. Ideally, this shared base of knowledge serves as a common platform for discussing and considering risk.

Employees at all levels should have a common view of risk-taking and risk-awareness. They should understand basic concepts and terms, and they should understand—at least at a rudimentary level—how the firm addresses key risks or what to consider in each employee's respective function.

People should be broadly familiar with the institution's risk appetite. In other words, it's important for everyone to understand the overall "risk picture." People should understand which types of risks are off-limits and where approvals are required. They should also understand the nature of limits and thresholds.

Some might ask, "What value is generated by expanding this level of knowledge of risk to the broader workforce?" My answer is this: Immense value can be gained. Risks can be prevented efficiently. Events can be handled more rapidly and more effectively. The organization's ability to spot, analyze, and resolve issues rises enormously. Sharing knowledge and understanding about risk also is crucial for developing and embedding the risk culture we discussed previously.

DEVELOP CAPABILITIES AND APPROACHES IN LINE WITH THE SIZE, COMPLEXITY, AND CULTURE OF YOUR ORGANIZATION

Right alongside "know your risks," there should be an awareness of the capabilities required to manage those risks. These would likely be flavored by the type of risk culture that is in place today.

The board and senior management must develop a sensitivity for the techniques being applied and how they compare to other approaches and techniques. They should continually challenge the measures, models, and processes.

It is especially important to consider the techniques required to support the institution's strategies. If a particular asset class is small today but is slated for aggressive growth, it's important to put in place risk management capabilities that are in line with that vision, ideally *before* the aggressive growth occurs.

Although this may sound like a quest for "best practices" capabilities, regardless of the institution, it's really not. For many firms, advanced risk models and commensurate capabilities are not necessary and may even be detrimental. Many organizations have run aground by trying to be too sophisticated. Some methods are beyond the capabilities of the people charged with managing them.

For example, back in relatively early days of risk modeling, some top executives at Citigroup decided to build "the mother of all risk models." They wanted to bring all of their exposures from all over the world, along with their subcomponents and sensitivities, into *one model*.

So they assembled a team of Ph.D.s who went ahead and built the model. But there was a problem: the outputs were extremely difficult to explain. As a result, the team of Ph.D.s had to be called in to explain the results. As you might imagine, management became frustrated, and lost faith in the model. The project was scaled down and partially decommissioned. In hindsight, we can debate whether the model was properly implemented, but the lesson is clear: Sometimes a model can be *too* complex. I have no doubt that the Citigroup model was an excellent and accurate tool—probably far better than anything previously available. But it was too impractical to be considered useful.

Some institutions develop risk management strategies that leverage the inherent strengths of their cultures. Those with a stronger, more pervasive, and well-embedded culture are often able to respond with less restrictive limits and controls. They may be more inclined to provide a certain degree of latitude to business lines and their teams, bracketed by broader guidelines of risk/return measures or by higher limit structures that allow teams to manage risks more collectively.

One example of this was a bank, now merged into a U.S. mega national, which had been located in a small town. They granted enormous loan approval authority to their relationship managers, which is normally a big no-no. But in this case, they had instilled a very strong credit culture. That combined with a view that a book full of bad credits would damage or even kill a career (in a small town where this was far and away the best job around, this was a very credible threat) was enough to ensure that relationship managers made very sound and well-analyzed credit decisions. As a result, they had one of the very lowest default rates in the United States for many years. It's not a model that would likely work as well in many companies, but it certainly demonstrates the power of culture and the right incentives.

MAKE IT TRANSPARENT *AND* COMPREHENSIVE

Too often, processes and measures are separated from the idea of transparency. In reality, we want to marry the two ideas. Both risk positions and risk management activities should be conducted with transparency.

In establishing transparency, a firm must consider how the details of the models, measures, and systems are presented to those outside risk-analytics teams. Reporting should assess the adequacy of models. They should be routinely validated and the results reviewed at senior levels and reported to the board. Periodically, the assumptions applied within the models also should be reviewed, even discussed. This may include robust discussions at the board and senior management levels about the models' key assumptions, inclusions, or limitations.

This may sound like too much detail at such a high level, but it is failure to discuss precisely these types of details that most frequently causes unwanted surprises within institutions. Boards and senior management should be fully cognizant of the limitations of the models and measures. Equally, this places a burden on risk-analytics teams to ensure that models do not take on "black box" qualities and to learn to explain the nature and details of the models in a way that makes their workings clear. This also ensures that the teams understand the models themselves. Too often models age or become so complex that even those who oversee them lose track of the details within.

The measures at minimum should include certain characteristics. They should be comprehensive, covering the full complement of business, products, customers, and risks. There also should be measures of economic capital and other risk factors, which may include provisions, expected loss, or even defaults, charge offs, and recoveries. Measures also should take into consideration the balance of risk and return.

A case study here would have to include the entire U.S. credit crisis, or at least most of it. One of the key issues of this crisis was that models were frequently lacking. They weren't comprehensive enough. For those companies that participated heavily in securitized assets, the large majority failed to include the risks built within these asset packages. This type of modeling is called "look through modeling" as it forces the modeler to literally look through the shell of the securitized asset and into the underlying asset pools. Another similar issue was that many institutions had failed to consider the assumptions they were using within their credit models. The business cycle had been benign for so long that the history being used to support the models was a very low default history, which, in turn, suggested that all credits had a lower default probability than they otherwise would have.

CONSTRUCT CLEAR LIMITS AND CONTROLS

No matter the culture, capabilities, or maturity in risk management and measurement, at some point it is important to construct limits and controls to manage the portfolio within the articulated risk appetite.

Limits and controls should be clearly rooted in economic capital and loss expectations and cascaded down to every level of the organization— across products, portfolios, customers, and risk classes. They should be constructed so that every individual position-taker and portfolio manager has a clear view of the limits to which he or she is managing and the rules associated with those limits.

Measures should be aligned to support the controls and limits, and reports should clearly articulate these as well as the current position on limits. The management information systems should support this process so the generation of reports is timely. Consider how long it would take to identify and react to an impending threat and mitigate it. That should define the system's response time. If it typically would take a whole quarter before a risk event could play out, and it would be easily mitigated in that time, then quarterly reporting may be good enough.

But if the portfolio is changing more rapidly and/or positions are likely to escalate more quickly, it may be necessary to move to a faster reporting cycle. Systems and reports should be tailored to the users receiving them, the decisions they are making based on them, and the nature of the risks that are being monitored.

At minimum, limits and controls should be established around each of the institution's core risks and reflect both the individual risks that make up a risk portfolio and the portfolio concentrations themselves. This includes operational risks in the form of capital consumption, event tracking, and any changes in exposure profile. Reports should be generated highlighting any exceptions.

Senior management is responsible for enforcing limits. They must monitor adherence to limits and periodically review position-taking, ensuring that limits are not exceeded. There must be a clear procedure for managing positions as they approach limits and actions to take if limits are breached. In addition, senior management should make periodic reviews of the institution's overall control systems and its capital-assessment processes and procedures.

Think back to the Banker's Trust example in the Introduction. Limits were put in place, but not enforced; in fact, it was senior management that allowed the limits to be waived in order to take on additional exposure.

ALIGN PERFORMANCE AND INCENTIVES TO RISK AND REWARD

This may be one of the most important and challenging of all the basic principles. Why? Because when this principle is followed properly, *almost everything else takes care of itself.* Financial institutions should develop a performance-management framework that establishes clear risk-adjusted metrics, and they should manage the organization to those metrics, *both through portfolio performance targets and through direct links to compensation.*

Measures should be established that link risk, return, and growth. Many organizations utilize metrics such as risk adjusted return on capital (RAROC) and/or economic profit. Return metrics may be married with growth targets to ensure that portfolios are not cherry-picked and marginalized into stagnation. More mature organizations should consider multi-period versions of these metrics in order to capture future earnings streams and to ensure a longer-horizon view by management rather than a short-term view. Metrics should be based in economic capital, rather than in simple assets or regulatory capital because it provides a closer link to true economic behavior.

Ultimately, the metrics should be established at each level of the organization and across each portfolio segment. Some organizations may ultimately evolve to consider customer segments and individual customer relationships or transactions. Institutions should seek to drive the metrics to the lowest possible level, pushing accountability to lower levels and supporting the analysis of outcomes. Ultimately, transactions should be evaluated for their individual return characteristics, their stand-alone value, and their contributions to the broader portfolio.

Pricing models should be rooted in the same performance metrics and should always consider a multi-period view. Ideally, pricing capabilities should include well-constructed inputs that consider the full range of risk behavior over time at every line item.

Compensation should be tied to portfolio performance on the same basis, and executives and managers should be compensated relative to their risk-adjusted performance from the top down to the lowest levels of decision-making. Individual performance also should be evaluated based on support and conformance to other risk related factors: adherence to policies, processes, regulatory requirements, and even values, cultural norms, and education requirements.

Performance metrics must be carefully monitored over time. Point in time and averages should be considered, with performance trends identified and understood. Equally, compensation ideally should be tied to long-run portfolio performance with compensation deferrals and knock downs considered in the framework, particularly for senior executives.

DEVELOP COMPREHENSIVE FORECASTING, STRESS TESTING, AND CHALLENGE PROCESSES

Here's something that almost always gets us into trouble: the inability or unwillingness to test and challenge the risk measures and systems we have put in place. All too many times, we've heard that "Our systems are excellent. After all, we survived the last crash . . . " Or, "How can we predict what will actually happen?"

Complaining won't help. Every effort must be made to capture what we can, and to challenge what we cannot capture.

This means financial institutions should project risks based on strategies, new business, and growth expectations. They should consider mergers and acquisitions and business cycle, managing scenarios against upturns and downturns in the cycle.

In addition, models and measures should be stress-tested. This means a range of methods should be applied to project potential extreme events and the effect they may have on capital, reserves, and liquidity. Stress testing should really be what it says—*stressed*. All too often stress tests fall short of what a real stress would look like and may not even come close to relatively frequent market movements.

Stress tests should consider a wide range of events and include the assumptions baked into the models. They also should consider business cycle variances. The tests should evaluate effects on capital, reserves, and the dynamics of how specific instruments or asset classes are affected: Which are more or less sensitive to stresses? Which provide stabilizing diversification benefit? To what extent may those diversification assumptions change in the event of a stress?

In addition to reviewing the effect of stresses on models, the institution should challenge other aspects of its risk management processes and systems. Consider where weaknesses lie, which processes may no longer suite the nature of the business, which methods could be improved. This should be a process informed not only by audit but by periodic external reviews as well.

A simple challenge may involve a review of risk-investment spending versus size and growth of the institution's overall balance sheet. Risk expenditures should broadly grow relative to and ahead of balance-sheet growth.

Beyond challenging and stressing, financial institutions should routinely forecast risks. This, as discussed earlier, may be considered part of the planning and budgeting processes but also should be updated and revised as part of the standard budget tracking processes. Periodically, long-term forecasts also should be conducted to consider the behavioral life of both asset and liability products. This ensures adequate preparation for business cycle downturns and sufficient planning for capital management activities, which may include capital raising or securitization that would require months of lead time.

PROVIDE ACTIVE LEADERSHIP AND DIRECTION

Here is a question I hear often: "What exactly constitutes active leadership and direction?" For many boards and senior executives, the phrase "provide active leadership and direction" is vexing, particularly when referring to risk management. However, when things go wrong, understanding this term can be very helpful.

"Provide action leadership and direction" basically means that the board and senior management are knowledgeable about techniques, approaches, and even risk models. They must be aware of the assumptions employed, broad techniques, and in some cases, alternative methods. They should be part of all key decisions.

They should take on a continuing-education program that ensures new team members come up to speed. Certification is one concept that can ensure a minimum level of knowledge and can be deployed to all levels, including the board.

Beyond this point, it is the board's and senior management's responsibility to take an interest in the resources and skills available at the institution. They must ensure that appropriate resources are provided and that employees with appropriate skills are obtained and retained and that they, too, are provided a means to keep up with changes in the field.

The board and senior management also must ensure that the risk-management personnel have sufficient seniority and integrity to assess risks, manage risks, and interact with the rest of the organization at such a level and with such impact that the appropriate outcomes are achieved. Those personnel must have the ability to cease trading and/or reduce positions and portfolios if necessary.

In addition, the board and senior management need to ensure that the risk-management team operates with independence from the business lines. This ideally should include positioning the chief risk officer as a direct report to the CEO.

Equally, the board and senior management should consider the positions of the institution and be willing to reduce positions and portfolios. This should be a conscious part of their role and not solely one that is reactive to management recommendation.

This means that both executive- and board-level committees may need to be reconsidered. The entire board and the entire senior management team should be involved in a number of decisions associated with risk management. In turn, this may result in more time spent on risk-management related matters. For some, this means longer meetings or more frequent meetings held in both committees or full board or executive-committee sessions.

More specialization should also be introduced. Boards should consider using an independent advisor or even taking on to the board an experienced risk professional. Independent professionals should also be utilized and mandated to conduct reviews of various aspects of the financial institution's risk management framework, beyond those areas that would naturally be covered by routine audit or other assessments. In particular, the adequacy of controls and of operational processes should be reviewed, along with the adequacy of capital to support risks.

Policies, limits and, of course, the risk appetite, should be discussed and approved at board and executive levels. Those officials also should become involved with reviews and approvals of models and stress-testing results. They should be aware of the particular vulnerabilities of the firm. It is important equally that they read and are able to interpret management reports including risk and capital needs. They should seek out information on exceptions to policies, limits, and exposures and understand their genesis.

Finally, it is critical to construct a strong Chief Risk Officer (CRO) role. This executive should report directly to the CEO or board. The risk-management organization must be clearly independent of other business lines, and the CRO must be seen as a strong leader who has a notable voice at the executive committee and board levels. The CRO should support the balance of both reward and risk and be a champion for the risk appetite within the firm.

CONSTRUCT STRONG GOVERNANCE AND OVERSIGHT

Development of a strong governance and oversight framework becomes a key tool for all levels of management. It supports the appropriate implementation of risk appetite and the risk-management framework, the dissemination of activities and positions, provides a means for the organization to adapt or adjust its strategies, and provides a vehicle for rapid escalation.

To that end, the reporting and committee structures put in place should be clear. Everyone in the institution must understand roles, responsibilities, and scope of each department and committee. For many organizations this may mean clarifying and rationalizing roles. For others, committees may need to be expanded to include a clear and separate risk-management committee. Risk and capital matters should be separated from audit committee discussions and given their own forum. A risk and capital committee should be present at the top of the house to address the management and maintenance of the institution's risk appetite. It also must ensure that adequate capital and reserves are available to support the risk position and the *potential* risk position.

In addition, separate points of responsibility and decision-making must be clear. Individuals in key roles must be held accountable for their actions and decisions. Their roles and responsibilities to the committee to which they report must be clearly laid out. The committees themselves must ensure those lines of accountability and avoid devolving responsibilities to committee decisions.

Maintaining a balance here is critical. The role of a committee is to provide oversight and guidance as well as to ensure that policies and strategies are successfully structured and acted upon. They may veto directions of individual managers, but they should avoid making specific decisions where it is otherwise the responsibility of a single individual.

What we're trying to avoid is "groupthink." This occurs when a cohesive group is more interested in avoiding conflict and maintaining unanimity than in realistically appraising various courses of action. Groupthink can lead to a litany of negative consequences, including minimizing the risks at play and forming biases.

Committees frequently tend to make more extreme decisions than individuals acting on their own. This tendency can be exacerbated if the committee becomes larger, or is less diverse. The key is to leverage the committee's strengths without allowing the committee to become overconfident or "loaf" behind the comfort of a group. It is important to focus committees on specific points of input.

Oversight of the risk-management framework also must consider validation and review and how this specifically plays out within the organization. The greater focus on risk models throughout most organizations means these models, their assumptions, and applications must be routinely reviewed and validated to ensure their on-going appropriateness. This may put an enormous burden on an organization, particularly where strong technical resources are limited. The organization may need to consider creative applications of independent review teams drawn from different roles throughout the institution or consider the use of external, third party expertise.

In addition, the role of audit may need to be reviewed and deepened to accommodate a better knowledge of risk-management capabilities. This may even include adoption of more technical-assessment capabilities focused on modeling issues or other technical risk-management items. Audit may find itself required to take on a more expansive, consultative role to help identify areas where improvements may be required.

The organization also should consider a more random review approach. This may not be coordinated through audit and most likely would be conducted by the board or CRO. Bringing in third-party expertise or seeking risk-management advice to address key issues and weaknesses where strategies or the external environment may be changing is often a great way to provide fresh insights and to ensure the right level of support to risk-management teams.

Finally, a key element in developing a strong oversight capability is to ensure a strong reporting framework. There must be an emphasis on reports that are focused, clear, and comprehensive. This doesn't mean that more reporting is required but that it has to be good. It also must be focused to the receivers of the information so it supports their best decision-making.

Management reporting on risks and capital needs should be comprehensive and be constructed so each area of the institution is covered and so it is possible to drill down to each of the business lines and sub–business lines into lower levels of the portfolio. The information included should be sufficient in detail so senior management and the board can assess risk performance. It also needs to send clear messages about the position of transactions, portfolios, processes, and internal controls. Timeliness is also a key factor in reporting. Every effort should be made to ensure the timeliness of reports so information can be reviewed and acted upon before it's too late. There also must be a mechanism for escalation, so new and emerging issues can be addressed before they expand into a major event. Reporting also must include monitoring of policies, strategies, and internal controls. This should include the tracking of exceptions.

MAKE CONTINUOUS IMPROVEMENTS

Ultimately, the organization should evolve to a point where it establishes a culture of continuous improvement. The organization wants to be described as one that continually challenges current norms and adapts and evolves its capabilities to support and bolster weakness and push forward to develop capabilities *ahead* of strategies and portfolio growth. It should consider changes in direction, in mix, and complexity to ensure that new challenges are met head-on with awareness and preparation. Risk management should be supported with resources and a budget that grows ahead of new strategies and increasing asset base.

This means the risk-management team must be at the table when strategies and forecasts are being established, even in their earliest stages.

The organization also should keep an eye on external activities and movement in the risk-management field. It should ensure training and continuing education of the workforce. It should periodically look to external expertise to challenge internal norms and periodically seek outside hires to bring new perspectives. The institution should be aware of best practices. It may not need to adopt each one, but it should be aware of the options and possibilities and continually evaluate what may be appropriate for the firm.

The audit function should serve as a partner to the risk management organization, not only to provide a means of review but also to examine risk management processes and capabilities and help to identify deficiencies and areas for improvement.

This principle probably sounds like an ad for consulting or a justification for big risk budgets. However, the issue here is one of decay. Too many times organizations make big investments—maybe yours is or has done so for Basel II or Solvency II? But after the big spend is over, senior management and the board wipes their hands of it, calls it "done." And of course, given the principles of entropy, the capabilities rapidly decay. What a few years ago was a leading practice had disintegrated and is now just plain bad practice.

Unfortunately, I have too many stories of working with a financial institution, taking it to the forefront of leading capabilities—or at the very least to a framework of sound practices—only to have it report a problem five years later. I go back in and discover that the investment stopped a few years after I left and nothing has been done since.

CHAPTER 3

Building the Risk-Management Framework

EXECUTIVE SUMMARY

Successful risk management strategies are built upon four foundational components:

1. Organization and governance
2. Policies and processes
3. Models and measures
4. Data and systems

Eliminate any of these interrelated components, and the strategy becomes largely meaningless. This chapter introduces the critical processes required to build a practical risk management framework and make it work over the long haul.

ALL THE RIGHT ELEMENTS

For many organizations, the biggest challenge is establishing a risk management framework that works for them. That means ensuring that all the right elements are present and that they are implemented with sufficient depth and skill to support the institution's current and near-future needs—those within the organization's near-term strategic grasp, say next three years or so. This also means striking the right balance so the organization has not over invested nor under invested, that the capabilities established can be maintained with the current skill levels within and that the right risks are addressed to the right depth. It also may mean establishing the best level of integration with the rest of the organization to support decision-making at every level.

Most organizations will safely say, "Sure, we have risk management that covers all of the big risk categories." But few can say that they really feel it's working for them in the way they would like it to; that it is balanced, that it establishes the right perception of "return" on the investment in risk management assets, that it supports and helps rather than overburdens.

One key question to ask is, "Do you have risk management capabilities in place because they are *required*, or do you have them in place because you believe that they add real value?" If your answer is the latter, then you're probably in great shape and your biggest challenge will be maintaining a state of continuous improvement. And in keeping with the spirit of continuous improvement, it's a good idea to revisit the question periodically. In other words, self-examination and reflection should be part of the corporate risk management culture. It's perfectly OK to ask questions such as:

- Do we have confidence in our risk management capabilities?
- Do we feel safe?
- Do we achieve optimum returns *because* of our risk management strategy or *despite* our risk management strategy?
- Do our risk management capabilities add value, or are they a drag on the enterprise?

As shown in Figure 3.1, creating a practical risk management framework is an essential and foundational step toward implementing a risk management strategy. Successful risk management frameworks have four key components:

1. Organization and governance
2. Policies and processes
3. Models and measures
4. Data and systems

As straightforward as these may seem, each component has numerous dimensions that must work together to support the institution's profile as a whole and its specific business lines and products. They must support the level of control the organization desires, as well as the degree to which the organization plans to leverage the risk capabilities to support its businesses. These also will be influenced by the organization's risk strategy and risk appetite.

We'll discuss each of these foundational elements at greater length, but here is a brief introduction to each component:

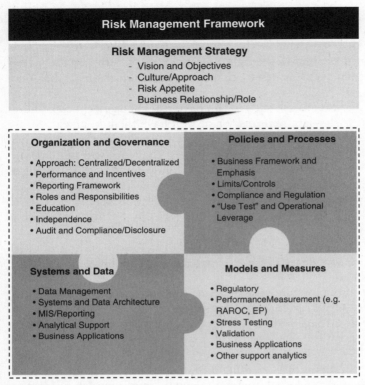

FIGURE 3.1   Developing a Risk Management Framework

Organization and governance is required to establish the specific roles and responsibilities within the risk management framework and to set the proper tone for the enterprise. The governance model itself "sends a message" to the business lines, quietly signaling what is considered important or unimportant to senior management. The model also may "send a message" to outsiders, such as equity analysts, bond holders, and regulators.

Resist the urge to think of the organization and governance model as some sort of inert structure. Its very presence will send signals to various audiences, within the enterprise and beyond its traditional boundaries. It establishes the kind of decisions that will be made and identifies who will be involved in making those decisions. It sends signals regarding the importance of such decisions and indicates the organization's willingness to establish points of control and responsibility within the formal risk management framework.

The very act of creating an organization and governance model represents a major step forward. It sends a powerful signal to multiple constituencies. In some organizations, it telegraphs significant changes in corporate culture. For these reasons, the organization and governance model may be the most important aspect of the risk management framework.

Establishing policies and processes is the next key step in the construction of a viable risk management framework. The degree of command and control expected, the willingness of the organization to empower, and the relative support and culture of the firm all will influence the approach to establishing the policies and processes required to support a successful risk management strategy. These policies and practices will determine the degree to which risk management concepts are embedded in the corporate culture and become part of everyday life. Think of polices and processes as the grassroots, nitty-gritty level of risk management. This part of the risk management framework will be dynamic, evolving over time as conditions change internally and externally.

Models and measures is the next critical step, for reasons that will be familiar to any modern manager. I'm sure you've heard the phrase, "If you can't measure it, you can't manage it" at least a thousand times. It also holds true for risk management. The success of your strategy, policies, and processes will depend on your ability to keep track of how well you are doing and how far you need to go to achieve your goals. Many organizations, particularly those struggling with new and tighter regulatory environments, tend to forget this extremely basic fact of business.

Models and measures are the tools you need to achieve goals. They also can play significant roles in developing new strategies, because they provide the solid information needed to make good decisions.

Data and systems are the guts of the risk management framework. They are where all the critical processes of risk management are executed. They are also the topics of heated debate and argument—especially when the company is trying to determine the appropriate level of investment in the technology required to collect, store, analyze, and report information. In today's enormously complicated global economy, information management is more than merely a basic requirement—it's often a competitive advantage.

Successful organizations consider their need for risk management information and establish clear investment strategies to ensure that information technology does not become an issue.

Now that we have looked briefly at the basic components of a successful risk management framework, let's return to the overarching questions: What sets apart the best institutions? What are the hallmarks of success?

From my perspective, there are four defining characteristics.

The first revolves around the company's culture and its attitude toward risk. Those companies that see risk as an opportunity, rather than a threat, *and* that have managed to establish a partnering role between the business lines and the risk management organization are generally those that have made the most progress and have most deeply adopted and embedded risk management capabilities.

The second characteristic is a commitment to governance models that ensure transparency at every level, establish clear leadership and set the "tone from the top," as well as striking a balance between business imperatives and risk management at all levels of the organization and in all departments.

The third characteristic is the establishment of a strong capability around risk-adjusted performance metrics. This capability enables management to factor risk into every decision, at every level and across every product line and business. Achieving this capability requires investing wisely in the development of systems and technologies that support the collection, storage, analysis, and timely reporting of critical information that can be leveraged to make the right business decisions.

The fourth characteristic is the ability to combine all of these capabilities and behaviors with a clear strategy that acknowledges the need for integrating risk management into all of the company's processes, at every level. This ability to promote and support a global discussion about risk management across the enterprise is the clearest indicator of success, even in rocky times.

YOUR RISK MANAGEMENT ORGANIZATION

One of the most important things a firm can do to establish a strong risk capability and culture is to give careful thought to the roles, responsibilities, and reporting lines of risk management. These provide strong cues to the wider organization about the role of risk and the intentions of the board and senior executives.

Creating new roles and responsibilities doesn't require the organization to indulge in a hiring spree. Nor does it presage the creation of a powerful new department within the enterprise. But these new roles do send important signals throughout the organization.

The most important role and clearest of all signals in the organization is the designation of a Chief Risk Officer (CRO). Many financial institutions have adopted a CRO function, but acceptance has not been universal and there are still some holdouts. Not all CROs are created equal; some have more authority and more clout than others.

Whatever the job description says and no matter to whom the CRO reports, the role should have several characteristics.

It should stand out as the key individual responsible for risk across the entire institution and all of its activities and holdings. The role should stand above chief credit officers, chief actuarial officers, and other similar roles. The CRO must be a senior officer and should have sufficient seniority, voice, and *independence* from business management to have a meaningful impact on decisions and to stand unencumbered from those business decisions.

Ideally, the CRO should report to the CEO and/or a risk committee of the board. It is critical that the CRO not report to any one business line, nor to the CFO, a historically popular choice.

The rule of thumb is that, much like the audit function, risk management must be independent of those who will be taking (or responsible for taking) positions on behalf of the institution. This generally disqualifies the CFO, who plays a key role in managing the company's balance sheet.

The CRO also should be considered with respect to other reporting lines. Of late, the CRO's role has increased in importance and may even take on responsibility for functions not traditionally under the umbrella of risk management.

Many organizations find that the CRO's role has become increasingly strategic, particularly given the more recent emphasis on articulation of risk appetite and risk strategy. But even before this, enlightened organizations have found value in establishing the CRO as a highly experienced and well-respected member of the senior executive committee—spending time in the CRO role might even be good training for any CEO hopeful. Companies that see the CRO as a strategic player may also consider having corporate strategy report directly to the CRO. In any event, the CRO should build a risk strategy team that can work closely with the corporate strategy team.

The increasing need for centralized analytics that are closely associated with risk measures, coupled with the need for independent validation capabilities for models, are driving many institutions—to adopt a corporate analytics team—one headed by a Chief Analytics Officer who may also report to the CRO. The team's responsibilities may include consolidation and monitoring of risk and economic capital. But they also may support performance-metrics development, implementation, and management, plus strategic analytics and technical validation of models used throughout the firm.

The CRO also makes sure that the organization has the appropriate human capital resources available to develop, monitor, and maintain risk analytics and models. Additionally, the CRO keeps an eye out for "key man risk" scenarios. The "key man risk" scenario is simply a situation in which an organization has invested one individual with too many critical responsibilities. Apart from creating issues of transparency, this kind of situation creates the potential for catastrophe if the "key man" is suddenly incapacitated or decides to leave the organization. In some situations, the unexpected departure of a "key man" has forced companies to shut down parts of their operation or change their business models.

The CRO's relationship with the audit function (Audit) can also affect the company's performance. More and more, Audit is providing a significant role in the review of the risk function. For this reason, Audit should be a direct report to the CEO and board, much the same as the risk function. But the traditional relationship between the CRO and Audit should change to accommodate a deeper understanding of the risk management function and the measures and models that are applied. That understanding should provide improved insights and feedback, plus a potentially deeper role in the validation of models.

In recent years, as the emphasis on risk modeling has increased and as regulatory reform has more deeply imbedded its linkages to capital, we find that the roles and relationships between the finance organization and the risk management organization have come closer together—particularly around capital management and performance metrics.

Although Finance has traditionally played the lead role in forecasting and establishing required capital level, including regulatory capital, the role of risk management is growing in this critical area.

As with most organizational choices, there is no one right answer. But most organizations find that it's best to have risk management teams managing the models that rely on risk information. In some organizations, the chief analytics role is a shared function between the CFO and the CRO, and includes the management, analysis, and dissemination of the risk-based performance metrics.

Other critical aspects of the risk organization should include the consideration of a role that supports risk strategy and strategic risk issues. This role may also include attention to the risk classes that may be less developed in terms of discrete modeling and analysis, such as reputation risk—and may consider consolidation and analysis of economic capital across all risk positions of the institution. The role should include stress testing and scenario analysis of the consolidated portfolio, must be able to work closely with all risk and finance teams, and have sufficient seniority to support executive-team and possibly board-level discussions. The role may be consolidated with that of the chief analytics officer or may be separated.

The risk management organization should incorporate direct reporting lines to the CRO for all risk personnel, including those who are embedded in business lines. This maintains independence through all risk-related decision-making. The organization should include clear roles across all major classes of risk evident in the institution and clear relationships to all business lines and products.

This brings us to the next key decision: the age-old question of centralization versus decentralization. Here again, there is no single right answer. It appears clear, however, that when the risk management organization becomes too far removed from day-to-day decision-making processes, it is difficult to maintain an energetic risk culture. Under these types of circumstances, nasty surprises may occur.

EXAMPLE

When National Australia Bank (NAB) suffered an overnight loss of roughly $350 million, it was attributed primarily to two traders who took advantage of weak controls and a small gap in data systems that allowed an unaccounted window of time. Subsequent reviews cited the trading area's poor risk culture and lax management attention at virtually every level. In other words, the traders ruled. They were aggressive and disrespectful of anyone or anything that challenged their domain, including the risk management teams. Risk had little control over what happened and was reduced to little more than a reporting team. Management removed itself from the situation and allowed this behavior to run rampant.

Ultimately, NAB realized that the failure they experienced was not so much about systems failures or gaps in processing times but largely about culture and the rampant disregard for controls. The only way to change such a broken culture rapidly was to demonstrate that it was fully unacceptable behavior. Heads rolled, from the trading desks up through every level of management. Ultimately, nearly the entire management team and most of the board was replaced or resigned. In addition, a fully redeveloped control framework was put in place along with improved reporting and monitoring of all sorts, including improved risk models.

The economic outcome exceeded the $350 million and impacted the bank at many levels. It was sanctioned by the regulator and had to carry additional capital for several years and its trading capabilities were restricted. Strained relations with the regulators extended beyond the trading area. NAB was put under scrutiny in nearly every aspect of its dealings. It invested millions of dollars in remediation of systems, models, controls, and in the search for new teams and executives.

Overall, a key aspect to establishing a well-functioning risk organization is ensuring that the individuals within it have sufficient authority in key roles and are supported with the necessary resources, including management attention. They need access to ongoing education and the ability to hire, develop, and maintain skilled professionals in various specialty functions, and they must be perceived as having a voice and weight in the organization. They need to have both the savvy and courage to occasionally and appropriately say "no" when it is required—and to have it stick.

YOUR RISK CULTURE

The risk taking and risk management culture an organization adopts can be the most important, most defining aspect of its risk management framework. For many organizations it is *the* factor that establishes the way they do business and their ultimate success or failure when faced with risk adversity. It also may define the level and type of investments that the organization chooses to make—or needs to make. There is no single "right" culture, but there are many examples of "wrong" culture.

Culture can often be thought of as the risk-taking style of the institution coupled with the awareness and acceptance of risk management within the institution. It's about how the organization perceives and utilizes risk and risk-related tools and techniques among other things.

Establishing a risk management framework must consider the organization's culture in the way the framework is implemented, the approach to risk management and mitigation, and the extent to which the broader risk culture of the institution must be actively changed or molded.

The first task in establishing a risk culture is assessing the organization's range of risk-taking behaviors—both present ones and potential alternatives (see Figure 3.2). An institution can be inherently risk-seeking yet maintain a very strong risk culture and capability. Conversely, it may be a highly conservative institution that has never given much thought to risk in an explicit sense.

Whether the nature of the organization is conservative or more risk-taking, the awareness of risk is generally a good thing. One of the great dangers occurs when an organization has been successful for many years and yet is unaware of its risk profile or abilities. It may even believe that it is "good" at risk management on the basis of its success. Too often, organizations of this type drift into riskier business (I call this "dangerous indifference"), or are simply caught unaware at the next downturn. Awareness is important.

An excellent example involves a large financial group mainly composed of insurance holdings. The irony of this group is that it is inherently

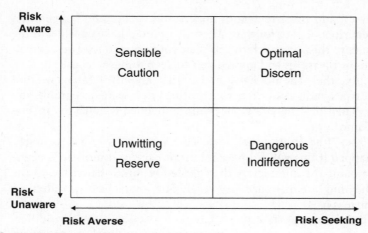

FIGURE 3.2 Risk Culture Dimensions

a very conservative organization yet allowed itself to get into a problem. The company tended to have a very low risk profile, and therefore, was fairly successful over time. However, that low risk profile also meant the firm's risk systems were fairly simple and less formal. During an economic and development boom, it took on increasing exposure to commercial real estate holdings.

Thanks to the boom, the company initially did well in this sector. So much so, that the board and senior management began to believe they were excellent at commercial real estate and that it was a core competency. This may sound strange for an insurance group, but it happened. Success increased their hubris, and the group took on exposure even more aggressively. Management evidently thought they could never lose.

Actually, they knew very little about commercial real estate and so, when the market turned, they discovered that many of their exposures were quite poor. Consequently, they lost a great deal of money. The losses looked especially bad for the company—it was difficult for it to explain to the market why an insurance company had such large exposures of this sort. Beyond the immediate loss, the group drew scrutiny from its regulators. So it experienced a triple whammy—direct loss, shareholder discomfort that drove share price down, and increased regulatory burden.

How could the company have prevented this? It's tough when management and the board are blinded by dollar signs. However, in a perfect situation, they would have put in place improved monitoring of their positions, scenario analyses, and stress testing to understand what could happen in a worst case scenario and plan for that. They also should have considered the overall exposure to this sector relative to their entire portfolio. These are all reasonably simple measures and approaches to keep things in check.

Additionally, they should have had a risk appetite statement that explained the types and sizes of macro exposures that were acceptable and unacceptable. Then they may have been more inclined to curb the investment as it became large.

There is also "the front page" test. This is where you ask yourself, "What will happen if this winds up on the front page of tomorrow's newspapers?" The company completely disregarded reputational risk and the effects that they might experience as a result of a loss. These can often be worse than the loss itself.

Overall, the most important trap to avoid is plain and simple indifference. Some organizations regard risk management—and risk management professionals—with disdain. Some executives are not respectful of risk, and may even aggressively defy risk requirements. Organizations with this type of management culture inevitably set themselves up for major problems.

Don't let this become the mindset of your organization, at any level. It can rapidly spread if left to fester. Send the right message by establishing firm risk management policies and supporting whistle blowers.

Regardless of your organization's particular risk appetite, it is crucial to set an example from the top and to support awareness, continuous improvement, and an information-seeking attitude. Leadership must demonstrate that the risk organization is a valuable partner with an important role.

Although buy-in and support from senior management is essential, the success of a risk organization will depend on its ability to demonstrate its value to the enterprise.

As shown in Figure 3.3, some risk organizations, particularly at institutions where risk management is in its early stages, function as organizational police officers. They see their role as upholding important institutional policies and, like traffic cops, frequently yelling "Stop!" In some instances, this type of organization represents an essential first step in the journey toward a fully-fledged risk management strategy. In other cases, however, it represents a heavy-handed approach that creates more problems than it solves.

Successful risk management organizations eventually find ways to partner with the business. That doesn't mean they give up their independence or yield authority to their peers on the business side, it just means they build more collaborative relationships with the rest of the enterprise. They leverage their skills and capabilities to support better business decisions at every level of the enterprise.

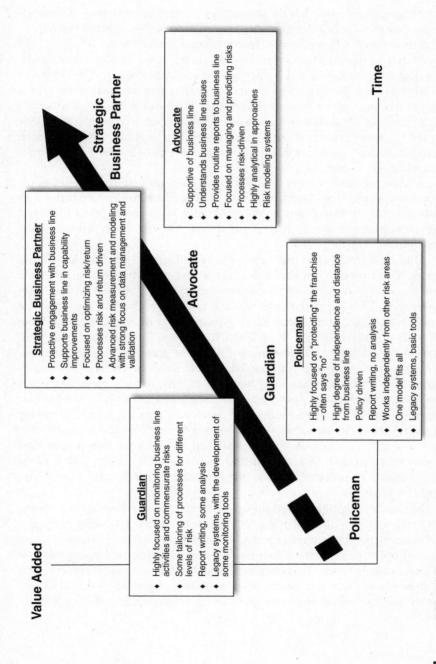

Value Added

Strategic Business Partner
- Proactive engagement with business line
- Supports business line in capability improvements
- Focused on optimizing risk/return
- Processes risk and return driven
- Advanced risk measurement and modeling with strong focus on data management and validation

Advocate
- Supportive of business line
- Understands business line issues
- Provides routine reports to business line
- Focused on managing and predicting risks
- Processes risk-driven
- Highly analytical in approaches
- Risk modeling systems

Guardian
- Highly focused on monitoring business line activities and commensurate risks
- Some tailoring of processes for different levels of risk
- Report writing, some analysis
- Legacy systems, with the development of some monitoring tools

Policeman
- Highly focused on "protecting" the franchise – often says "no"
- High degree of independence and distance from business line
- Policy driven
- Report writing, no analysis
- Works independently from other risk areas
- One model fits all
- Legacy systems, basic tools

Strategic Business Partner

Advocate

Guardian

Policeman

Time

FIGURE 3.3 The Risk Management Continuum

51

YOUR GOVERNANCE MODEL

Even organizations that have a seemingly strong organization and capability set can rapidly fall down in the area of risk management governance. When bad things happen, governance is often a crucial factor.

A strong governance framework starts with a clear and well-socialized statement of risk appetite. We'll discuss this further in more detail, but it is important to understand that this statement creates a framework and an anchor to ensure that business decisions don't spin out of control. The risk appetite statement sets an advanced agreement regarding how much risk the organization is willing to take—both through direct position-taking and in the event of market downturns and other risk events.

All too frequently, it is the lack of such an anchor and similar guidance for specific risks and businesses that leads many organizations to ramp up risk to dangerous levels, particularly in the light of fantastic return opportunities. It forms the basis for the limit and control framework.

One great example of this was Banker's Trust. In its day, Banker's Trust was both an icon of innovative risk management techniques and at the same time the source of some of the worst examples of poor risk culture and governance. This particular case was the last straw, the one that took the bank down. It had, along with many institutions at the time, taken on large positions in Russian bonds. Post-Soviet Russia was booming, and the bond positions were making fabulous money. As in our previous example, management saw dollar signs and continued to double down on the position. Needless to say, it did not take long before their risk models rang alerts that they were indeed overexposed. But they continued not only to retain their positions but to increase them. The bank was making fantastic money on these—at least on paper. Its senior market-risk executive built case after case of continued warnings, escalating them to the board level, but he was rebuffed with "Stow it, or find the door." Ultimately, you may recall, Russia's finances collapsed, down went the bonds, and with them, Banker's Trust.

In this case, sophisticated models were in place, reporting was done, and there was escalation of the issue. But all of the bank's own governance and warning measures were effectively ignored at every level. There were no firm limits on the ultimate risk appetite and commensurate upper-end capital levels to help ensure that decisions stayed in line. As many of these sorts of disasters do, this one came down to issues of governance and clarity around the likelihood and consequences of a collapse, and the inability to construct clear limits—not on the actions of a trader but on senior managers and board members themselves.

If the bank had had in place a risk appetite and a strong governance process, it would have been less likely that these sorts of decisions would be made—not on a continued basis, anyway. In addition, the use of stress testing and scenario analysis might have further underscored to the board the degree of risk they were taking. Would they have kept it up if they had: a) blown their own top level portfolio and capital limits; b) understood that they could easily bring the bank down; and c) known that it was imminent?

The idea here is to establish a clear position that guides the organization—as well as its committees and even the board itself—and to stick to that position, even when facing excessive returns that may distort judgment.

The organization's committee structure should support not only the risk appetite but also the limits and controls that cascade from the risk appetite. Like other aspects of a risk management framework, the committee framework can be varied, but it must ensure that each of the key risks and management activities most commonly described within the institution are addressed with strategic consideration.

For most financial institutions, there is good justification for setting up committees associated with each core risk the organization faces: asset/liability management (ALCO), market risk, operational risk and, in the case of a bank, credit risk.

Some institutions have more recently tasked their risk committees to consider strategic and business risks in a separate committee or as a headline item within one of the other committees. A consolidated risk and capital committee may also address strategic risks and should preside over the other committees to provide both a final appeal and to specifically address consolidated issues across the portfolio—particularly those that threaten the risk appetite. This committee should be separated from the ALCO and also should be differentiated from even the most senior credit committee.

A key aspect of the committee structure is the level of individuals included. Most if not all of the risk committees should include most of the senior officers of the company. If the organization tends to devolve decisions to lower levels, a subcommittee structure may be useful. The senior executives from key business lines, strategy, risk, operations, and other functions should be highly engaged in the issues and decisions of these committees.

For many institutions, this likely will require an initial round of education to ensure the appropriate level of participation and discussion and to safeguard against "hijacking" of meetings by a knowledgeable few who hog air time or intimidate through their deeper knowledge and comfort with subject matter.

Many organizations will find that, at the onset, ongoing education, and possibly coaching sessions could be required to ensure that there is equanimity among committee members and that the desired level of discussion and agreement is ultimately obtained.

Equally, it is critical to establish a separate risk committee of the board. Too often, risk items are addressed within the audit committee or other subcommittee and not provided with sufficient air time to establish even the most rudimentary basis of understanding of risk management activities within the institution.

The board's risk committee should become involved with issues such as the establishment of the risk appetite. It should ensure the independence and voice of the risk management organization, and it should become involved in incentives and remuneration of key executives to uphold the alignment to the risk appetite and risk culture within the bank. This should be considered across the organization to align the view of businesses, even those that may function in different jurisdictions. The board risk committee also should perform a role in the understanding and use of risk models, including the review of the validation of models, stress testing, and forecasting.

Reporting on risks also should form an integral support component to the governance process. Reporting on risks should support the decisions that are being made by way of careful thought put into the type of information that is being provided to each committee or level within the organization. Reports should consist of clear and concise format so that information can be obtained easily and without much page-turning. Consider the maximum length that any given executive can tolerate. This is usually something under five pages. That means key messages and issues should be addressed on the first page, with simple supporting points following. Clear points for attention or decision should be spelled-out up front.

All of this may seem obvious, but it is the pursuit of a concise risk-reporting framework that completely stymies even the best of institutions. For this reason, many organizations have moved to establish the "risk dashboard." This constitutes what now often is a web-based interface with simple reports and metrics available on all key risks and key business lines, portfolio segments, and the like. It allows users to rapidly find the information most important to them and to "drill-down" to lower levels of detail. It also supports views of trends over time, comparisons to budgets and thresholds, and other detail.

Finally, reports must be constructed in terms that everyone can understand. This may require some education, but it's usually worth the effort. Remember, the goal is furthering the cause of transparency, management attention, and urgency when it's required.

EXAMPLE

Credit Suisse is another institution that has had a famously strong risk-management capability built on practical measures and strong reporting and monitoring. One of its institutional traditions was the two-page risk report. This may sound nearly impossible, but the bank pulled it off. The key was to keep focus on the most important messages, cover each major risk class succinctly, and clearly highlight trends and changes. This approach forced teams to create the ultimate in succinct, clear messaging and transparent communication. Credit Suisse pioneered the concepts of "top ten risks"—a simple list of the most concerning risks the organization faces at any given time—and the "risk dashboard"—the simple executive's display of the individual risk classes, their consolidated position, and their contributory elements by business line.

Focusing on keeping the report size down forced risk teams to think and consider only the most important issues of the day. It also forced them to create simple, clear explanations that management could understand. In addition, senior management did not become overwhelmed. They were able to focus on the core issues so they could isolate them and deal with them.

YOUR POLICIES AND PROCESSES

At the most rudimentary level, institutions have a framework of basic policies and processes for conducting ordinary business. These will inevitably control the approach to conducting transactions and will place guidelines on the types of transactions and qualifications for individual transactions. The risk management function should set and monitor those basic policies and guidelines.

In today's complex and highly competitive business environments, however, institutions need a framework of policies, controls, and limits that are reconcilable from the top of the house to the individual transaction level. These should be driven from a basis in reserves, provisions, economic capital, and the risk appetite, then cascaded to each major portfolio and sub-portfolio and downward to customers and transactions. Typically, we would expect the framework to consist of the following broad types of limits:

- **House limits.** These set total financial institution limits, typically on portfolios. However, they may describe total cross-business-line activity with or exposure to a single customer, single type of activity, or even an industry that crosses business lines and geographical entities. These should consider consolidation of exposures across types of risk (e.g. credit, market) as well as other factors.

■ **Portfolio limits.** These set limits on specific portfolios or sub-portfolios. They generally describe the limit set on exposure to industries, geographies, or products and may be set at a consolidated or sub-portfolio level. They are frequently set as limits associated with one risk category, such as credit risk or market risk.

■ **Transaction limits.** These are generally set with business or product lines and are specific to single transactions. They usually describe the level of exposure that may be granted.

■ **Customer limits.** These are limits placed upon a single customer or group of related customers (such as a corporation with multiple legal entities or subsidiaries). Limits of this type should be placed on the consolidated exposure to the entire group as well as potentially any one entity with it, depending on its legal relationship and reliance on the group for financial support. The limit should include all exposures to the institution, including trading, credit, investment, or other transactions.

A great example of this was what the financial world experienced after the collapse of Enron Corp. It seemed virtually every financial institution on earth had exposure to the energy giant. Many didn't know just how much exposure they actually had. Although many were aware of their larger exposures that clearly carried Enron's name, many also had numerous smaller exposures buried within legs of transactions or under different special purpose vehicle (SPV) names that Enron owned. I know of several organizations that were still finding Enron exposures years after the collapse.

For this reason it is important to diligently manage your log of names and related entities and ensure there is a mechanism to link them and roll them up to a consolidated view. Many policies consider only direct relationships and can be unclear about certain subsidiary relationships, particularly when the parent does not provide support. Worse, they may allow for some of these positions to be netted out against each other. That works great for taking a conservative view over obligations and what is allowable for underwriting. But it does the exact opposite for understanding the concentrated risk of being exposed to numerous small entities that are unrecognized as part of a larger entity.

The risk-management organization should monitor adherence to limits and, ideally work with business lines to support the development of transactions that can be managed within limits. This may be accomplished by understanding the contribution of individual transaction characteristics to the overall risk of the deal and how it, in turn, would be constrained by the limit framework.

The risk function can facilitate the evaluation of trade-offs and development of sound deal-structuring. In this fashion, risk management teams can best ensure that transactions are sound and sensible, both to the institution and for the customer.

This is an important concept that goes beyond the simple management of policies and limits toward developing the culture of the organization and how risk management is perceived within it. It supports the education of the front line in risk management concepts while keeping an eye toward developing good business. It also establishes the risk organization not as a police function but as a partner in developing good business. It is important for business lines to see this role as such and for the risk organization to realize its role in serving the organization, rather than purely acting as "gate keepers." This approach does not have to compromise the independence of the role but should serve to enhance its overall effectiveness.

In addition, the risk management organization should have the resources to monitor the overall portfolio for not only adherence to limits but for broader trends as well—customer preferences, credit quality, economic shifts, business-line-acquisition strategies, and others. They should develop a view toward trigger points and thresholds to support transaction-taking and also customer interactions and portfolio decisions.

Processes should be constructed so that each step and the graduation from one step to the next are clear. Processes associated with transaction-generation should be set up with clear "go/no-go" decision points to ensure clarity for business lines, customers, and risk officers. This also minimizes operational risks which often become most apparent when the organization is under stress. Ideally, the decision points should be established with a clear basis in policy and aligned to the overall risk appetite framework.

In more sophisticated institutions, the performance framework should also align to this level of decision-making, so hurdle rates, valuations, and the general view toward profitability at the customer and transaction levels are also rooted in risk-adjusted performance considerations. This also supports clarity of message and an unbroken link from the top of the house to the most discrete transaction.

This thinking also supports what we call the "Use Test." The Use Test is a concept included in the Basel II Accord for the regulation of capital measurement in banking. The idea behind the Use Test most simply suggests that the models, measures, and rating systems that are used for risk and capital should not be constructed simply to satisfy the capital regulation. They should be put in place for their *use* in managing the institution's day-to-day business.

For many organizations, this may seem like a non sequitur. Those that have been building risk capabilities all along—before Basel II—would have built these capabilities for exactly that: for use in day-to-day risk and business management. The intent is to ensure that the capabilities are embedded into the management of the institution and not set up as a stand-alone means of satisfying a new regulation.

Many regulators and their institutions have used this as a means to embed risk measures and related metrics more deeply in the institution. Performance measures are being reconsidered and revitalized throughout many institutions, and they are being driven down all the way to lower-level business lines, individual account officers, and to pricing.

Many institutions are applying the metrics to ensure that each transaction meets minimum standards but also to remunerate account officers, to evaluate individual customer relationships, and to remunerate at each level of business management, particularly where there is direct responsibility for transaction-taking.

YOUR DATA AND SYSTEMS

As the role of analytics and modeled views of risk and capital become more important in most financial institutions—whether due to regulatory pressures or in response to competitive pressures—it is certain that the importance of data and of technology increase in lock step. Here again, those institutions that have responded by actively planning and investing have been able to respond to markets and to regulators with greater agility, often becoming market leaders in their ability to drive a risk-adjusted performance culture throughout their respective institutions.

Data—accessing it and ensuring its general quality or integrity—has been a key concept in risk management circles for quite a while. With the onset of Basel II and its sister framework, Solvency II, the focus on data is growing stronger.

As a practical matter, there are five key points to keep in mind when assessing data requirements and capabilities:

1. **History.** Most modelers will tell you they want all the data they can get—and it's true that it is desirable. Realistically, most models require at least three years of data to get started. Regulatory requirements dictate the use of up to seven years of data. And to make matters worse, requirements for models to reflect business-cycle adjustments could mean 15 years or more of data in some countries.

The best way to deal with this issue is to get started with whatever you have, clean it, and make preparations to start storing it carefully. It's generally a bad idea to wait until history is collected before attempting to build or use models because often, it never happens. There is often enough data, albeit weak in some cases, to get the ball rolling and build rudimentary capabilities. This will usually inspire the organization to take greater care of data as it is initially entered and stored and will begin the institution on a tradition of data management awareness.

In some cases, data can be purchased or models can be purchased and adapted to the local institution. These are also good ways to get started, but they can't replace internal data. No two businesses operate in exactly the same way, and chances are that nobody knows your business as well as you know your business. So it's important to accept these approaches for what they are—stop-gap measures that will suffice until better internal data is collected.

Some financial institutions have gone so far as to hire squads of retired bankers to manually enter data from files. This sounds like an extreme approach but can work wonders toward filling in gaps and extending data history just enough to get the job done. An institution considering this path would be better served by hiring professionals more familiar with relevant files than general data-entry people. Those that have tried the latter often are sorry, because it often takes twice as long and generates more errors than it might be worth.

2. **Integrity.** On the surface, it may sound obvious that data needs to be good, but this is the biggest issue for many organizations. In many cases, data may be stored in aggregate format or may be incomplete or manually entered. All of this means the data could have random gaps, be unavailable at the level of granularity where it is required, or just may be untrustworthy.

There are a few ways of dealing with this problem. It's often difficult to repair files if they have already been damaged or are incomplete, but as with data history, it is possible to re-enter data if it is deemed worthwhile. Those that are considering a more complete system build should consider the infrastructure to support data integrity, including entry checks that ensure that erroneous information isn't entered and that all important fields are populated. In addition, databases should be constructed as fully referential to support the manipulation of data, and storage must be managed to support long-term storage at the most granular levels.

3. **Completeness.** This goes hand-in-hand with integrity and refers not simply to the elimination of data gaps but also to the completeness of

information being captured. It embraces a wide range of information regarding the customer or transaction. This must go beyond simple transaction amounts to include industry information, customer details, geography, payment behaviors, and even the storage of risk information over time, including the retention of changes and the details supporting the changes.

4. **Storage and availability.** We've hinted at this already, but storage needs to be managed, not only to ensure that granular details of files and transactions are not lost but also to allow ready access to the individuals and teams manipulating the data. Some organizations have been known to send off data to disk in storage warehouses that, at best, may take days or weeks to retrieve. At worst, data can be frequently lost or destroyed using these methods. Groups responsible for using the data need to have ready access and input into the development of policies for long-term data storage and management.

5. **Ability to manipulate.** Here again, a seemingly obvious concept but not to all. Data fields must be supported with referential capabilities, and interfaces must allow modelers and analysts to query and analyze large quantities of data. This must support not only the efficiency of teams but also long-term traceability and auditability. It also must preserve the integrity of the data itself from its very users—for example, not allowing accidental overwrites.

For many institutions this level of data care can become a nightmare—for both investment management and for organizational ownership and co-ordination. Each group handling data must take ownership or data rapidly falls to disrepair. This starts with the front line and those that are conducting initial data entry. Increasingly stricter policies for the accuracy and completeness of data entry and its longer-term manipulation are essential. This must be accompanied by audit, and in some cases, strict consequences—particularly in cases of flagrant disregard.

The concept of a Data Steward or Data Czar has been successfully implemented at a number of institutions. They are companies with an executive role supporting the development of data policies, the assurance of their implementation, the quality of data long-term, and the clean-up of any notable data vacuums. This role frequently also carries a budget to support the development of systems, plus storage to support the management and long-term care of data.

In short, data has now moved into the light as one of an institution's most valuable assets. Where only a few short years ago many analysts and modelers found their data environment characterized by pot luck, now they feast on a high-quality asset that is given formalized care and feeding.

Data is only one piece of the puzzle. Alongside data are the technology and systems that support a wide range of applications. These often start with the data warehouses and data-marts discussed earlier. But we must consider a broader array of systems and their linkages. Today, the risk management environment is intricately woven through the overall systems infrastructure of the institution. It does not stand alone and must consider its requirements, interfaces, and linkages alongside the rest of the infrastructure. It includes:

- Warehouses and marts
- Models and calculators
- Transaction origination
- Portfolio monitoring and tracking
- Reporting and user interfaces

Institutions that are considering rebuilding transaction systems or even core banking systems now must examine the requirements of the risk management organization. In many instances, these requirements may even drive much of the decision process. Key considerations in the decision process should include:

- Build or buy
- Centralized warehouse versus decentralized data marts or hybrids
- Degree of redundancy
- Degree of analytical and reporting automation
- Integration across and within systems, including modeling capabilities: specialization versus integration; needs for stress testing, particularly institution-wide
- Lowest level of use
- Links to external data sources
- Features: user interface; live reporting; web-interface, etc.

Of these decisions, three often create the most consternation for institutions:

- **Build versus buy.** For many years, the best risk-management organizations really had only one choice: build. But over the past two decades, risk systems have improved dramatically, including off-the-shelf models and modeling tools. In many cases today, except for the smallest or the most sophisticated institutions, the answer is easy: buy.

  The key is to find a system and a support group that is best positioned to cover your needs today and to grow with you. The working relationship with the vendor may be the most important aspect of the decision.

But as is always the case whether building or buying, ensure that assumptions are transparent and that any model is supported through open architecture and accessible code. Those that built the engine may not be around in five or ten years when you're ready for an upgrade.

■ **Specialization versus integration.** Today, many risk capabilities are built into straight-through processing systems and even core banking or finance systems. This is still a tougher question than the previous, but it is fair to say that many integrated systems have now evolved to a point where it is finally worth considering their risk capabilities. Only a few years ago this would have been acceptable to only a handful of organizations, but now it is worth a hard look. Ask yourself if the system will support the organization's immediate needs and future aspirations, and can the organization work long-term with the vendor team supporting it?

■ **Lowest level of use.** Of a slightly different ilk, but no less important. This point is one that has frequently surfaced and resurfaced over many waves of systems' capabilities and theories in risk management. It is now back on the table with increasing interest because of the regulatory attention drawn to risk-adjusted performance management and its deeper level of use within organizations. In the end, many institutions are limited by their ability to link risk measures and performance metrics to individual customers, transactions, and even sub-products and business lines, not only due to their analytics, but more commonly due to their systems.

As a result of increasing interest in stress testing, egged on by the global financial crisis, there is an increasing need for risk analysts to construct a variety of stress tests. These are being required at both deeper and broader levels and on institution-wide results. This is a dramatic departure from the compartmentalized approaches of years gone by. It requires modelers to reach deep into portfolios with the ability to simulate broad economic shifts and reach across business lines and risk classes to account for extreme and sweeping consequences that trigger highly correlated outcomes across institutions.

This ability is upon us now, and with demand for it increasing, debate has begun on the pros and cons of more integrated risk systems. The form this may take and the ability for organizations to adopt it are unclear. It defies other tenets that advocate for more transparency in models and clarity of assumptions. Organizations that have attempted such endeavors have found outcomes too complex to unwind and understand. Remember that Citibank built the ultimate model only for it to become too unwieldy? The need for improvements in stress testing is evident, but the solution may be tied to more simple approaches or concepts rooted in clear structural frameworks that support a degree of consistency at every level.

This may drive decisions regarding new infrastructure investments (including data warehouse architecture) so key information can be rolled up or rolled down for routine monitoring, management and for performance review.

Overall, it is now increasingly important to tie risk management interests to a broader range of decision-making. Risk organizations need to be included in discussions of IT strategy alongside other business lines, even in areas where they may not have participated in the past. With fast moving and ever-changing regulations, organizations are relying increasingly on the deepening of data, modeling, and use capabilities. So they must plan a longer-range systems infrastructure for their risk organizations with a viable budget demonstrating commitment and reflecting growth.

CHAPTER 4

Measuring Risk and Capital

EXECUTIVE SUMMARY

What holds true for most business customs also applies to risk management: If you can't measure it, you can't manage it. In this chapter, we take a deep dive into risk measurement. We also look at the value you get when you have systems and processes in place for measuring risks accurately. Remember, risk isn't just about the downside—it's about the upside, too! We examine how measuring risk is fundamental to managing risk, and how companies that do a better job of measuring risk can leverage their knowledge to make business decisions that result in more profits and fewer risks. We also look at how regulatory processes are built around measurement, and we make a strong case for using risk-adjusted performance metrics to get a much clearer picture of where profits really come from. This is a crucial chapter, so get out your highlighter.

WHY MEASURE RISK?

It really wasn't all that long ago when risk wasn't often measured. Even as late as the early 1990s, relatively few financial institutions were trying to measure risk and link that to measures of capital. So, if we lived that long without it, why do it?

Measuring risk has become an all-important aspect of risk management. It is not the end-all and be-all, but it is a center point of managing risk now. Through Basel II and Solvency II, it now has been embraced by regulators as a key component of risk management.

It provides a means to assess relative risks, understand their materiality, and identify and apportion treatment strategies for them. It allows us to develop analytical means of assessing transactions, customers, and investments and manage them throughout their life with increased efficiency. It supports the overall quality of the balance sheet through measures of liquidity and interest rate risk, and it also supports the ability to establish appropriate reserves and capital to support the institution's risk.

Done properly, risk measurement not only can support the assessment of the current book of business but also support the analysis of future risks and issues. It also allows the market to assess the relative soundness and financial strength of the institution on that basis. AAA-rated institutions are perceived to be safer and, in turn, far more likely to hold higher levels of capital than BBB institutions.

Whatever the size, complexity, or sophistication of your dealings, however, there is no doubt that measuring risk on some level can yield important insights into the way the institution is managed.

LAYING OUT THE FUNDAMENTALS, FROM THE TOP DOWN

Several core concepts provide the basic foundations for applying risk measures within the financial institution. We have already touched upon these in Chapter 1, but it is worth taking these deeper because they are among the most important concepts in risk measurement.

There are two key measures, each linked to the two core financial mitigation techniques:

- Expected loss (linked to reserves)
- Unexpected loss (linked to economic capital)

As mentioned earlier, expected loss is the mean loss rate that we would expect on any of our transactions or on our operations. This is the amount we can reasonably expect to lose, and therefore, we establish provisions to ensure we have a sufficient financial backstop to support that loss.

Hand-in-hand with expected loss is unexpected loss. It is the *volatility* of losses and represents the "true risk" of an institution, portfolio, or transaction. This is the "unknown" part. Think of it as the degree to which loss will vary from the expected or mean loss. This concept we link to capital—the shareholder equity that is held to support loss.

For many, it is this last concept that is the most curious, but in some ways it is the simplest. It is shareholder equity that absorbs unexpected losses within the institution. Quite simply, it describes the difference between assets and liabilities and how these may ebb and flow as the financial institution takes risks and is, in turn, remunerated for the risks it takes. This further links to the financial solvency of the institution: the ability of the institution to support its own obligations—that is, its debt rating. So, unexpected loss is scaled up according to the institution's target debt rating to determine how much capital is required to support its financial strength.

Let's discuss how this works in a simple practical setting. A bank has $100 million in assets (loans) which carry an interest rate of 6%. It has funded those loans through $6 million in shareholder equity (capital from investors) and $94 million in liabilities (deposits and bank-issued bonds). These liabilities carry with them an expected return of 4%. At the end of one year, the bank hopes to receive $6 million in return from its assets. If this happens, the bank would pay its depositors and bondholders the 4% they were expecting—$3.76 million, plus their principal—leaving a very healthy return of $2.24 million, or 37.3%, for its shareholders.

However, the bank management knows that, historically, about 2% of its borrowers default on their loans, and those can't be recovered. That is the *expected loss*. If the bank is correct in its assumptions, the amount returned to shareholders decreases to $120,000 and 2% return—far less attractive and dangerously close to losing money. If however, the bank's assumptions are wrong, then the amount returned to shareholders may change—perhaps disastrously.

For example, what happens if it's an unexpectedly tough year and defaults on that $100 million in loans increase to 8%? That results in a total yield of $97.52 million—not enough to cover the $97.76 million liability-holders were promised. So, the bank defaults, and the shareholders lose all.

If it had set provisions at $2 million to cover expected losses, the bank would not have been able to protect its shareholders from a poor return, but it would have had enough to pay its bondholders, thus would not have defaulted and would have survived. Likewise, if sufficient capital had been assured to cover all, or most, of the potential loss scenarios, then the bank would not likely fail even under extreme loss scenarios. It would be able to ensure that it would not default on its own obligations and, in so doing, support its debt rating. How much capital would be required? The specific amount depends upon the target debt rating of the institution.

A financial institution needs to establish sufficient capital and provisions to ensure it won't default on its obligations. Capital also must support the specific debt rating that the debt-rating agencies have assigned or the rating the institution hopes to achieve—that is, its target debt rating. Capital must be aligned to the debt rating. If the bank has a high amount of risk and a low amount of capital, we can see a high probability that things could go wrong—that the institution could go bankrupt or default on its external obligations. With that level of capital, the bank most likely would receive a low debt rating.

However, a low debt rating has an advantage: The bank can take on a higher level of risk and potentially yield a higher rate of return for its shareholders. But keep in mind that debt holders will want a higher rate of return in order to be compensated for the risk that they are taking. Conversely, a high debt rating, such as AAA, would need to be supported with a high amount of capital proportional to the risks the bank was assuming. Bondholders would not demand as a high a return for their investment; shareholders would more likely achieve a lower return but one with greater certainty. The higher the debt rating, the lower the probability that the bank will default on its obligations and, therefore, the higher the amount of capital required relative to its risks—or unexpected losses.

Of course, a real bank is much more complex, but the principles all hold. It is important to understand the difference in expected returns—or losses—and in cash flow requirements between our assets and our liabilities. In addition, it is important to consider establishing funds for both provisions and capital based on both expected loss and unexpected loss. It is not a far cry to begin to understand that provisions need to be kept in relatively liquid form and that at least a portion of capital needs to be established as high-quality capital. That is, common equity and retained earnings that are unencumbered by other requirements, cannot be redeemed and have no requirements on their dividend or return expectations.

So, in this simple example we have:

- Learned the importance and the role of provisions and capital
- Touched on the concept of bank liquidity and asset/liability management
- Touched on issues associated with capital quality
- Touched on the idea of target debt rating and capital to support the debt rating
- Touched on the trade-offs in balancing risk, return, and funding choices (debt, equity, and liabilities [e.g., deposits])

As we progress through this chapter, we will drive deeper into each of these concepts to lay out the mechanics that support them.

PROBABILITY, EXPOSURE, AND SEVERITY

Besides expected loss and unexpected loss, there are three more core building blocks of risk measurement. These are *probability*, *exposure*, and *severity*. We will see these concepts used repeatedly in measuring each type of risk, individually and in portfolios.

Probability is, quite simply, "likelihood." The two words in fact are used interchangeably. In a risk context, we think of it as the likelihood of loss or of an event that may result in a loss. A good example of this is default. In credit-risk examples, we frequently discuss the probability of default and what it would portend for different assets and at different points in time during the life of a loan.

Probability is generally obtained by examining the number of events over a period of time. The key issues with probability modeling are the ability to obtain sufficient data to observe enough events to form a predictive view of event drivers; and understanding how the probability may vary over time. That begets a concept we often discuss, particularly in credit-risk circles, called "through-the-cycle modeling." The simple issues are: How do we identify how the probability of a loss event varies through an economic cycle; and where, at any point in time, might we be relative to that economic cycle.

These issues are core requirements in Basel II and have garnered a lot of discussion about approaches to modeling and applications in day-to-day decision making.

Exposure defines literally how much money the institution may lose at a point in time of a loss event. When considering exposure, the key is to consider future value. Consider the example of a loan. When granting a loan, for example, it is fairly easy for an institution to work out how much exposure it has at a point in time: it is the amount of principal and interest not repaid. We like to include both principal and interest in this calculation to take into account the ramifications of lost cash flow on interest payment. We saw how important it is to preserve that in the previous section when we discussed risk in the calculation of making $100 million in loans.

However, if we consider that a loan could default at any time in the next year, we may need to model the likely principal and interest payments that could be incurred as well as any draw down on credit lines. To be safe, we often use current exposure plus any draw down on lines. The most conservative position could include the full value of a credit line, plus the current outstanding principal and interest.

Similar examples can be identified for each type of risk. For example, traded instruments, exposed to market risk, are similar, albeit a bit more complex than loans, and must include the full value of options and other structured arrangements that may increase exposure as part of a market event.

This brings us to *severity*. Severity is basically what it sounds like. It is the amount, usually expressed as a percentage of total exposure that could be lost as the result of a risk event. It includes reasonable efforts toward any recovery. So, the modeling exercise associated with severity focuses on those drivers of recovery. These may be the risk of a borrower, the underlying collateral on a trade or loan, any insurance—even the efficiency of a recovery unit in collecting on certain types of loans or other transactions. Basically, it is whatever loss mitigation may be in place and on which the financial institution can rely.

Severity modeling has two main issues.

The first is the ability to extract reliable information on loss and recovery across a sufficient number of situations. Many types of losses are very infrequent. Even in financial portfolios, certain transactions may be unique or few in number and so are not well represented in the loss history. Also, the specifics of the recovery exercise may be drawn out over a long period and therefore not well captured. The true amount of recovery, the cost involved, and the time involved are often difficult to pin down.

The second issue with severity is the variance associated with it, particularly over time. Basically, it is the uncertainty associated with the recovery itself and how this may vary, particularly during a downturn. A housing market downturn is a great example. Under normal circumstances, recovery on mortgages may be relatively simple to estimate and could exhibit strong characteristics tied to the underlying equity in the home and the amount of total equity in the transaction—the loan to value, or LTV. However, during a housing downturn, home values may drop precipitously, and this may vary wildly across the market. Borrowers may even find themselves in a situation of "negative equity"—when the value of the home is less than the outstanding balance on the loan. That makes collections and recovery more complex, more costly, and less fruitful.

These concepts will replay in each risk class in varying ways and have become central issues in regulation of risk modeling.

Hand-in-hand with these definitions is the concept of the "probability distribution." This describes how probability, exposure, and severity come together to generate a range of outcomes.

PROBABILITY DISTRIBUTIONS

We frequently use probability distributions to understand how losses will behave over an extended period of time and in groups as portfolios. It generally takes multiple years of data to accumulate enough loss history to determine what the probability distribution looks like. We need long data histories supported with high quality data. Probability distributions are a key tool for risk analysts because they reveal enormous amounts of

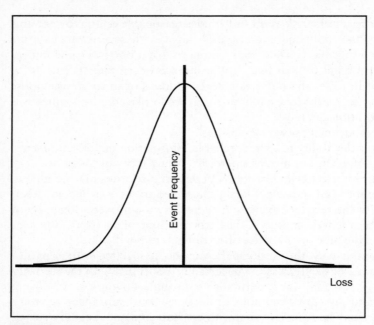

FIGURE 4.1 Normal Distribution

information about the nature of a portfolio and its risks. Probability distributions generally describe the range of probabilities over which different levels of loss are likely to occur. So we graph a probability distribution as probability on the y-axis and loss on the x-axis.

Broadly speaking, probability distributions come in two types: normal distributions and skewed distributions. The *normal distribution* (see Figure 4.1) is also known as the Gaussian distribution or bell curve. It is the most commonly understood distribution in general but is the one least applied to risk measurement. It is, however, most commonly used to describe traded market risk—changes in the underlying factors such as interest rates, exchange rates, and equity and commodity prices.

In *skewed distributions* one tail of the curve is considerably longer or drawn out than the other tail. They include a number of specific types of distributions, including the log normal distribution, gamma, Weibull, and beta (see Figure 4.2). These types of distributions often are used for many risk-modeling activities. This is important because in the modeling of losses, the mean and standard deviation are just the beginning; many modeling issues require understanding the nature of the distribution and its tail.

Skewed distributions have two notable qualities: their skew and a concept called Kurtosis, or "fat tails." Skew is basically the measure of

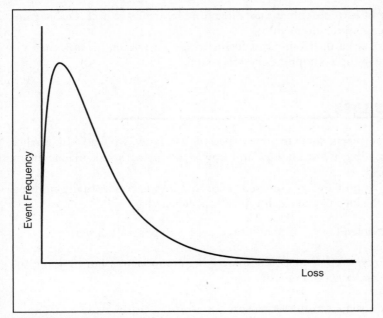

FIGURE 4.2 Beta Distribution

asymmetry of the probability distribution. The degree of skew can be positive (long tail to the right) or negative (long tail to the left) or even undefined. When referring to risk measurement, losses may be depicted as either positive (amount of loss) or negative (amount of negative profit). That quite simply means the distribution can be shown with the long tail pointing left or right. It typically doesn't matter which, as it's virtually always loss that is being described.

If distributions are built from real data, the specific skew often is undefined. The details are largely unimportant, other than to a modeler. What is important is to get used to looking at these sorts of distributions, particularly noting how long or short the tail appears. The more skewed—the longer the tail—the greater the likelihood of a catastrophic-loss event. That is, more of the distribution is extended out to the tail. Therefore, more capital generally is required to support the potential of loss or unexpected loss.

Kurtosis is another concept which broadly describes the degree of the distribution's "peak" and consequently the degree to which the tails of are fatter or thinner than typical. For most risk situations, we experience what is called "leptokurtotic distributions." These distributions are more peaked than typical and their tails are fatter. Basically, it means there's a higher probability of extreme values than one normally would expect. Once again, this raises capital requirements.

So if we see a distribution of losses with a very long, fat tail, then we know we're in for a whopping capital charge.

EXPECTED LOSS

We've already spent some time on expected loss. Now, we'll go a bit further in understanding its mechanics and how it fits in with risk management techniques.

As we've previously discussed, expected loss is conceptually nothing more than the mean loss rate. It typically is depicted as:

$$\text{Expected Loss} = \text{Probability of Loss} \times \text{Exposure} \times \text{Severity}$$

We've reviewed some of the underlying components, but in doing so, new questions have been raised:

- Is there variance around exposure?
- Is there variance around severity?
- What happens over time as a result of the economic cycle?

The upshot of these questions is that expected loss often becomes a more complex equation. Probability, exposure, and severity all can vary. So expected loss (EL) is more accurately expressed as a term:

$$\text{Expected Loss} = \text{Probability of Loss} \times \text{Mean Exposure} \times \text{Mean Severity}$$

From a practical perspective, most financial institutions develop more complex models to manage the outcomes of these variances and to project expected loss as the result of cyclic expectations. The outcome of this modeling is what is more frequently applied to provisions.

The most complex modeling of expected loss typically occurs with credit-portfolio issues, although the same thinking applies to many types of risk and across many industry sectors. More recently, these have been amended for their use in provisioning, to avoid earnings management. There is a fine line between conservative provisioning and earnings management, with several cases coming to public attention.

The implementation of International Financial Reporting Standards (IFRS) has further amended the use of more aggressive provisioning approaches. Under IFRS, statistical provisioning has been reduced or

EXAMPLE

SunTrust Bank in the United States was notoriously accused of earnings management as the result of similar practices. The bank was holding increased reserves against future losses as a conservative position. However, the Securities and Exchange Commission (SEC) saw it as a borderline case of "earnings management," meaning, the bank was subduing the recognition of profits and understating their return. The SEC forced the bank to restate years of financial statements. As a result, a number of other banks followed suit.

As one might imagine, this raised a cry within risk management circles as a counter-intuitive signal to financial institutions about their ability to manage their financial positions prudently and conservatively. This was particularly vexing to risk managers since, in response to recent downturns, the Federal Reserve and its sister agencies at the time were encouraging this very behavior.

Note: SunTrust was accused of earnings management in the fall of 1998. The issue was settled in 1999.

eliminated in some countries to restrict through-the-cycle estimation of expected loss for provisioning purposes. Provisions still can be modeled through expected-loss methods in most locales, but they are restricted to point-in-time estimates of expected loss—those over the stated accounting period. All of this may change as the result of Basel III (see Chapter 9), but the specific form will likely play out across individual jurisdictions for at least a little while.

The Spanish method for loan loss provisioning has attracted much attention over recent years, in part because of its seeming defiance of this approach and in part because of its application to reducing a modeling concept called "pro-cyclicality."

Pro-cyclicality is much talked about because of its effect on troubled institutions and financial systems during bad times. The general idea is that provisions and capital rise in line with increased distress of the financial system and, in turn, are likely to further exaggerate or exacerbate an economic downturn. Here's how it works: Financial institutions require more and more provisions and capital as the economy moves into a downturn—their individual transactions appear riskier as markets become more volatile and borrowers become less reliable. As a result, they increasingly limit lending and other risk-taking business.

In turn, the banks are perceived as increasingly risky themselves, further amplifying downturn effects. Some experts even postulate that requirements for provisions and capital can generate an economic downturn, contending that financial institutions are forced to seek increasingly new and risky means of generating enhanced profits. This drives increased riskiness within the system and increases systemic concentrations in risky activities, which further amplifies the downturn's effects when it occurs. There is merit in all of these arguments. Nevertheless, it is likely that more help than harm can come of using provisions and capital.

The Spanish method minimizes pro-cyclicality by allowing financial institutions to set aside more provisions in good times and release them in bad times to support specific defaults and risk events. This idea may be a bit over-exaggerated in the press, but the idea is sound. More specifically, the method works on the basis that Spanish banks are allowed to set aside general provisions to be held during good times. The collective provision is established based either on a bank's internal models or a model provided by the Spanish central bank.

The model was developed by accessing losses over roughly 15 years. Its design is more backward-looking than forward but tries to leverage off past loss experience to establish a basis for the degree to which loans can go bad during a strong downturn. Once a loan does go bad, provisions are moved from collective to specific provisions to support the specific event. The nature of the approach allows a level of transparency for how specific assets are treated and characterized and is supported through clearly documented historical basis. It also avoids the slippery slope of "earnings management."

This and similar methods have been keenly studied recently in exploring new approaches to establishing a sounder, safer basis for financial-system management. Along with credit risk, provisioning for other risks also has been considered and is starting to take hold in different locales. The approaches and issues are largely the same, however.

UNEXPECTED LOSS AND VALUE AT RISK

Our real measures of risk are unexpected loss (UL), which we've discussed, and its cousin, value at risk (VAR). They try to establish a parameter around the degree of uncertainty in loss estimates. They also are the basis by which we establish measures of capital. Although it seems simple, the complexity in measuring UL lies with three broad issues:

1. The degree of variance that can occur naturally within the specific components required for modeling and how those play out across any given instrument

2. Identifying the correlations and relationships between each of the underlying risk factors
3. The ability to utilize past experience to infer future behavior

Recalling our discussion of expected loss, unexpected loss is similarly modeled as a function of probability of loss, exposure, and severity. Each of these factors varies over time, in relation to each other and in relation to other market factors. Now, imagine piecing each of those factors together with their variances, the drivers of their variances, and doing so across the myriad of instruments that might be present in any given financial institution. Now make that predictive, rather than fully backward looking. There lies the conundrum.

As a starting point, it's useful to know that there are a few methods available to measure expected loss and VAR. Many institutions these days choose one of several options for vended models. We'll discuss the key forms of these under each of the specific types of risk. More broadly, there are two classes of modeling: "closed-form" and "simulation." Most of the models that can be purchased are engines that generate a simulation solution (called simulation engines) and are not closed form.

The closed-form solution refers to one solved by a single equation or set of equations and does not involve generating a loss distribution. Instead, it assumes a loss distribution. The closed-form solution does not always generate the most accurate representation of a financial institution's portfolio and may be accused of oversimplifying assumptions. Nevertheless, it can be a great solution for smaller institutions or portfolios. It also can address specific issues in the applications of risk and capital measurement, including further allocation of capital.

The alternative is to use a simulation engine. The simulation engine—through several possible methods, depending on the type of risk being modeled—generates a loss curve. The loss curve attempts to simulate the institution's specific portfolio. Once the loss curve is generated, the mean and standard deviation can be determined, along with other attributes of the curve. Thus, the standard deviation, UL, or VAR can be identified. We'll discuss these types of methods a bit later when we address each risk class.

The greatest issue with simulation engines is their "black box" effect. It is quite easy to lose track of how the engine was set up or to try to incorporate too much within a single model and lose track of how it actually works. This often can result in key man risk (only one person knows how it all really runs), increased staff and expense to maintain the model (an army of Ph.D.s required to manage the inputs, outputs, and reporting), problems with trouble shooting, interpretation, and general maintenance. Transparency is key, and it must be made transparent not only to modeling professionals but to senior executives and the board to ensure their confidence in the information and their ability to support decision-making and disclosures.

In one instance, I worked with an institution whose capital position literally doubled overnight due to a modeling problem. It took days to work through the cause: The model was complex; documentation was slim and not detailed enough to glean many fine points of the assumptions used; and few individuals who had knowledge of the system's original setup were still around.

Ultimately, it was found that the underlying cause was due to rounding—some of the setup parameters had been constructed in a way that limited the decimal points allowed. This seemed benign when the institution was smaller, but as the portfolio grew, its attributes approached their limit. Overnight one of the setup parameters ticked over its rounding threshold, causing the output to move from 1—where it had been for years—to 2, having the effect of doubling the capital position on that sector of the portfolio. The fine points of this are tough to explain, short of an academic white paper, but the idea is clear enough.

There was no process for reviewing and challenging assumptions. Worse, the inheritors of the model were running it with little or no understanding of what was inside and how it worked. It had been reduced to a black box.

Unfortunately, this is an extremely common problem that I've seen repeatedly in even the best of companies. In this case, without any reasonable level of documentation, it became very difficult to unlock the black box to create transparency. The company had to conduct a comprehensive review of the model, its workings, assumptions, and their impacts. After documenting the findings, the company put in place a process of yearly review. This served two purposes. Firstly, it ensured that the model was checked and working as intended and that it was adapted to address new positions and new economic developments. Secondly, it ensured that those individuals responsible for the running of the model actually understood it.

ECONOMIC CAPITAL

Translating from unexpected loss to capital is the next hurdle. There are two common approaches: the *confidence interval* approach and the *capital multiple* approach. In general, the confidence interval approach is far superior, but the capital multiple is a great way to get a quick and dirty number. Each approach leverages off the same general concept: that capital is a function of the institution's unexpected loss and its target debt rating.

TABLE 4.1 Typical One Year Financial Institution Probability of Default Estimates/Solvency Standards Per Credit Rating

S&P Rating	One-Year Default Probability/Solvency Standard (bp)
AAA	1
AA	3
A	7
BBB	10
BB	100
CCC	1100
Default	10000

The *target debt rating* is the projection of safety and soundness the board wants to establish in the market—its ability to support its external obligations. We discussed this concept earlier and how debt rating may play out in the context of extreme loss. The concept hinges on a *target* as it may not be the debt rating currently assigned by rating agencies. In the case of a diminished credit rating or a sovereign limit on the debt rating, it may be higher than the debt rating assigned to the institution.

Both approaches are based on the concept that an institution's public debt is rated in line with its likelihood of institutional default. The market measures this likelihood through analysis of historical financial institution defaults at each credit rating, and then adjusts for a one-year time horizon. Although the specific default likelihood can theoretically move around over time, and in practice is quite difficult to observe, the approach has become so commonly adopted that there is some convergence in the typical default probabilities assigned (see Table 4.1). In fact, even Basel II refers to a 99.9% confidence interval as the regulatory target, likened to roughly a BBB/BBB+ credit rating. Most institutions adopt a standard table of default probabilities and stick with it to avoid any confusion.

In the *confidence interval method*, the implied institutional default probability literally becomes the confidence interval applied to the loss distribution. It defines the amount of total capital and reserve an institution must hold to absorb losses up to the point of the confidence interval that is required to support the target debt rating (see Figure 4.3). So, in the case of an AA institution, a 3bp confidence interval would assume a .03% institutional default rate—in other words that 99.97% of the institution's risks would be covered by its financial resources. This is sometimes referred to as the "maximum probable loss" or MPL.

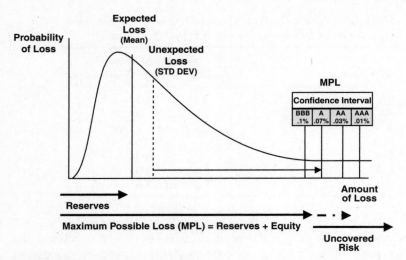

FIGURE 4.3   Estimating Economic Capital Using the Confidence Interval Method

So, an AAA institution would hold considerably more capital, roughly twice more, than an AA institution; an AA institution would hold more capital than an A institution, and so on.

With the capital multiplier approach, the idea is the same. It is simply the MPL—the distance on the institutional-loss curve between the unexpected loss (standard deviation of the loss curve) and the confidence interval—expressed as multiples of UL (see Figure 4.4). This method is a bit old fashioned and less often used these days, mainly because it suffers from notable inaccuracies. The loss curve can shift in shape and specific form, and the capital multiplier method cannot easily accommodate those changes. In fact, it can sometimes dramatically underestimate required capital, especially on riskier portfolios.

Once the total capital, or MPL, is obtained, economic capital—or equity required—is determined by adjusting MLP by EL, or provisions.

$$MPL - EL = \text{Economic Capital (Equity)}$$

For most institutions, a single loss curve does not exist as such. Most measure loss curves across each of their core portfolios or across each distinct risk class. It is not uncommon to see separate loss curves and capital estimates for three, four, or five types of risk. In this situation, there are several methods for consolidating risks and capital.

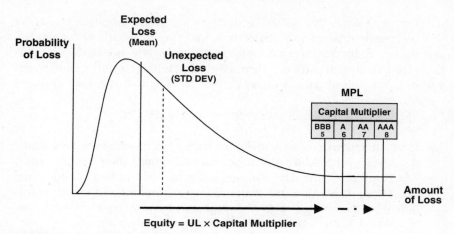

FIGURE 4.4   Capital Multiplier Method

First, it is important to point out that capital, as an expression of volatility, is additive. But UL and VAR are not easily added. So, once capital is obtained for each class of risk, it is simple enough to just add them up. For the vast majority of institutions, this is the preferred approach. It is clear and transparent and recognizes that in a severe downturn or stress event, the behavior of even seemingly unrelated risks tend to become closely correlated in their behavior.

More and more financial institutions, however, are examining other approaches for aggregating economic capital. Many use simple estimates of correlations between risks, simulation approaches, and copula methods. Although these tend to be notionally supported by logical observation, all are extremely challenging to justify and manage. Simulation and copula particularly suffer from black-box syndrome. In addition, they are often highly reliant on correlation assumptions which are rarely more than assertion. For board and senior management, they may be a tempting method to reduce implied capital requirements, but any foray into these methods should be carefully managed and well understood for their limitations.

THE ROLE OF DATA AND ASSUMPTIONS

I've mentioned the importance of data several times, but it's worth revisiting the topic in the context of developing and managing models. The bottom line is that risk measures and models are fundamentally dependent on historical data. We use this data to ascertain long-run trends as well as specific relationships, behaviors, and specific details of the models themselves. Risk measures and models are only as good as the assumptions and data that support them. Yet developing sound assumptions and obtaining good data is always at the forefront of risk-measurement issues.

There are a few rules of thumb for managing this:

- **Start somewhere—don't make excuses.** Many organizations make the mistake of holding off on risk measures until their data is better. The irony of this is that without some sort of burning platform for addressing data issues, the issues are never resolved and the organization never has enough or good enough data to move forward. It's better to start with whatever is available, recognize its limitations, and support its improvement while measures are being developed. Once the broader organization sees how serious the intent to develop measurement capabilities is, the group often will fall in line to support the effort. In fact, once the measures are applied to the organization as risk-adjusted performance metrics, the organization likely will demand improvements.

- **Establish clear assumptions and documentation.** This point is extremely important. Very often, few individuals—including those conducting the modeling themselves—understand the core assumptions being applied within a model, let alone specific details of decisions involving important concepts like aggregation and rounding of numbers. Models can hang around in an organization for five to ten years or more, and in that time, it only takes one change of personnel to lose track of what is in a model. This can lead to dire consequences, such as the previously discussed rounding error that falsely doubled my client's capital overnight.

- **Get involved and understand the assumptions.** Boards and senior management often believe they shouldn't get involved with modeling issues. But they should be aware of many key assumptions that would dramatically change if they could influence them directly. Models often have numerous limitations that might alter decisions at the top of the house. A portfolio issue that seems minor to a modeler may be of deep strategic importance.

- **Get as much as you can however you can.** You can never be too young, too wealthy, or have too much data. If possible, utilize and set up capabilities and storage to capture as much data as you can at its granular level. For many organizations, this may mean starting out by going back to paper files to reconstruct data history or missing fields. As painful as this may seem, it is usually worth it, particularly if there is a regulatory burden hanging over your head.

I've worked with a number of institutions that found themselves in dire need of better data history, particularly when preparing for Basel II. Some threw up their hands, some tried to purchase it from outside, some tried to cleanse the data they had. Several had teams of data-entry clerks keying in data from paper files. Their success was mixed.

One such organization quite successfully used retirees familiar with the files to enter data. The firm was rightly reluctant to use standard data-entry clerks who were unfamiliar with complex credit files and would have introduced as many errors as they were trying to fix. Instead, the company engaged teams of ex-bankers, gentlemen who had been familiar with credit files as a core part of their jobs in the past. They were ultimately dubbed distinguished older gentlemen (D.O.G.s). This practice increased both efficiency and quality because *these* data-entry clerks understood the details.

MANAGING ACROSS THE ECONOMIC CYCLE

Hand-in-hand with obtaining data is the issue of estimation across the economic cycle. This has become a hot topic in recent years as regulations expect "through-the-cycle" estimates of risk, stressed estimates meant to emulate severe economic downturns, and, of course, for organizations to apply lessons from our most recent large economic downturn.

Estimating risk in downturns and across an economic cycle presents three challenging issues:

1. **Data.** It's difficult to obtain sufficient history in general, let alone across an entire economic cycle. A further complication is that the portfolio mix likely will have shifted across time; even the nature of instruments and their usage are likely to have changed. That fundamentally changes the risk profile.
2. **Point-in-time.** It is very difficult to identify where we might be in the current economic cycle at any given point-in-time. Unless there has been a very recent crash and it's clear that the economy is in recovery, it's almost impossible to sort out.
3. **When it applies.** Although the broad concept may seem sensible, it is not always completely obvious when it's sensible to apply an economic cycle or stressed estimates and when it's not. Regulations have provided some clarity for measuring regulatory capital. But for day-to-day use and even for provisioning, there is little guidance. Provisioning is a

good example. We've already discussed earnings management. For some years, the trend in best practices was to develop expected-loss models to extend beyond the basic calculation to consider historical trends and how these relate to future economic expectations. This helps predict future trends and relationships between variables and then to adjust expected loss for use in collective provisioning. The Spanish method is exemplary of this approach, but many went much farther. Changes to accounting standards and backlash around earnings management has complicated the issue and created—at least in some jurisdictions—confusion about what precisely is allowed.

Another area where this can be a problem is in application to pricing models. Which expected loss and capital estimate do we use? One that is based on current, point-in-time estimates or one that is based on long-run estimates? The simple answer is that it may depend on the specific instrument itself. Instruments that have long lives and expect to be held through their maturity—such as a portfolio of 30-year mortgages, may benefit from long-run estimates. Most instruments, however, have fairly short lives on book (even most mortgage products have on-book lives of less than six years) and likely may be uncompetitive when priced using higher loss estimates.

All in all, this creates a burden for analytics teams to manage multiple sets of loss estimates for the same products.

There are a number of ways that through-the-cycle estimates and stressed estimates may be determined. Of course, the best are rooted in actual data that occurs over the course of the cycle, barring the complications we've mentioned. Realistically, there are few methods that have any great level of accuracy, although, some may be better justified than others. Normally, the current portfolio point-in-time estimates are simply adjusted upward or downward against an estimate of where we are in the current economic cycle. So, if we believe we are at a peak in the cycle—or at least a strong economic period—then loss estimates are adjusted upward to reflect an average against bottom-of- the-cycle estimates, during which there would be high loss rates. Some cycle average usually is sought. Similarly "stressed" estimates may be applied, particularly for regulatory purposes, by estimating the loss profile at the bottom of the cycle and adjusting current estimates to reflect those relative factors.

All in all, this should not to be confused with stress testing. Through-the-cycle estimates and cyclically-stressed estimates are designed for day-to-day use. This is unlike stress testing, which attempts to emulate more severe events as well as determine the thresholds at which a financial institution may fail.

STRESS TESTING

Stress testing is what it sounds like, but there are no fixed methods of doing it. There are, however, some methods that are better than others and some that should be considered together. There are generally three types of methods:

1. **Factor.** This involves moving a single or several risk factors to determine their effect on risk: expected loss, unexpected loss/VAR. Factors should be stressed at multiple levels and in multiple ways—yield curve movements, not only up and down but inversions and twists.
2. **Economic/scenario.** This tries to simulate the effects of specific market or broader economic scenarios. They could be as broad as "What happens if China collapses?" or as narrow as "What happens if there is a sudden drop in the Argentine currency?"
3. **Reverse stress testing.** This approach attempts to identify the types of movements and level of capital and provisions at which an institution would collapse.

The methods share general similarities: It's all about identifying a factor or group of factors that might affect the value of the portfolio, deciding upon some level to move them, then reporting the results on the key portfolio risk results—expected loss, unexpected loss, and capital.

A few common pitfalls must be managed:

- **Not stressing enough.** Many times, what seems like a significant rate movement is not really so significant on observation. For example, many regulators for years recommended an interest rate movement of about 400 bp for stress testing interest rate risk, while others recommended movement of only 200 bp. In many locales, it turns out that in standard trading and on many instruments, interest rates can fluctuate well beyond that movement even in the course of a year. It's important to find a level that really jars the portfolio—something that would not occur very often (if ever).
- **Correlations.** These often are overlooked. Many of the models establish assumptions about correlations between risks, risk factors, portfolio segments asset classes, and other things. These are developed typically as long-run averages or recent observations. That may be fine for day-to-day use, but under stress, these correlations generally shift. It's common for most factors to become highly correlated in a stress event. So it is important to consider this when evaluating stress testing. For some models, this may present practical problems in how to make those changes; for other models, it may be fairly easy. For less frequent

scenario testing, it is likely that modelers and analysts can retrofit adjustments for correlation at the very least. It's important to try.

■ **What scenarios.** It often is challenging to determine which economic scenarios are useful to an organization and whether they provide sufficient coverage of issues to be tested. A great way to deal with this is to create an organizational event around economic stress testing. Determine from a wide range of stakeholders, including the board, what they are worried about. Typically, this will identify the key weaknesses in the portfolio and which issues could make them most apparent. Exercises such as war-gaming are another method of getting a similar outcome. The other benefit of these sorts of approaches is that they engender buy-in by the broader organization and key stakeholders.

■ **What to do with results.** Results often seem both obvious and at the same time unrealistic. We can all guess that if we stress key risk factors in the portfolio, it will result in increased EL, UL, and capital. Stressing at higher and higher levels inevitably reveals that more and more capital is required. Boards and senior executives too often throw up their hands and say, "We're not holding that much capital, so what's the point?" The point is to find conditions where the institution would fail and signs that may lead to such a failure.

As the scenarios play out, watch the shape of the loss curve. Are there signals within the changes to that shape that can help forecast events better? We often can identify increased movements in EL, which of course ties to provisions, leptokurtosis, skew, and "heteroskedasticity," a condition in which mini-distributions appear within the larger distribution, creating bumps in the tails where events become more likely and more severe. It's as much these "tells" as anything that define the value of stress testing.

VALIDATION OF MODELS

The basic concepts of model validation have been around for as long as models have. However, they are under scrutiny now because regulations have taken on the use of models. The basic idea is pretty simple: Verify that the model in fact predicted what it said it would—how close to reality did we get? There are a few key basics to consider when embarking upon validating models:

■ **Validation is an iterative process.** It isn't done once, then ignored. Validation has to occur regularly, for most models, at least once a year. If market conditions are moving, it may be useful to do so more often.

■ **There is no single method.** Validation requires the use of multiple tests and metrics because models aren't one dimensional. They must describe various aspects of how instruments and events will behave. For example, we're concerned not only about a model simply predicting the correct amount of loss; we also want it to predict the right amount of volatility, the order of riskiness of events or transactions, and more.

■ **Quantitative and qualitative.** Validation should encompass both quantitative and qualitative elements. It must assure the quality of data and the underlying processes for generating inputs to models—the correctness of the coding (it's easy to make mistakes, even typos, when building a big model) and the quantitative natures of the models themselves.

■ **Review of the process.** Validation processes and outcomes should have independent review. They must be included as part of audits and should be periodically reviewed by third-party experts.

■ **Management's role.** The board and senior management must be involved. They need a fundamental understanding of the models and their conditions. This is necessary not only to ensure compliance with regulations but also to understand the weaknesses in their institution's capabilities and the information on which they make decisions.

Validation usually encompasses several components or steps. The validation policies and processes the organization establishes should be built around these core components and made clear and transparent, along with the expectations for each step. Validation is no longer a back room exercise conducted by the modelers and analysts who built and administer the models. New regulations have put validation in the spotlight (see Figure 4.5).

The components include:

■ **Data.** Beyond the information itself, this comprises data specification, storage, and controls in each step of the process—including data used to build models, inputs to models, and the data required to validate the models. Data must be well defined and documented. Clear descriptions of techniques are required for sampling, cleansing, interpolation, and/ or extrapolation. Even data storage and the data architecture must be clearly described and reviewed.

■ **Build of models.** This includes *estimation*—initial identification of the model's form and key coefficients—and *calibration*—the adjustments made to those coefficients to meet observed outcomes. Calibration may be done as part of the initial build of a model, but may also be conducted periodically over the life of a model. Basically, it's like doing a tune up on a car: set the timing, then adjust it at tune-ups. Usually,

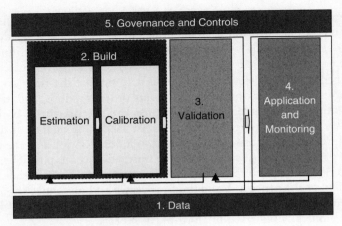

FIGURE 4.5   Model Validation Framework

Re-calibration is a component of a technical validation process. Models are tweaked as a result of their relative accuracy to adjust for current conditions.

As part of the review of estimation and calibration, the overall integrity of the modeling process is reviewed. Detailed documentation must be done. Models are reviewed for relative conservatism and for their adjustments to "through-the-cycle" requirements or stressed/down-turn requirements.

- **Statistical validation.** These are the technical parts. Models are tested for their ability to predict future behavior through comparisons to actual, or benchmark, data. They are tested for discriminatory power, that is the ability to discriminate one risk from another and the relative order of those risks (highest to lowest), accuracy, and stability (yes, models definitely drift over time).

- **Application and monitoring.** This part of the validation process assures that processes and controls are in place around the use of models and the monitoring of models in use. It seeks to ensure that ownership, responsibilities, and authorities are in place and that there is sufficient independence between those that are building models, using models, and validating models. It also seeks to ensure that models are monitored routinely for calibration and rebuilding.

- **Governance and controls.** This component ensures there is rigor and appropriateness of people, processes, and systems and that approvals are in place for each step in the process. It seeks to ensure that there are enough of the right resources targeted at the right activities, that policies are being followed, and that there is appropriate documentation, education, and training.

MODELING CREDIT RISK

Much of our discussion about the modeling of EL and UL holds true for credit risk. There are, however, a few twists and definitions particular to this class of risk.

Credit-risk portfolios generally are modeled off of the same concepts of EL and UL. However, at least half of the model processes—if not more—is tied up in the underlying, support models. Those define the probability, exposure, and severity. In credit risk terms, these concepts are referred to as:

- **Probability of default (PD).** PD is the probability of an asset defaulting over a defined time horizon, usually one year.
- **Exposure at default (EAD).** This term is exactly the same as previously described. It is the exposure to loss (foregone principal and interest) at the time of default, and it may be augmented by the existence of credit lines. It is important to check the definition being applied as some institutions do not include foregone interest payments in the exposure amount. Most regulations include *both* principal and interest, but there are sufficient gray zones in this to warrant being careful about definitions.
- **Loss given default (LGD).** This is the percent of loss against the expected exposure (or 1 − recovery). It includes all costs of recovery and the time spent on it. That is the net present value (NPV) of all recovery less all costs.

$$LGD = 1 - NPV\,[\text{Recovery Amount} - \text{All Costs to Recover}]$$

As discussed, these components are multiplied to yield EL or modeled more discretely to understand variances and to address linkages to economic factors, such as home-price index.

Two common methods are used to generate UL. The first is a closed-form equation. It is useful to get a feel of this if for no other purpose than to understand the kinds of relationships between variables and the assumptions that may be applied to the consideration of UL.

The closed form equation typically starts with a few key assumptions:

- **That at the end of the one-year time horizon, any given transaction is either in default or not in default.** (This seems obvious but is mathematically important for derivation purposes).

■ **That there is no variance in the exposure at default.** In reality there may be some, as the time of default may not be specifically known or if there is variance in the draw-down on limits. But if we assume conservatively on these points, we can safely simplify.

■ **That there is no variance in severity.** Also a leap, as recovery values tend to vary dramatically, even within closely defined groupings.

■ **That there is no correlation between probability, severity, and exposure.** (Also not strictly true but useful for simplification purposes.)

Then, we can derive the function:

$$UL = \sqrt{(PD - PD^2)} \times EAD \times LGD$$

If we take more conservative assumptions, then we can expand the equation as follows:

$$UL = \sqrt{((PD - PD^2)\, LGD^2\, EAD^2 + PD \times (\sigma_{EAD}^2 LGD^2 + \sigma_{LGD}^2 EAD^2 + \sigma_{EAD}^2 \sigma_{LGD}^2))}$$

It is common to use a form that assumes no variance around EAD but retains variance in LGD to yield:

$$UL = \sqrt{((PD - PD^2)LGD^2\, EAD^2 + PD \times (\sigma_{LGD}^2\, EAD^2))}$$

Where σ denotes standard deviation. Using this approach, once the UL is obtained, it can be multiplied by the capital multiplier (CM) for credit risk that is applicable to the bank's credit rating in order to yield a capital estimate (see Figure 4.5).

$$Capital_{\text{Target Debt Rating}} = UL \times CM_{\text{Credit Risk@Target Debt Rating}}$$

If the capital multiplier method is chosen, it is important to recognize that each risk class and each target debt rating will require its own multiplier. This is because each risk class has a different loss distribution curve and, therefore, will have a different multiple (a different distance) between the standard deviation and the confidence interval implied by the target debt rating (see Figure 4.4).

Alternatively, the EL and UL can be applied either to a loss distribution assumption—generally a beta, gamma, or log normal distribution because they represent general distributions that more closely mimic the way credit losses frequently are exhibited and how recovery patterns tend to look. With this approach, the confidence interval can be used to directly ascertain the required capital. This method is by far preferred over the capital multiplier because it is computationally simple—it can even be done in Excel— and is far more accurate. If the concept of a capital multiplier is attractive this method can also be utilized to present a capital multiplier for reporting purposes. Many institutions like it, feeling it is transparent and simple, although it's wildly inaccurate and fraught with danger.

UL is most commonly modeled for credit risk by applying a simulation of all of the PDs, EADs, and LGDs along with their individual variances to generate a loss distribution. Once a loss distribution is obtained, the UL can be identified and confidence intervals can be applied to seek capital much in the way that we did previously under the beta-distribution approach. The only difference here is that the distribution—rather than assumed—is discovered based on simulation of the actual underlying portfolio. It is a far more accurate method and is far more supportive of decomposition for smaller portfolios and for stress testing. It is, however, far more computationally intense and generally requires the purchase of a vended model or the development of one from within the organization. Usually it's better to buy one of these than to build, but there are exceptions.

Scorecards and Rating Systems

It's tough to spend too much time discussing probability and severity without making at least a mention of scorecards and rating systems. These are the predominant means by which we identify probability and severity within a portfolio.

For credit risk, we generally start with rating systems that estimate probability of default. There are typically two general types: scores and ratings. There is little difference between these two conceptually, but the terminology is separate. Scoring systems are typically applied to retail portfolios and are built on the concepts of determining "odds." Yes, this is the same type of odds we think of in horse racing: they denote the number of "bads" versus the number of "goods." The term "rating system" more commonly is applied to middle-market and corporate rating systems and generally is constructed on the basis of probability, number of bads versus total number. As you can guess, there is little difference between these two ideas other than their names.

The main difference is that scoring systems tend to be more statistical in nature. They assign specific scores to attributes as they contribute to the propensity of default. They do this based on information such as demographic data and past payment history of a borrower, and they draw from external data—such as that provided from a credit bureau—as well as internal data or data taken at the time of application. Scorecards themselves fall into two categories: application scorecards and behavioral scorecards. The application scorecard utilizes information on the borrower available at the time of—you guessed it—application. The behavioral scorecard utilizes information that is acquired on a borrower typically as the result of the borrower's performance–payment behavior—after being on book for a period of time. That period is generally anywhere between four to six months and thereafter. These are successfully used to determine the PD of any given borrower and to track it and the total portfolio over time.

Scorecards typically are constructed on a scale from about 350 to 850, rating each borrower with a granular score along this spectrum. Higher scores indicate higher credit ratings.

Rating systems have the same function, but may not be as statistical as scorecards. They often include more qualitative information about a company, such as quality of management. Having said this, rating systems can become very statistical in nature by using the specific financials of a company to contribute to the factors used within the rating system. The best rating systems typically take advantage of both qualitative and quantitative information. Although rating systems based purely on either can be very robust, they're harder to use and it's less likely to obtain strong results. Rating systems also can be more varied in their format than scorecards because they often vary from eight ratings, or grades, to as many as 25 grades. Most institutions settle on something around 12 to 15 because this level of differentiation is easier to manage and explain.

With both scorecards and rating systems, individual models are built for each product and sometimes even sub-product or asset class. For example, it's common to see several used for different data, borrower, and facility conditions within a single corporate portfolio. So expect that any given bank or lending institution could have upwards of 20 to 50 different models just for PD estimation in credit—I've seen a few with more than 100. That fact often is the most startling to senior management. Many folks don't realize how many of these models are proliferating nor the burden associated with building, validating, and recalibrating them. Consider that all of these models need to be validated yearly and that most retail models will be recalibrated at least yearly as well. Rating systems tend to require less recalibration but may require recalibration roughly every two or three years.

But don't fall prey to the temptation of eliminating all of these scorecards just to simplify. It seems like a good idea—and sometimes is—but, more often the differences in scorecards allow modelers to distinguish distinct customer behaviors to achieve a greater level of accuracy and predictiveness. So, although simple is usually good, it is important to understand the framework of risks.

Master Scale

The *master scale* is another important element of rating systems. A master scale often is used to align all the varying credit-grading models to a single scale tied directly to PD. So, for example, the retail score of 750 may inherently align to a specific default probability that, in turn, can be mapped to a master scale that describes a credit grade of—let's say—4. All credits in an institution can be aligned in such a way and discussed relative to each other. This is particularly handy when individual assets or portfolios of assets are discussed at the senior executive or board level. Folks at this level only have to understand one main scale and the relative PD associated with each grade. It can also be used to facilitate certain portfolio-modeling operations.

Rating systems also exist for measuring severity or LGD. These are called "facility ratings." They seek to score the characteristics of a facility or product in order to identify those factors that contribute to recovery behavior. In scoring collateral, for example, different collateral types and arrangements may tend to yield better or worse recovery situations. Equally, so do the characteristics of the product or specific facility itself, such as payment terms. Facility scores generally take the form of alphabetic grades from A to G and are constructed to link directly to LGD. Risking order tends to denote higher LGD and may span a range from 5% to 125%. It is important to note that it is possible to lose more than the EAD value of a loan, given time and expenses associated with their recovery.

Unlike the rating systems and scorecards used for PD modeling, facility scores rarely employ the concept of a master scale because most organizations align all assets to the same scale from the outset, although in larger institutions it is certainly possible to employ the same sort of approach.

Facility scores can greatly improve the ability of an organization to classify loans, sort through the myriad of differences in their recovery patterns, more easily assign LGD and track its variances. It can also be a great tool for improving loss mitigation as well.

Credit Portfolio Risk

Measuring and understanding portfolio risk require other considerations. The measurement approaches we've discussed work well if we have a single asset or a group of assets that are nearly identical. But these measures must be more closely considered if we have several very different portfolios. If we want to discover the total risk of a mortgage portfolio and a corporate lending portfolio combined, for instance, we need to understand the concepts of *correlation* and *covariance*.

There are a number of specific modeling techniques for addressing these, but first, let's get a grip on the basics. When portfolios are combined, the correlation between portfolios needs to be considered. If we hark back to high school math or statistics, we remember that squared terms or standard deviations are not simply additive. That means the portfolios must be combined by using the correlations between portfolios as follows:

$$UL_P = \sum \sqrt{\rho_i}\, UL_i$$

Where UL_P is the UL of the combined portfolio, UL_i is the UL of each individual portfolio, and ρ_i is the correlation between portfolio i and the combined portfolio.

The concept of unexpected loss contribution (ULC) is often used and is worth noting. It is defined as:

$$ULC_i = \sqrt{\rho_i}\, UL_i$$

The reason we bother with this at all is that it often provides a handy method of shorthand that often comes into play for adding capital and for allocating capital to businesses, products, or transactions once the consolidated portfolio calculation is achieved.

$$UL_P = \sum ULC_i$$

This is a common approach when the portfolio capital is calculated using a calculation engine that models the entire portfolio. Then it is necessary to use this term to decompose capital to its sources for separate tracking and performance management.

Of course, the devil is in the details, and it's the correlations in this case that cause quite a hubbub in the risk world. There are many, many ways of trying to estimate these, and most are lousy. Unless the institution is fairly large relative to its market and can then estimate correlation directly from its own portfolio experience, it's quite hard to obtain reliable correlation information. If your financial institution falls into this category, then encourage risk teams to conduct this research. If not, be wary of correlations from estimates based on other markets or from equity correlations. There are several approaches based on traded market correlations of equities or bonds. They work passably well for large liquid markets, but rapidly break down in smaller markets—most places outside the U.S. markets and major European markets.

This also goes for the purchase of vended systems for modeling UL. Consider that most of these systems are fairly similar from one to the next, but their key point of differentiation is their approach to generating correlations. So, if your organization is in the mind to make a purchase, pay careful attention to this point above all others. It will be the key defining point of differentiation and the one that may be hardest to live with if you get it wrong.

Different Models for Different Portfolios

Anyone who's spent even minimal time in a bank or financial institution that lends is probably aware that different types of products have very different types of characteristics for many reasons. These may be due to the construction of the product itself (term, payment profile, etc.) or due to the type of borrower and its uses (consumer versus commercial). In a nutshell, this means that each portfolio and sub-portfolio is likely to behave very differently—often so much so that we need to construct the models differently.

Many of the models sold to date have focused on middle market and corporate lending portfolios—usually those that are fairly vanilla on the whole. It's important to recognize this as the organization considers how to model for credit risk. Retail portfolios often require separate loss-distribution modeling because the structure of the portfolio and factors that drive them are sufficiently different from those in a corporate-lending portfolio. Similarly, more structured transactions generally require different types of engines to account for the many moving parts that can affect exposure and recovery value.

Moreover, two types of portfolios specifically require special note: credit risk in the trading portfolio and securitized assets. Both of these portfolios are so uniquely different that they require special focus. In the trading portfolio, most organizations initially focus on market risk, and rightly so because that is far and away the biggest risk. Credit risk, however, can become substantial, so it's important to understand its behavior and provide for its calculation. Generally, the best way to do this is to either build or buy an add-on to the market risk VAR engine. This is because exposures in a trading portfolio can vary greatly over time, and these already are being modeled with the VAR engine. So it's a relatively easier process to address that behavior as part of the same system. Alternatively, some organizations try to pull this form of credit risk into their centralized credit-risk modeling activities, but that's generally an unwieldy approach that either ends up missing critical information entirely or requires an enormous amount of coordination.

Securitized assets often create problems for many banks. Many of these instruments are held in a financial institution as off-balance-sheet items. This causes much of the risk to be ignored. At best, they may be addressed by including their exposure as a single exposure to the headline credit rating on the instrument. But recent years have proven this approach is fraught with danger. Securities of this type generally are constructed by consolidating groups of sub-portfolios that could be built out of many different types of assets—many of which are not of headline-credit grade. To make matters worse, some of these assets include embedded options of varying form that can change the exposure, value, or effective grade (probability of default) overnight. So it is important to understand what lies within each securitized instrument. Modeling securitized assets in this fashion is called *look-through modeling*—so named because we are looking through the shell of the asset and the credit grade it represents into the underlying behavior of the asset.

Once the organization chooses to come to this point, much of the basic concepts are similar to those we discussed previously. Other, more sophisticated ideas—such as the use of copulas—are beyond the scope of this book.

MODELING MARKET RISK

At a high level, modeling market risk is similar to modeling for credit risk. But there are a few notable differences, mainly the types of approaches to modeling market risk.

There are three different types of techniques for modeling VAR. Often, all three methods may be present in the same modeling package and are best applied when all are used as a suite of analyses. Each approach has different strengths and weaknesses, so individually, they come up short. But together, they form a solid modeling platform. Individually, each suffers because it attempts to model future behavior by assuming that risk factor relationships from the past will continue to hold. If those relationships break down— which happens frequently during a crisis—all three methods are likely to break down, at least to some degree. In addition, all three methods require some degree of historical data, and where markets are thin, weak, or discontinuous—when trading may stop, then start or become thin—the information becomes less reliable.

The three methods are *Parametric VAR, Monte Carlo simulation,* and *historical simulation.*

Parametric VAR is known by several other names: linear VAR; variance-covariance VAR; Greek-normal VAR; delta normal VAR; and delta gamma normal VAR. It is the simplest of the three approaches and assumes that the probability distribution is normal. The method quite simply identifies sensitivities of each instrument in the portfolio to a set of risk factors (such as a foreign exchange (FX) exchange rate). Then it applies historical data on the risk factors to identify their standard deviations and correlations between them, and then applies the sensitivities of each instrument to the standard deviations by multiplying them together. This generates a loss distribution for the portfolio, and capital can be derived in the same way as we've discussed (see Figure 4.6).

VAR (single instrument) = Sensitivity of Instrument to Risk Factor Value
× Probability of a Market Change

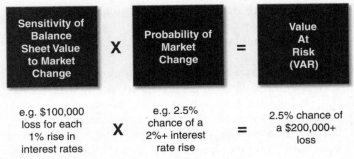

FIGURE 4.6 Calculating Value-At-Risk (VAR)

The beauty of this method is that it's relatively simple and computationally fast. The downside is that it does not adequately address situations where there is a lot of optionality in the portfolio. So it doesn't adequately capture tail events or complex transactions.

Monte Carlo simulation is an approach that uses the same underlying risk factor relationships. But it creates many scenarios by applying randomly created future rates, then applying them to nonlinear pricing models to estimate the change in value for each scenario. Its advantage is that it can test many possible outcomes and can capture the non-linear behavior in options and other more complex instruments. Its main disadvantage is that it can be computationally intense and often takes thousands of calculations to arrive at the outcome for a single instrument. Multiplying that over the entire portfolio can be extremely time-consuming and, depending upon approaches, can devour computer power. It also has the disadvantage of assuming quite often that the risk factors have a normal distribution.

Historical simulation is a method often favored by regulators because it tends to avoid some of the computational pitfalls of the other two methods, although it has issues of its own. This method takes historical market data, calculates the percent change of each of the risk factors on each day, and then applies those changes to the institution's current market portfolio. More specifically, it applies those changes to the non-linear pricing models, like those utilized in the Monte Carlo approach. Historical simulation avoids many of the non-linearity and non-normality issues of the other two methods. But it can still be computationally complex, and it introduces a new problem: it assumes that relationships between risk factors will continue to behave as they have in the past.

This is why some analysts will save historical series and apply different time series to their portfolios to analyze what might happen under differing conditions. Some of these analysts even trade historical series like kids swapping baseball cards. Some systems allow the user to make up scenarios and apply them. So historical simulation engines often are coupled with scenario-generation engines.

It's important to keep in mind a couple of more pieces of information about market risk measurement. First, it's necessary to specify what we call a "holding period." This is what it sounds like: the amount of time an instrument may go untraded in the event of a rapid market disruption. Regulations assume 10 days. But depending on the instrument and the market, it easily could be longer, so it's useful to have an engine that allows the user to change holding period assumptions. VAR calculations initially are done on a one-day basis, so to meet regulatory minimums or to calculate economic capital, we need to translate from one day upwards. The approach to doing this often is referred to as the "square root of time" rule. It's an easy derivation that can be found in any statistical textbook or VAR text. It suggests that adding up the number of standard deviation events to account for any amount of time can be reduced to the square root of time multiplied by the one day standard deviation.

$$VAR_t = \sqrt{t} \times VAR_1$$

So for regulatory capital, we simply multiple the one day VAR (at 99% confidence interval required by regulation) by 10 to adjust for the holding period. Regulations also typically require an additional multiplication of three to five times in order to adjust VAR from 99% to the solvency standard required by the specific regulator. This is much like the capital multiplier approach previously discussed.

For economic capital, a full year is required. A year has 250 trading days in most jurisdictions. So we multiply the institution's VAR at the confidence level dictated by its target credit rating by the square root of 250, which is 15.8. For an A-rated institution, whose multiplier is roughly similar to the regulatory minimum, we would find that the amount of capital implied between regulatory capital and economic capital would be almost 13 times higher.

Difference in capital between regulation and economic capital for an

A-rated institution $= \sqrt{t_{250}} - \sqrt{t_{10}} = 12.7$

There is, no doubt, merit in the arguments that management would intervene before a complete loss of capital and that in a trading book, this could be subverted more rapidly than in other cases and result in potentially lower capital at risk (and a lower capital adjustment). But the conclusion is clear: Significantly more capital is required to adequately account for and support capital needs under an economic-measurement approach than under regulatory requirements.

This can clearly be a significant difference that many institutions choose to ignore. Many tempt fate by relying strictly on regulatory capital when it comes to market-risk calculation for precisely this reason.

Interest-Rate Risk

So far the methods we have discussed pertain mainly to traded market risk. You may recall from our taxonomy of risks that there are also interest-rate risks and liquidity risks included in those items considered under the market-risk approaches. These risks are those used to measure risk within the balance sheet of the portfolio, generated by the mismatch of behaviors between assets and liabilities.

Starting with interest-rate risk, the approaches for measuring it are a special subset of those applied to traded-market risk. It is an important risk class, however, for both banks and insurance firms, as it is typically one of the larger risk classes. This is particularly true in markets or businesses where there are quite a bit of fixed-rate interest rate instruments that create a mismatch between assets and liabilities. That is, the inability to perfectly match or fund assets with liabilities.

Interest-rate risk is also an area where regulators have been slow to define required approaches to economic modeling. There have been attempts by the Fed and a few other regulators acting independently from global regulatory bodies, but there has not been any strong consensus.

There are four types of interest-rate risk that we attempt to measure:

1. **Re-pricing risk.** The risk that assets will have a different maturity characteristic than liabilities and will "re-price" to create a differential in value at some point during their life.
2. **Option risk.** The risk that liabilities and/or assets could have embedded options that causes their value or maturity to change during their life. This is usually due to things like prepayments of loans, withdrawal of deposits, the existence of lines or limits, or other products with indeterminate maturity, such as a credit card.
3. **Basis risk.** This risk crops up when the rate basis varies between assets and liabilities. For example, a loan may base its rate on the London inter-bank offer rate (LIBOR), and a deposit may base its rate on the local treasury rate, so the two rates may change in proportion to each other over time.
4. **Yield curve risk.** The risk that the yield curve itself will change over time, thus changing the expected value of the portfolio.

Three methods can be used to measure interest-rate risk: *Rate shock method*, *Monte Carlo simulation* and *historical simulation*. The latter two are basically the same approaches that we discussed in the section on modeling market risk. The only notable difference worth mentioning is that some of the details of how the engines are constructed are different, so it is generally not desirable to use a traded-market risk engine to value a balance sheet portfolio. That is because assets and liabilities on a balance sheet are structurally different than those in the markets and so must be managed differently in the engines.

The rate shock approach quite simply captures the sensitivity of assets and liabilities to an interest-rate shock. Shocks are generally conducted at various levels, such as at 100 bp, 200 bp, 300 bp. Most institutions assume a parallel shift across the length of the yield curve as a starting position. Some jurisdictions have a regulatory minimum on interest-rate shocks, generally about 200 bp. This corresponds to about an 85% probability rate shift, so it's a very poor approximation to economic capital or even regulatory capital, which generally seeks a 99.9% confidence interval. A more appropriate number for basic safety and soundness is about 400 or 500 bp. In addition, a parallel shift is limited in its effect and should be coupled with simulations of dips and twists in the yield curve. These are all pretty easy to manage analytically.

Regulatory sentiment is rapidly moving to the adoption of VAR engines, much as in traded market risk, so the adoption of these should be expected. It is already the case in some jurisdictions.

Liquidity Risk

Liquidity risk measurement is the close cousin of interest-rate risk measurement. It quite simply attempts to discern the difference in cash flows between assets and liabilities. It's generally managed by the same group that manages interest rate risk and often uses the same calculation engines since, in both cases, differences in exposures across time are being calculated and assessed. The problem is much the same, although liquidity risk is specifically flow-related.

The approach to liquidity measurement attempts to calculate the expected funding requirement across different points in time and under different scenarios, taking into consideration the optionality of products on both sides of the balance sheet and other assets and liabilities. This must include an analysis of loss on sale of assets in order to factor in the reduced value of certain instruments when a crisis occurs. The standard deviation from the mean funding expectation defines the risk in the same way as our other risk metrics previously discussed.

Although this may seem pretty straightforward and rational, relatively few institutions measure liquidity risk on this basis. Most manage liquidity through a series of ratios constructed at different levels of the balance sheet. The simplest is the loan-to-deposit ratio (or an asset/liability ratio in non-banking institutions). This describes the macro funding position of a bank. It is simple and can be used as a rule of thumb for checking the consolidated position of the institution. In general, any position greater than 70% suggests the institution has a reliance on external markets for funding—the higher above 70%, the stronger that reliance. During recent market-liquidity squeezes, virtually all institutions that failed or relied on government bailouts had high loan-to-deposit ratios. The UK-based Northern Rock Bank's was more than 300% when it failed, and most of the UK banking system was more than 150%.

As with interest-rate risk, it is important to identify the behavior of assets and liabilities on the balance sheet to try to model the variance that these behaviors create and the risk to liquidity management that these present. Behavioral life, particularly where optionality exists, is a key component of prudent liquidity risk modeling.

One of the great conundrums with liquidity risk measurement and management is simply convincing senior management that it's important enough to invest in. Many institutions assume that it is simple enough to manage in normal environments and that as long as it is well positioned for those market situations, then it is unlikely that it needs anything further. Although they are largely correct, it's the highly unusual situation that we're managing for—that one-in-a thousand event we're trying to understand and manage our resilience to. This is what has caught many institutions off guard.

In several notable situations, I have sat at asset-liability committee (ALCO) or senior-management meetings where the subject of liquidity risk and the institution's potential investment in liquidity risk has come up. The discussion simply revolved around the binary nature of liquidity risk. That is, when times are good, it's fairly easy for most mature and well-run institutions to manage liquidity without a sophisticated system or capabilities. When things go very bad, the institution can rapidly become insolvent. This situation is relatively rare under most market conditions, however, and in most cases, other institutions in the market would be experiencing the same set of problems. The upshot is that these and many other institutions have come to the view that regulators and central banks would likely provide some form of support and that it is in their shareholders' short term interests to "do nothing." Clearly, this attitude begs questions regarding corporate responsibility, institutions that are "too big to fail," and other concerns. Basel III aims at addressing at least some of this, but the thinking is still prevalent—and worrisome.

Another dimension to this conundrum is whether economic capital is in fact the correct measure for liquidity risk. There are several methods of generating the number, and all relate to measures we've just discussed. But the more important point is whether having capital alone is sufficient or whether it's the quality and specific type of capital that's most important. Therefore, it's important to capture not only the variance but also to consider the organization's ability to convert that need into immediate funding to support its external obligations.

Capital must be high quality *and* fairly liquid in these instances. So the relative liquidity of the sources should be rated to ensure that they are sufficient to support the institution in a crisis. Key to liquidity-risk measurement is calculating the loss on sale of assets to support liquidity requirements in a crisis. This is much like conducting period analysis, which we discussed earlier. In addition, the diversity of the forms of liquidity also should be considered. Dependence on a single form of liquidity easily can be a show-stopper if that particular source dries up—such as when the securitization markets seized and banks that were dependent on selling their packaged assets to support liquidity requirements were unable to meet their obligations.

It is also important that institutions utilize scenario analysis to plan for worst-case liquidity scenarios, such as a bank run or creditor call and to analyze the consolidated liquidity requirement, the loss on sale, and ability to sell assets to support those requirements.

MODELING OPERATIONAL RISK

Modeling operational risk is possibly the trickiest of all risks, as it is so different from firm to firm and so amorphous in its nature. Although it may be the oldest risk class, it is among the newest to be measured. Operation risk has existed in business for millennia and in organized activities since the dawn of man. So there are many aspects well understood and even intuitively managed, but specifics of how to pinpoint operational risk and measure it are incredibly challenging.

For this reason, many measurement methods have been developed. All of them ultimately lead to the generation of a loss distribution and the identification of capital—just as all of the other methods we've discussed. But how we reach that point can be highly varied. It's probably safe to say no two institutions will have exactly the same approach, even now that Basel II is providing some unifying thinking.

Our dear old friend data is one reason. Internal data is difficult to come by and for most institutions had not been captured in an organized way before formal modeling attempts—perhaps not even until it was dictated by regulators. Important loss events are also inherently infrequent, so they don't lend themselves to yielding a nice, tidy distribution. Likewise, external data, although available in several ways, is often difficult to interpret and often not readily applicable to the institution at hand. Most external databases are simply lists of events that have happened to others and what sort of losses they incurred.

Nevertheless, there are expectations of what constitutes a robust operational risk measurement and management capability. This includes *all* of the capabilities as follows:

- **Internal data.** As difficult as it may be to collect it and use it, it's better than nothing and is required by Basel II regulation (five years of internal data must be utilized and categorized across a set of specific factors/supervisory categories). As a result, most organizations that are serious about measuring operational risk have implemented an internal data-collection system and developed processes governing that system and the collection of data within it.
- **External data.** Also required by the Basel Accord, regardless of its relative relevance. Organizations tend to apply it in several key ways. Many attempt to parameterize external events to their institution, sifting through the various events to determine if and how they could occur within their own organization and scaling it to their situation. These can then be directly applied to the loss distribution. Alternatively, external events can be used to inform scenario analysis and/or facilitate sessions with management about potential risks and the ways they could play out within the institution.
- **Scenario analysis.** Also a requirement of regulation, scenario analysis was one of the most commonly used techniques even before the Basel II authorities got involved. It can be applied in several ways. Most organizations generate mathematical scenarios much in the way the VAR engine generates scenarios. In addition, specific scenarios often are identified through a process of work-shopping potential events with key managers throughout the organization and applying these scenarios to the potential loss distribution.
- **Scorecards, key risk indicators, and self-assessment techniques.** These are often referred to as *business environment and internal control factors* (BEICFs), the regulatory catch-all term to describe these techniques. Here again, organizations are likely to use any one or all of these in order to generate a view toward the underlying propensity for a risk event to occur and its relative severity. They are the same concepts we described in credit risk for scorecards and rating systems. They try to identify a series of potential specific risks and assess, or "score," the

organization on the likelihood of their occurrence. Similarly, the severity of the event—or range of severities is determined. Some presence of these sorts of approaches must be evident in the process of measuring operational risk for regulators to accept the use of the internal approach to modeling operational risk in Basel II. We'll discuss these later.

■ **Operational risk VAR modeling.** Here again, there are numerous approaches. Probably the most prevalent is the two-distribution method, often referred to as the *loss distribution approach or LDA*.

For each portfolio, business line or event type, distributions of event frequency and of losses (or severity) are constructed. These two distributions are then combined, using a method known as convolution, to generate a total-loss distribution function. Modelers like this approach, as it allows them to use different types of assumptions for the shape of each distribution. It also allows them to separately analyze the shape of the tails of the distributions and make adjustments for anomalies in the tails, which are common in operational risk. In this way, it takes account of the underlying inaccuracies in establishing discrete losses and their respective frequencies or probabilities.

In addition to the complication of simply generating a number, one of the toughest things about measuring operational risk is *making sure that it is meaningful*. One big problem is that many of the catastrophic-loss aspects of operational risk often sit beyond the 99.9% confidence interval used by many financial institutions (BBB target credit rating and Basel II minimum) and can even sit beyond many other typical target credit ratings (see Figure 4.7).

This means that required capital isn't always large enough to catch anyone's attention until it's too late. Once capital is broken down and doled out

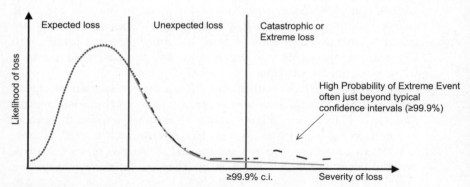

FIGURE 4.7 Operational Risk Loss Distribution

to different business lines to account for, the number can become so small that no one gives it much thought. It can also be very difficult to convince anyone to take action on shifts in measured operational risk when they do occur. The process of generating an operational-risk loss distribution can become so remote and removed from most activities that it is hard to get senior management and the board to take it seriously.

Ultimately, the best methods to create urgency use the underlying scorecards, key indicators, and assessments. Senior management must ensure that these are developed in such a way that they are meaningful enough to be used for making business decisions.

JUMP DIFFUSION AND EXTREME VALUE THEORY

Two special concepts are worth mentioning before leaving this chapter. Both are methods designed to achieve better estimates of the tails of the distribution and to emulate what can happen when things go wrong.

The first is *jump diffusion.* In risk management in recent years, the term almost has become a household item. The concept leverages from an idea mentioned earlier—that there is an expected behavior of risk factors. If we recall, there typically is an assumption that changes in risk factors are distributed normally. Jump diffusion suggests that under crisis, the typical behavior in risk factors can change. The crisis distribution is applied to the estimates of VAR by assuming there is a probability that the normal (non-crisis) distribution is applicable a certain percentage of the time (P) and that the crisis distribution is applicable the rest of the time (1 − P). That way the results can be readily combined.

It allows organizations to attempt to include more extreme events and generate an enhanced estimate of the fat tails of the distribution. Of course, the devil is in the details here, and estimating the crisis distribution can often be difficult.

The other concept is *extreme value theory, or EVT.* EVT attempts to estimate the shape of only the tails of the loss distribution. This is done by assuming a different distribution and applying it to the data in the tail. As with jump diffusion, the specific parameters can be extremely difficult to estimate, particularly since extreme events occur infrequently.

Many models also suffer from a related but almost opposite problem—the underestimation of risk as the result of long periods of good times. This can be true of almost any risk model and becomes particularly problematic the longer the history of good times continues. In some cases, the historical sampling period can become so long that even the analysts lose sight of what periods of hard times may look like, and they begin to believe the good times will never end. This phenomenon can be a major issue, whether data treatments using weighting factors that put more reliance on recent data are used or whether all data is considered equally. The best way to handle it is to ensure that analysts include data series from tougher times gone by or, if those are hard to come by, using scenarios that simulate a more volatile or higher-loss environment. These may be mixed within the data series, or more likely, called out as specific scenarios, albeit less extreme than some we might examine in stress-testing cases.

CHAPTER 5

Managing Trade-Offs Between Risk and Reward

EXECUTIVE SUMMARY

In this chapter we continue our journey toward the upside of the risk equation. We'll discuss managing for reward, and we'll focus on using performance metrics to improve your business—and make more money. We'll consider which metrics will help you and examine the trade-offs between risk and reward. We'll see the very real dangers of focusing on excessive short-term gains and discuss achieving the tricky balance between growth and safety. We'll look at the difference between being smart and being lucky, and we'll examine the fine line between investing and gambling.

THE CEO CHALLENGE

Ultimately, the chief executive officer (CEO) and the board are responsible for managing the balance between the safety and soundness of the institution; its stated business objectives; the interests of regulators, rating agencies, and bond holders; the interest of analysts and other influencers; and the interests of shareholders.

Managing this balance is a complex and difficult task requiring the highest levels of business acumen and leadership skills.

Protecting financial solvency involves identifying and understanding the institution's overall risk appetite and target debt rating, as well as its implications on the firm, its strategies, and general business. It also reflects on the company's funding abilities. So the decisions about risk, risk appetite, capital, quality of capital, and funding are closely intertwined and must be considered together.

To make matters worse, risk and risk appetite often reflect significantly on the ability to grow. So it's not only the quality of earnings that we're concerned about. A firm's sustainability and growth trajectory also are critical. With this point of view, it may now become more obvious why the risk-management team must be a part of strategic decision-making. These concepts work like levers: Pull one, and another moves.

To examine the implications further, let's look at an AAA institution and a BBB institution. AAA is the epitome of safety and soundness. BBB is rated as "junk."

The AAA institution must demonstrate strength of management, consistent, stable earnings, and a strong capital position. Let's consider what that means from a quantitative point of view. Earnings need to be stable and consistent. That means the volatility of earnings must be low, so the company itself has to be low-risk. In measurement terms, that typically would mean expected loss—and particularly unexpected loss—are proportionally low relative to the company's asset base. This is a proportion that must be maintained over time. In addition, the capital base must be proportionally high.

Going back to our measures, an AAA institution must hold roughly 52% more capital than a BBB institution with the same risk profile. Capital also should be "high quality," meaning it would be dependable in a crisis. So the capital should predominately comprise common equity and retained earnings to provide a stable, tangible base. It also should be held as a high proportion of liquid assets so it doesn't generate additional risk of loss upon liquidation. Therefore, it should be held in cash or other high-quality, cash-like instruments.

For this extra margin of safety an AAA institution receives some benefits. Its bond holders don't require higher returns for their risk, and it is allowed to pay a low rate for its funding. That rate often is only a few basis points over government treasury rates.

The BBB institution is a different story. Its earning streams are likely to be more volatile, less certain, particularly over time. So less capital is expected proportional to risk. Because its institutional probability of default is higher, investors demand a higher rate of return. That necessarily makes funding costs higher.

There are some upsides to lower credit ratings and downsides to higher credit ratings. Since higher credit ratings require more capital, they leave more money that is not deployed, making it harder to realize growth rates

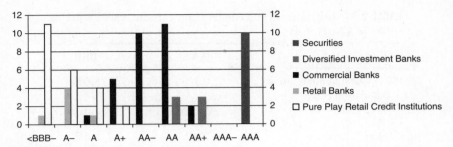

FIGURE 5.1 Financial Sector Credit Ratings

the market may expect. This may further disadvantage specific business lines or mixes of business.

Consider how financial institutions receive funding and make money. Those that are mainly in retail lines tend to receive money directly from consumers, in the form of deposits, as a means of funding. This is often a good way to obtain relatively cheap funding. But it requires a distribution network, thus higher entry costs and a capital investment basis, plus risks associated with individual consumers and a greater reliance on large transaction volumes and diversification within the consumer population in order to manage risk. It does, however, provide avenues for high growth. Required rates of return and growth rates in the market tend to be higher for retail-based businesses. This often drives those businesses to deploy more capital and carry a lower credit rating (see Figure 5.1). It all works because they don't have to seek as much funding from market sources. Conversely, an AAA business must show stability and, therefore capital. It can achieve funding in the market at low cost but can't suffer the volatility that a consumer-based business naturally would incur. So this type of institution often will have greater diversification of earnings sources and likely will get much of its earnings from wholesale types of businesses that trade with other high-quality institutions.

Notice how some of the fundamentals look very similar (see Table 5.1). Sometimes it can be difficult to spot the differences, especially if we're not sure what to look for. It's possible for the AAA and BBB to carry nearly the same levels of capital, despite being fundamentally different businesses with very different risk profiles.

The upshot of all of this is two-fold:

1. The approach to setting the firm's target debt rating and risk appetite is a strategic exercise and must be considered with the weight that it commands.

TABLE 5.1 Risk, Capital, and Funding Comparison: AAA Institution versus BBB Institution

	AAA	BBB
PD (Typical Lending Book Population Avg.)	0.1%	5.0%
EL%	0.05%	2.5%
UL%	0.25%	1.3%
Capital	7.8%	7.8%
Capital Multiple	31.2	6.0
Funding Rate	4.0%	6.8%
Funding Source	Capital Markets	Internal/Direct
Business Mix	More Institutional	More Retail

2. The best way to manage the firm to meet these objectives is to establish a performance framework that targets, tracks, and manages return *relative to* risk.

PERFORMANCE MEASURES—THE BASICS

Financiers generally are fascinated with numbers. So it's not surprising that financial institutions spend lots of time and energy tallying up all kinds of metrics, including risk-adjusted performance measures. That might seem well and good, but in my mind it raises two critical questions: Have they established the right *set* of measures? Are they really measuring risk-adjusted performance in a meaningful way that can help the institution?

Why am I raising these questions about risk-adjusted performance measures? Because when I look at a bank or other financial institution that's failed, I usually find that on some level, it was measuring the wrong set of risks. And I think to myself, "Gee, if they had the right set of risk-adjusted performance measures in place, maybe this collapse could have been avoided."

There are two broad types of risk-adjusted performance measures: return measures and contribution measures. The first provides a percentage measure, and the second, a dollar measure. These may seem like trivial distinctions, but they are important.

Typically, it's the return measures with which institutions feel most comfortable; they're the most intuitive and easiest to get a handle on. Percentage is an easy thing to understand, remember, and compare. The downside of percentages, however, is that they provide no relativity in terms of the contribution a business line or transaction makes.

Two equal-size transactions would compare well with return estimates—but what happens when they are not equal in size? Is it always better to go with the best return, even if the actual size of the return is tiny? Does that kind of strategy provide the appropriate portfolio profile? Will it drive the institution toward limiting its dealings to higher and higher returns, potentially whittling down the desire for larger deals or riskier deals to the point of stunting growth?

I've seen this happen. Business line managers will reduce growth and eschew more complex transactions in favor of those with lower risk and higher return. At the outset, this practice seems like a good thing, but it can send a business line—or the institution itself—into a death spiral.

In many cases, the return measure can be augmented with other measures, such as growth and revenue—simple risk-adjusted profit. For some organizations, it takes a wholesale shift to a new metric, such as economic profit. Several common measures should be understood and used according to their relative strengths and weaknesses (see Figure 5.2).

Risk-Adjusted Return on Capital (RAROC)

This is the standard basic risk-adjusted return measure and the place where most institutions start their journey to risk-adjusted metrics. If this one is well understood, the rest follow easily. The simple equation for risk-adjusted return is as follows:

> Revenue (both interest and fee revenues)
> − Expenses
> − Cost of Funds
> − Expected Loss (this may be provisions in some institutions)
> + Capital Benefit
> − Taxes
>
> ---
>
> = Risk-Adjusted Profit
> ÷ Economic Capital
> = RAROC

- **Revenue.** This is all revenue, from interest, fees, and other sources.
- **Expenses.** Likewise, this is all attributable expenses. When measuring RAROC at the top of the house, this measure is simple. But when measuring business line, product, or transaction returns, expenses easily can descend into a debate about whether corporate overhead should be allocated into this number or not, and what method should be used for other allocations. As for the allocation of corporate overhead, it's often useful to examine both. For general comparison purposes, this

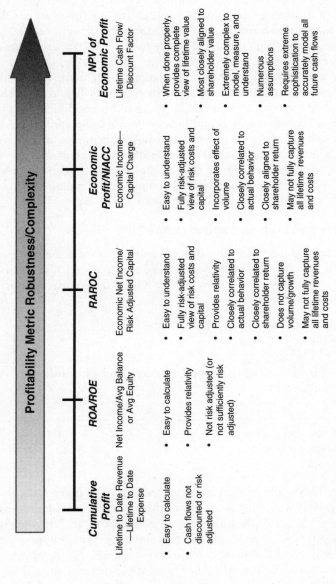

Profitability Metric Robustness/Complexity

	Cumulative Profit	*ROA/ROE*	*RAROC*	*Economic Profit/NIACC*	*NPV of Economic Profit*
	Lifetime to Date Revenue —Lifetime to Date Expense	Net Income/Avg Balance or Avg Equity	Economic Net Income/ Risk Adjusted Capital	Economic Income— Capital Charge	Lifetime Cash Flow/ Discount Factor
	• Easy to calculate	• Easy to calculate	• Easy to understand	• Easy to understand	• When done properly, provides complete view of lifetime value
	• Cash flows not discounted or risk adjusted	• Provides relativity	• Fully risk-adjusted view of risk costs and capital	• Fully risk-adjusted view of risk costs and capital	• Most closely aligned to shareholder value
		• Not risk adjusted (or not sufficiently risk adjusted)	• Provides relativity	• Incorporates effect of volume	• Extremely complex to model, measure, and understand
			• Closely correlated to actual behavior	• Closely correlated to actual behavior	• Numerous assumptions
			• Closely correlated to shareholder return	• Closely aligned to shareholder return	• Requires extreme sophistication to accurately model all future cash flows
			• Does not capture volume/growth	• May not fully capture all lifetime revenues and costs	
			• May not fully capture all lifetime revenues and costs		

FIGURE 5.2 Performance Measures Compared

difference rarely matters, but for pricing purposes it can matter greatly and is generally NOT included. It is important, however, to understand which form is being used and why and to consider total overhead to ensure those figures are in line with competitors and are being sufficiently covered. Some institutions can even achieve sufficient sophistication to understand marginal expenses, which is ideal.

- **Cost of funds.** This is the funding cost of the bank or transfer rate to the individual products or transactions. We'll discuss further nuances of this later when we examine pricing. An important item here is that the funds-transfer price (FTP rate) typically applied to measures below the top of the house should consider interest rate and liquidity risk of the business line or product. So there is no need to account for that capital later in the equation. It is addressed here.
- **Expected loss.** These are provisions or actual expected loss for the business or transaction. We've discussed this previously. Please see Chapter 4 for a full explanation.
- **Capital benefit.** This is the "benefit," or return, earned by economic capital held by treasury to support risks—the risks of the specific transaction, portfolio, or business being measured. It is usually considered to be capital, earning the bank a level swap rate or treasury rate. This capital cannot attract risk itself and so earns a "risk-free" rate.
- **Economic capital.** We've also discussed this previously. Please see Chapter 4 for a full explanation. The term "economic capital" should address capital for all the risks associated with the entity being measured. For example, if we were measuring RAROC for a lending unit, it would naturally include credit-risk capital but also should include operational-risk capital and any other risk to which the unit is exposed. Transfer pricing should cover the market risk of the lending instrument itself and generally is not included in this term. But it's often necessary to check that the funds-transfer price is appropriately constructed.

RAROC is a term that has created its own folklore. The term often is misrepresented, and the specific definition can vary. There are two important concepts to remember:

1. The numerator is simply *risk-adjusted* profit. It must be risk-adjusted.
2. The denominator must be economic capital. This is not regulatory capital or any other definition of capital.

Return on Equity (ROE)

This one seems like an old standby but can be a complex item because its generality leaves much to specification. Every institution seems to use a slightly different definition; some differences have a very meaningful effect. For many organizations, it is no different than RAROC. For many others, it utilizes regulatory capital in the denominator. For still others, it can be a more standard accounting definition, with equity being the total balance sheet equity.

Economic Profit (EP)

This is the most commonly applied of the contribution-type measures. Economic profit is a simple concept that considers profit, less the amount of return lost on the holding of capital for risk. The equation is effectively a variant on the RAROC equation:

$$EP = \text{Risk-Adjusted Profit} - (\text{Cost of Capital} \times \text{Economic Capital})$$

Economic profit often is referred to as net income after cost of capital (NIACC).

PERFORMANCE MEASURES—MULTI-PERIOD CALCULATIONS

Multi-period calculations may be considered for certain analysis. These are particularly useful for determining the value of a transaction or strategy, but some organizations utilize them for even more. Pricing is frequently constructed based on multi-period measures. In addition, sophisticated applications may include the use of multi-period measures for understanding the overall economic value of the firm itself. These measures have been found to correlate to stock market returns, so they are often useful in evaluating senior managers' contribution of strategies or the managers' overall quality as it relates to the share value of the company. The most common of these measures are shareholder value added and net present value.

Shareholder Value Added (SVA)

As are many of the measures we've discussed, this one too, is often known by many names. It is often referred to as economic value added (EVA) or multi-period EP. In fact, that last term is just what it is: economic profit projected over several years (usually about five years) and discounted.

It is important to note, however, that some versions use a number of accounting adjustments. These methods must be carefully considered. They can be very useful for comparisons to competitors but are very difficult to apply internally because it's hard to use them to manage pricing or performance. They tend to create a nearly "black box" level of transparency and often involve too many adjustments for managers to effectively manage to the bottom line.

Net Present Value (NPV)

This method is commonly employed, particularly for evaluating investments and for pricing. The NPV approach, when properly applied, should yield the same results as the multi-period EP. The principle difference is that the NPV method considers all capital to be invested at the outset of a transaction, and then returned as principal. In the multi-period EP approach, the contribution of capital is considered each period. Assuming the same cost of capital, or hurdle rate, the two methods yield equivalent solutions.

In a financial services context—particularly when applied to standard transactions that are part of the typical risk-taking of an organization, such as lending or trading—the multi-period EP typically has a subtle advantage because it is far less likely to make material mistakes. For example, if the horizon time on a transaction is inappropriately estimated, multi-period EP still will tend to appropriately reflect the relative contribution of a transaction. NPV often will overestimate or underestimate the value of a transaction.

Figure 5.3 shows that, constructed properly, the two calculations yield the same answer. But we also can see that the NPV method shows far more volatility of cash flows year to year, thus introducing the potential for greater error if horizon time or other factors are miscalculated.

Discounting Methods

Discount rates are an important element of a multi-period measure. The standard method for determining the discount rate typically blends the organizational contribution of the cost of debt and the cost of equity to yield a consolidated cost of capital. For most standard investment decisions, this is an appropriate rate to apply. But for many organizations, particularly those in financial services, it is worth considering other options.

Financial-services firms, by definition, earn profits through returns on the money they put at risk. This means they must make a minimum expected return on their transactions to ensure that they will meet their shareholders' expectations. When considering the discount rate applied to multi-period performance metrics, as we just discussed, it is not always sufficient to simply apply the standard cost of funds. If we are evaluating the expected performance or pricing for a standard transaction (such as a loan or trade), then it is wiser to consider a minimum rate of return that is in line

Interest Rate	5.20%
Equity Rate	3.00%
Equity Credit (Capital Benefit)	5.50%
Hurdle Rate	0.18
Weighted Average Cost of Capital (WACC)	0.11
cost of Funds	3.50%

Example 1: Traditional Cash Flow

	Year 0	Year 1	Year 2	Year 3	Year 4	Year 5	Year 6
Revenue							
Loan Balance	1000	900	800	700	600	500	0
Principal		100	100	100	100	100	500
Interest Income		52	46.8	41.6	36.4	31.2	26
Fees		3	3	3	3	3	3
Equity Credit		1.65	1.485	1.32	1.155	0.99	0.825
Total Revenue		56.65	51.285	45.92	40.555	35.19	29.825
Costs							
Origination and Servicing		0.7	0.7	0.7	0.7	0.7	0.7
Cost of Funds		35	31.5	28	24.5	21	17.5
Expected Loss		20	18	16	14	12	10
Total Costs	0	55.7	50.2	44.7	39.2	33.7	28.2
Net Income		0.95	1.085	1.22	1.355	1.49	1.625
Taxes		0.3325	0.37975	0.427	0.47425	0.5215	0.56875
Net Income After Taxes (NIAT)		0.6175	0.70525	0.793	0.88075	0.9685	1.05625
Equity	30	27	24	21	18	15	0
Change in Equity	30	−3	−3	−3	−3	−3	−15
Net Cash Flow	−30	3.6175	3.70525	3.793	3.88075	3.9685	16.05625

NPV	($12.28)

Example 2: Economic Profit Treatment of Capital

Equity contribution	5.40	4.86	4.32	3.78	3.24	2.70
Economic Profit	−4.7825	−4.15475	−3.527	−2.89925	−2.2715	−1.64375

NPV Economic Profit ($12.28)

Example #3: When WACC is Different than Hurdle Rate

Equity Contribution (using WACC)	3.30	2.97	2.64	2.31	1.98	1.65
Economic Profit	−2.68	−2.26	−1.85	−1.43	−1.01	−0.59

Economic Profit NPV ($6.42)

FIGURE 5.3 Economic Profit versus Cash Flow Example Calculations

with the returns for that type of business as if it was a stand-alone entity. This is particularly important, given that corporate overheads and operating costs are typically not included in above-the-line expense calculations.

As a practical matter, however, this means that some firms will have many different hurdle rates in order to support their many business lines—wealth, insurance, credit card, corporate lending, capital markets, and numerous others. These differences can be difficult to manage, and can lead to wearisome internal debates over fairness. As a result, most organizations establish a minimum hurdle rate that all business lines must meet. This rate is typically one that supports cost of capital, plus an additional buffer to provide for insurance and some growth. An appropriate way of accomplishing this is to utilize the equity-return expectation for blended activities as a minimum to ensure that core business dealings meet market expectations.

CAPITAL ATTRIBUTION AND ALLOCATION

Capital allocation presents a fundamental challenge to the development of usable performance metrics. The allocation of capital is when measures of capital that are generated at a higher level of consolidation within the organization are broken down to more granular levels that apply to individual business lines, sub–business lines, products, customers, and/or transactions. The reason this is so tricky is that most risk models generate capital numbers in aggregate, mainly because they are designed to address the issues of correlation that we discussed previously. Breaking apart these aggregate calculations to lower and lower levels can become incredibly challenging, particularly if the correlation coefficients associated with those more granular levels have not been discovered.

The general approach involves refreshing our old friend, the unexpected-loss contribution (ULC). Remember that the sum of ULC for each of a set of transactions or sub-portfolios is the UL for the entire portfolio or institution, respectively. The economic capital contribution (ECC) works in the same way. For any given transaction i and portfolio p, the economic capital contribution is:

$$ECC_i = \frac{EC_p ULC_i}{UL_p}$$

This assumes that the transactions to which this equation is applied have relatively uniform capital and risk. So where risk may be uniquely different, a new ULC needs to be identified and applied. There are other simpler methods, but they tend to involve more rounding and assumptions of portfolio uniformity. So this one tends to be the preferred approach. It is straight forward and quite accurate within its limitations.

Another aspect of capital allocation that frequently thwarts institutions is the ability to capture and manage it through the information in systems. Many organizations do not have sufficiently flexible systems architectures or warehouse structures to support the addition of capital numbers at every level, nor to manipulate them.

Why should we care about capital allocation? As we've seen previously, it is a key component in any risk-adjusted performance metric and is often critical to other applications of capital, such as risk appetite and limit setting, which we will discuss later. Practically speaking, the capital term can make a notable difference to the return measure, depending on the measure and level of error. To explore this a bit further, let's apply a simple experiment comparing a one-period risk-adjusted return calculation and a one-period economic-profit calculation over a range of capital options (see Table 5.2).

Example: One-period metrics on a secured retail loan	
Outstanding:	$100
Interest and fee revenue:	3.75%
Cost of funds:	1.5%
Expenses:	$1
Expected loss:	0.35%

We see two things immediately:

1. There is a big difference in the impact depending on the particular metric employed. Return metrics are far more sensitive to the capital term than are contribution metrics.
2. Depending on the variance of capital, the difference can be more meaningful.

TABLE 5.2 Example: Comparison of Performance Measures Under Varying Capital Scenarios

Capital Scenarios	RAROC	Economic Profit
3%	30.00%	$0.86
3.5%	25.71%	$0.85
4%	22.50%	$0.84
9%	10.00%	$0.77

These capital numbers were chosen with specific forethought. A typical, well-secured, and relatively low-risk, prime portfolio of this sort would traditionally have a capital level of about 3 to 3.5%. However, depending on the portfolio's specific mix, 4% is certainly possible. And 4% corresponds to the traditional, Basel I regulatory requirement for residential secured loans. A typical subprime rate would be 9%, a rate more applicable to certain specific markets globally.

So the swing can be enormous, depending on location, portfolio type, and many other factors. The bottom line is that in some circumstances, the granularity of capital can be very important. Conversely, it doesn't necessarily need to be a show-stopper. If you know what sort of portfolio you have, it is fairly uniform and/or low risk, then it's quite possible to live with a higher-level estimate without any great ramifications. Risk-analysis teams typically can review scenarios like these and sample the portfolio to determine the capital impacts and ranges. So it's possible to rapidly assess the ramifications of the chosen approach and its respective issues to determine whether it is "safe" to go for less granularity or not.

Another issue in the pursuit of the right capital number is which sort of capital to use. The simple answer is that it should always be economic capital. But a surprising number of institutions use other metrics. It's not always as obvious as it may seem. There are still many organizations that do not hold sufficient capital in line with the true underlying economic risk, that is, economic capital. Many organizations simply hold the regulatory minimum. For them, it's not always an obvious choice whether to use regulatory capital in the return calculations or economic capital. Conversely, there are portfolios and situations, where regulatory capital can easily exceed economic capital. Here institutions often counter that they would prefer to ensure that they are achieving the right level of income relative to the capital they are required to hold. In this case, it may be prudent to examine *both* return on economic capital and return on regulatory capital. One to ensure that we understand the relative degree of risks and how those compare to other products, transactions, and business lines; the other to ensure that we are achieving sufficient profitability for the real capital that cannot be employed.

With the advent of Basel II, much of that is changing. Capital is more closely scaled to risk and many regulators are enforcing the use of economic capital as well as regulatory capital. Nevertheless, for most, economic capital should be a higher number because it not only is scaled to risk but also scaled to the bank's solvency standard. This generally yields a limiting number that should be applied.

Another fine point to keep in mind is that, unlike certain provisions, capital is not usually allocated. Few institutions create highly specific allocation mechanisms. It is *attributed*. So the capital numbers are notional to the specific business line, customer, or transaction being measured. This is important because they could conceivably change—very rapidly under certain circumstances. Outside of changes that can occur with the underlying transactions themselves, the mix of transactions can also drive changes. Remember that correlations can change—and more importantly, the mix of assets can change—in turn altering the diversification-contribution of portfolios. As a result, this can shift the capital that is attributed to any given portfolio or even business line. Within a portfolio, this is generally a minor point. Across business lines, however, this can add up to a substantial movement.

Consider a situation where there are two business lines. One business line traditionally services a retail clientele and naturally tends to have numerous small transactions. These transactions as a portfolio reflect the broad population of customers targeted by the institution. During any given period—quarter or even year—adding a few additional customers or transactions, even of any one type, is unlikely to shift the portfolio make-up dramatically. It's a very homogeneous portfolio.

Correspondingly, the correlation between transactions and the relative contribution of the business line to the rest of the institution tends to stay fairly stable.

Now consider the other business line. It is an institutional portfolio made up of very large transactions. Compared to the retail business line, it has significantly fewer transactions, so is more likely to see bigger swings in its risk profile as a result of adding one or two large transactions. This in turn, can shift correlations both within the business line and between this business line and the other. Overnight, our first business line—the very stable, homogeneous one—can find the capital assigned to it change dramatically because it is affected by the behavior of the other business line (see Table 5.3). Here's how this can happen:

Business Line 1: retail portfolio
Business Line 2: institutional portfolio

Business line 1 did absolutely nothing from one period to the next. It did not change volume or number of transactions, yet its economic capital contribution dropped because business line 2's activities changed the correlation between the two lines. In this case, the effect benefited business line 1, but that's not always the case. The effect can go both ways. The activities also created a big swing in the numbers that were outside the control of business line 1. Business line 2 managed to make this swing by only adding a few additional transactions, but in this case, we can see that business

TABLE 5.3　Capital Allocation Effects between Business Lines

	Period 1	Period 2
UL1	5	5
UL2	5	17
ULC1	4.5	3.4
ULC2	4.5	11.5
ρ	0.8	0.5
N1	50	50
N2	5	7
Total Outstandings 1	350	350
Total Outstandings 2	170	350
Stand Alone Ecap 1	25	25
Stand Alone Ecap 2	25	85
ECap Contribution 1	22.5	17.1
ECap Contribution 2	22.5	57.6
ECap	45	74.7

line 2's transactions are large and lumpy. In these cases, a business line of this sort can easily push capital and correlations around, readily affecting other business lines.

This kind of volatility can deeply frustrate the business lines trying to live within this system. Therefore, some organizations move to a system whereby changes in capital due to correlation changes are held out separately from the business lines being affected. This way, the businesses can pay attention to their stand-alone contribution as well as the correlation benefit that they create for the rest of the organization. In this case, business line 2 created a net increase of stand-alone economic capital of 60 but a net correlation benefit of roughly 10 to the entire institution.

There are pros and cons to this approach, like in many others. It creates more transparency and makes it easier for business lines to manage their stand alone positions. But it's not always clear how to manage and reward for the diversification benefit provided, particularly when there are multiple business lines creating correlation changes simultaneously.

APPLYING PERFORMANCE MEASURES

Applying performance measures successfully is often both an art *and* a science. Seemingly subtle differences in choices can make big differences. The right measure applied to the wrong level of the organization, for example, may mean the difference between success and failure.

EXAMPLE

One very good example of well-intended plans going very wrong involves a large financial group that had both banking and insurance operations. It had exuberantly decided to implement risk-adjusted performance measures and made two critical errors. The first problem was that management decided to implement EVA for performance management and remuneration. They used an approach that involved numerous accounting adjustments designed to help create "apples-to-apples" comparisons between business lines and between similar competitors. Although this sounded like a great idea on the surface, they decided to push this approach down to lower and lower levels of the organization. This frustrated managers who not only couldn't clearly understand the drivers of their own performance but couldn't influence most of them either. In the end, the approach served to annoy most of the organization.

The second problem was choosing to apply RAROC measures for pricing and other transaction decisions. This drove additional unintended consequences when many of the managers determined that they could optimize RAROC by reducing transactions and only focus on the very best, high quality deals. RAROC improved, but growth screeched to a halt, and in fact, in some areas the book shrunk.

Effectively, they managed to choose the worst aspects of each metric and apply them for the wrong applications. In the end, they had to scrap their whole program and re-introduce risk-adjusted performance metrics after a "break" of a couple of years, long enough for the institutional memory to wear thin. The second time around, they took a more cautious and step-wise approach. The approach ultimately was implemented and worked well, but it took them far longer to manage the implementation the second time than it might have under other conditions.

The key questions to consider are (see Figure 5.4):

- Which measures do we want to use, and why?
- Will the measures be applied at the top of the house only, or will they be cascaded to lower levels? What will the measures be used for and how will they be applied within the organization?

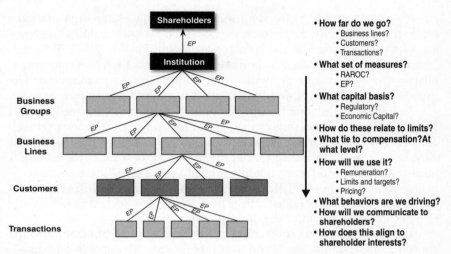

FIGURE 5.4 Risk Adjusted Performance Measures Key Considerations

When answering the first question, always remember that performance measures must emphasize return, risk, and growth. This is the all important "three-legged stool." So whichever performance measure is chosen, all three of these need to be evident. Otherwise, it is very easy to send an organization out of balance. If economic profit is the favored approach, then great! You're basically there. But if RAROC is more comfortable to use, then some sort of measure of absolute returns, volume, or growth must be factored into the mix. If not, it's too easy for the organization to become so obsessed with the quest for better RAROC that it seeks out better and better risks, to the exclusion of growth. It may even shrink the book while achieving fantastic returns.

The level to which the measures will be used is the next important question. Who will be using them? Top management? Business units? Transaction-level managers? If the measures become too complex, they will rapidly frustrate lower-level managers because they probably won't have control over the measures' various components. To avoid creating these kinds of no-win scenarios, strip the measures down to their bare bones. Sometimes removing the capital-benefit component also can make measures easier to understand and accept.

The last key question is, "What will the measures be used for?" The "stripped-down-to-the-bone" method may be effective for general performance and incentive management, but more complex, multi-period approaches will be necessary to evaluate strategies and price transactions.

It's possible to use a mix of measures successfully. As an organization's comfort and skill with the measures improves, it is easier to adopt improvements and derivations of the core approach without too much difficulty. Many organizations start with a single period view of RAROC (accompanied by a growth measure) or with economic profit used for monitoring performance of the major business lines, and then expand over time.

As both the depth and breadth of application expands, the organization typically becomes increasingly interested in ensuring that measures are well constructed and accurate. This, in turn, puts pressure on the risk and finance teams to ensure the quality of the measures. In turn, as the measures improve, they can be more readily applied. This begets the expansion of measures into more sophisticated terms and often into multi-period measures. It is, indeed, a snowball effect that occurs over several years. Expect two to three years for this behavior to occur.

The point of arrival is when the whole organization has embraced the concepts, understands them, and uses them in everyday speech and activities. This concept will come up again in discussion about Basel II and its expectations under the use test. Suffice it to say that this is the aspiration of the use test. It is why it is arguably the most difficult aspect of accrediting under Basel II because it is non-specific and highly particular to the organization.

It is useful for those embarking on implementing these capabilities to consider the applications a little more closely. What are they, what might they require, and in what order are they typically implemented.

Many organizations can fairly say that they already have elements of these capabilities, but until they are institutionalized and built into a framework that supports a broader set of organizational objectives, the concepts cannot be embedded. This level of socialization and institutionalization typically requires a stepwise process of top-down agreement, socialization, and reinforcement. The best place to start in this process is to establish the measures for performance monitoring. Once the measures are understood and have been observed in action, it is possible to begin to broaden out to applications that carry more weight.

The first application is in *remuneration and incentives*. This application may be one of the most important for any organization because, for some, it is the key motivator toward adoption of a real risk-based performance-management system. This is the point where lip service ends and people sit up and take notice. Once remuneration is tied to the metrics, the interest within the organization will increase enormously. People will want to ensure the quality of the metrics, and make sure that the metrics work effectively.

But building in incentive is a process. For some cultures, it is best to start slowly. The performance metric may be treated as a gateway or a hurdle. That is to say, managers are remunerated on their adherence to the measures and targets and their ability to meet a threshold. As the capabilities are better understood and better developed, the link may become tighter. Bonuses may be specifically tied to the numerical outcomes of the measures, rising and falling accordingly. Some of the underlying components of the metrics may also be considered for specific linkages to remuneration or, as well, gateways. So risk thresholds often are singled out, given their importance in ensuring a quality asset base. This may mean ensuring that net capital and provisioning charges stay within agreed bounds with bonus reductions held out as a consequence of failure to conform. For some organizations, meeting these thresholds may even carry more dire consequences, including dismissal.

Budgeting is another key area where the performance measures come into play. Many organizations find that it provides a means to not only manage capital but also the return structure of the business. Some may take a more passive approach, allowing businesses to meet thresholds and targets previously described, but others develop an active process whereby businesses must justify their position against alternative "investments" the firm has in play. If we consider the budget associated with the growth of each business line as an investment decision on the part of the firm, then the ability to justify that investment becomes a critical part of the budgeting process.

Business lines may enter an internal "bidding" process whereby capital is awarded to businesses that make the best cases. That means those businesses that contribute the best risk/return-growth profile or economic-profit contribution are those that get the richest budgets for the next year. This may be decided through track record or through the presentation of business cases that further establish a path for improved contribution and effectively "signing up" for a more ambitious target.

For many organizations, this latter process is better constructed through the development of business line balance sheets. This goes beyond a simple profit and loss (P&L) statement by establishing a complete balance sheet, including the control over capital and capital investment within the business. Clearly, this method is only efficient for the largest business lines where the operations can be established as stand-alone businesses. Nevertheless, it provides a level of clarity and control beyond that of more simple management methods. Businesses must take full ownership of their capital requirements and applications and must justify to their "shareholders"—the broader financial group—the value of continuing to allocate larger shares of capital to them. This also begets the issue of what to do with retained earnings. These may stay with the business in the event of capital reinvestment or may even need to be granted back to the larger company if other business lines justify a higher proportion of investment.

The notable downside of these types of approaches—beyond the over-head and initial complexity associated with the establishment of individual balance sheets—is that they result in over concentration of assets in businesses and products that are pro-cyclical.

Systems that support an approach in which the highest bidder wins or the most profitable and fastest growing segment of the business wins will always be biased toward growth—even when that growth is detrimental to the organization. The harsh truth is that businesses can grow too rapidly, exceeding the organization's ability to manage for their downside risks.

Focusing too much on easy wins can also blind businesses to deeper problems in their markets. Often, economic sectors become overheated, making them prone to sudden collapse. When organizations allow their business to over-invest in growth, they set themselves up for failure.

This brings us to another critical application: *asset allocation*. Asset allocation is a method whereby institutions can evaluate their portfolio mix and overall net portfolio position relative to their peers, based on a risk-return view. The performance metric allows them to assess the mix of individual businesses, their relative contribution to the whole of the institution as well as the net performance of the institution.

The objective is to establish a balanced mix of businesses with an appropriate risk return profile—so as not to overweight or overheat the overall institution through any one business—and to ensure that the institution as a whole stacks up against its competitors. We'll discuss this further in Chapter 8, but the bottom line here is that, although it's tempting to strictly allow those business lines with the best individual contribution to "win," it is important to keep an eye on the mix of the larger institution to ensure it is adequately diversified and that those business lines that are big performers aren't artificially heated up through an economic niche.

Pricing and decision-making are some of the most common applications of these metrics and often precede even the implementation of incentives and other applications of risk-adjusted performance metrics. These concepts are also those in which multi-period metrics become most desired. Having said that, it's not a show-stopper if they don't exist as such. If the organization is not yet ready to manage a multi-period metric or if systems cannot be constructed readily to support it, it's still better to go forward with a single-period metric and adapt it, either immediately or over time. The use of risk-adjusted performance metrics for pricing not only provides a strict link to the economics of a transaction but also links the mechanics of a deal to the specific portfolio performance targets being driven through the top-down incentive structures. It literally provides a bottom-up mechanism to ensure top of the house success.

We'll discuss each of these applications in greater depth later in this book. But the key here is to understand which applications the organization will take on immediately and in the future. Each requires a level of organizational acceptance and effort toward setup and implementation. Few firms take on all of these applications at once or in their most advanced form. It becomes a process of introduction of the concepts and a patient, stepwise approach toward achievement of the ultimate goal—ensuring their appropriate acceptance and use. An early decision to be made is the choice between adopting methods top-down or bottom-up. That is, will the process start with approaches that enlist metrics at the transaction level first or approaches that drive conformance from the top?

TOP-DOWN VERSUS BOTTOM-UP

The idea of *top-down vs. bottom-up* is a common construct. It means quite literally what it suggests. "Top-down" means estimates are constructed through aggregated data and modeling on the total institution or major business line, then broken down to business lines, sub-businesses, products, customers, and/or transactions. It also refers to the applications and approach to implementation. Top-down implementation applies broad measures to equally broad applications, such as remuneration and incentives and general performance tracking.

"Bottom-up" means that granular estimates are constructed for each transaction, then aggregated upwards. A bottom-up implementation suggests that granular measures are applied to specific applications such as pricing of an individual deal. The process describes starting at one end or the other and then moving up or down the organizational hierarchy and hierarchy of applications.

There are pros and cons to either method. Bottom-up measures often seem like they will be appealing and relatively simple to implement. But they often create the greatest measurement challenges because costs and revenue streams must be allocated, and risk measures must be constructed on the lowest level—which is not often the case, particularly in capital allocations. Top-down measures are often easier to construct but implementation can be challenging because they often end up in incentives and broad performance tracking that can have enormous ramifications on behavior.

Realistically, many institutions end up with a hybrid approach. Models required for granular decision-making at a transaction level apply a bottom-up method, and those required for large-scale performance measurement and incentive management may be constructed using a top-down method. As the organization increases in sophistication, it is ultimately able to reconcile the two and support both sets of needs.

CHAPTER 6

Understanding Your Appetite for Risk

EXECUTIVE SUMMARY

Your risk appetite tells you how much risk you're willing to assume given the return you're seeking. Sure, you'd love to have a 25 percent return on your investment—but would you love it so much if you knew that you could lose 75 percent of your investment every other week? This chapter gets down to the nitty-gritty of defining just how much you're willing to lose, and how fast you're willing to lose it. Defining your risk appetite is essential for two reasons. The first is that it enables you to align your strategies and tactics more clearly with your desired level of risk taking. The second is that defining your risk appetite is now increasingly required by regulators. In other words, what had been a best practice is rapidly becoming a common practice. In the banking industry, for example, regulators are pushing companies to articulate their risk appetite in a formal statement. It seems clear that the practice is going mainstream, but many managers don't know how to put together a formal risk appetite statement. This chapter shows you how . . .

IDENTIFYING THE RISK APPETITE

Successful risk management hinges on a company's ability to gauge its risk appetite and to work within the parameters established by that appetite. The risk appetite serves as both a benchmark and a reminder of the company's overall willingness to take risk. Senior management and the board use this critical tool to set the organizational tone from the top. They articulate how much risk the company is willing to take, in what areas, and for what kind of return. This *risk appetite statement* also describes the types and degree of risk a company specifically wants to take—and wants to avoid.

It's important, however, to think of risk appetite as more than just a benchmark or line in the sand. Risk appetite is also a process for identifying acceptable parameters of risk, establishing and agreeing on those parameters, and maintaining risk within those parameters at every level of the organization.

Risk appetite can be an extremely powerful driver of behavior when considered within this framework, and it becomes a significant activity within the risk management function and as part of the institution's broader business cycle. It's also a critical part of the *internal capital adequacy assessment process* (ICAAP).

The risk appetite statement itself, in its simplest form, is a statement of the target debt rating. We've seen in previous chapters how powerful this concept is. It defines the relative amount of capital the organization requires against its core risks and it is a critical element for economic capital modeling. But it goes beyond that. When constructed well, the risk appetite provides a broader statement to the organization about the overall eagerness for risk-taking and its boundaries. It also allows the organization to define and analyze its risk/return profile. To that end, it becomes a key tool for internal communication—to the board, shareholders, and other stakeholders. It also supports the ability to describe how the organization will set controls to manage within these tolerances.

The risk appetite statement identifies not only the overall level of capital, but also how capital will be allocated and the limits and thresholds to which capital will be managed (see Figure 6.1). This, in turn, allows the organization to set policies and strategies to support those thresholds and the specific types of positions it will take. Risks then can be reported against this framework, limits monitored, and capital assessed. To this end, it becomes a key tool for establishing broad strategies and to ensure tactical, operational decision-making.

For this reason, the risk appetite statement is appropriately more than a declaration of target debt rating. It describes the boundaries of risk within the organization, both numerically and in words. It establishes a mutual understanding of the overall risk the organization is willing to take, how that translates into capital, and in which business lines and risk classes capital will be directed or retracted. It generally describes capital in at least one or more methods—for example, economic versus regulatory. It may describe the buffer between these measures and actual total capital. It frequently describes implications of core capital generation, business forecasts, and provisions. It may also identify triggers and implications of capital decisions on performance.

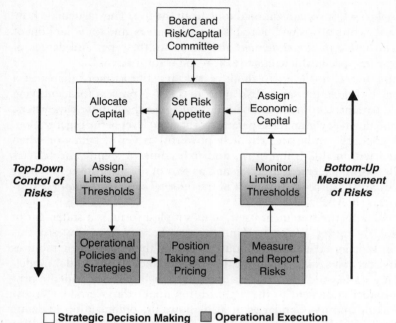

Strategic Decision Making ■ **Operational Execution**

FIGURE 6.1   Risk Appetite Framework

RISK APPETITE AND ICAAP

The ICAAP has become a core vestige of Basel II and new regulatory risk management frameworks globally. In many jurisdictions, it may even be required beyond the implementation of Basel II advanced approaches. For some more enlightened institutions, ICAAP is a process that has been in place, perhaps under different names, for many years. For some organizations, ICAAP and the risk appetite framework are virtually the same. For others, the risk appetite is a distinct sub component of the ICAAP framework. Realistically, as long as the key elements are addressed, then it's a matter of semantics. Of course this begs the question, what are those key elements?

The ICAAP framework starts with a comprehensive set of risk models that are validated and reviewed through formal processes (see Chapter 4). These models, in turn, are applied to the generation of economic capital—(and potentially regulatory capital in Basel II or Solvency II). Expectations for risk and capital models are broadly the same as the approaches we've

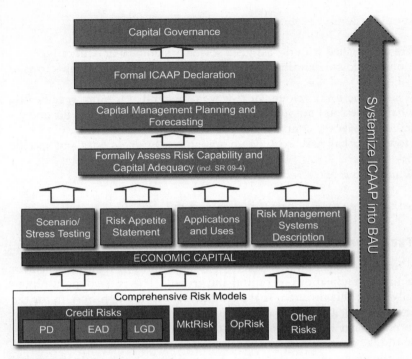

FIGURE 6.2 ICAAP Framework

discussed in previous chapters. The models are applied to a framework of stress/scenario testing, the risk appetite statement, and numerous other applications, many of which we've discussed. The framework also typically consists of a statement of risk processes and systems, plus the formal assessment of the overall risk management framework, including self-assessment. All of this rolls into the management and planning processes for capital and capital adequacy and the governance over these processes (see Figure 6.2).

BUILDING THE RISK APPETITE STATEMENT

For many organizations, constructing the risk appetite statement for the first time is a process tantamount to giving birth. To set the risk appetite correctly, it forces senior management and the board to come to grips with the implications of their actions and make specific trade-offs. It requires the board and senior management to engage in organizational introspection.

Start by asking the following key questions:

- Are we satisfied with the assigned solvency standard or debt rating?
- How would we describe our organization's relative willingness to take risk?
- What is the total amount of risk we can stand? Or more specifically, what is the total amount of money we could stand to lose in one instance or over the course of the year?
- How does that risk break down among our business lines and specific risk classes?
- What are our perceived limits?

Let's explore these concepts in greater detail.

The Target Debt Rating

Many organizations don't consider the ramifications of their current debt rating and its implications on capital and growth. This is the opportunity to formally think this through. Is the current debt rating appropriate for the business we're in, and our strategic aspirations? If there is a compelling reason to reconsider this position, then there may be an equally compelling reason to take a stand through the target debt rating reflected in the capital position the organization establishes. Many organizations set up the capital implications in a simple table that can unveil the most immediate ramifications of the decision to make a change (see Table 6.1).

For organizations based in markets where a sovereign debt rating creates obvious limitations, there's no reason to abandon this line of thinking. Consider comparisons to peer institutions, both domestic and foreign. With which institutions do we see ourselves most in line or aspire to be most like?

TABLE 6.1 Example: Capital, Funding, and Credit Rating Implications for a Single Institution

	AAA	AA+	AA	AA−	BBB
Solvency Standard/Confidence Interval	0.01%	0.025%	0.03%	0.035%	0.30%
Capital	3.35%	3.06%	3.00%	2.96%	2.25%
Capital Multiple	5.15	4.70	4.60	4.55	3.45
Funding Rate (spread over treasury)	0.68%	0.75%	0.78%	0.79%	1.51%

The Organization's Willingness to Take Risk

What is the reaction of the board, senior management, and external stake-holders—such as analysts, and regulators—to potential issues? What is the organization's reputation? Companies with a long history and reputation of safety, soundness, and predictability are more likely to be institutionally conservative. And the market and analysts tend to expect few surprises from these types of institutions.

The converse may also be true. The organization may have a bullish view toward risk, particularly when in recovery after a long economic down-turn or when faced with the need to execute do or die competitive strategies.

The Total Amount of Risk You Can Stand

This is not as obvious a question as you might immediately think. It's also not strictly about modeling. Of course, we can and should run some analy-sis to gain a better understanding of what type of risk can take down the institution. We discussed these techniques under stress testing. We want to enter this exercise armed with a strict understanding of the firm's capital limitations and the results of stress testing and reverse stress testing exer-cises. They provide a keen understanding of what risks can create the most havoc and the shape and size of those risks. But the exercise goes further.

How much loss can the organization truly withstand in supporting the expectations of stakeholders? Has the organization ever experienced a loss? How big was it, and what was the reaction? Consider the size of losses rela-tive to the economic capital base and how the market and other stakehold-ers reacted. For most organizations, it is unlikely that the answer is simply to preserve the full capital basis or even the economic capital requirement. The true threshold is usually a number far below that point. What kind of number would cause management extreme discomfort? Or worse, would cause the market to lose faith or cause a run on deposits?

Remember that many organizations fail long before their capital is wiped out. They go down because they have lost the faith of their deposi-tors, bond holders, or the market in general.

The Breakdown across Business Lines and Risk Classes

What businesses do we want to invest in or grow? Which provide the best return profile? Which will command the greatest growth through sheer momentum? These are generally the businesses where we consider the greatest allocations. But we must do this with caution. Be sure to consider the diversification benefits each business contributes and how they create a consolidated balance of total return across the institution. The same is true of risk classes. Which contribute to the growth of the businesses we've high-lighted? What diversification benefits do they provide? Do some risks create a core cost of doing business? For example, operational risks are often for-gotten, but it is critical to consider the general growth of the operational risk base along with the broader growth of business.

These aspects of risk appetite must be considered as an exercise in port-folio management. One of the greatest mistakes many firms make is to simply support the largest and fastest-growing businesses with the largest capital allocations without further consideration. It's important to consider these in context of their contribution to the broader portfolio position. A large and fast-growing portfolio will at some point create a concentration that could outweigh its short-term value.

The Limits

It's also important to set a series of limits and thresholds to protect the orga-nization from spinning out of control and, in the event of a serious problem, to buy time for senior management and the board to shore up additional resources. Generally, the best approach is to establish a series of limits that start with business lines, possibly even risk classes or sub-portfolios within those business lines. Devise a set of maximum limits. These may be the total allocation to the business or a level a bit beyond. Set up triggers or buffers that signal the approach of the limit. Triggers may be based in capital con-sumption or other measures, such as provisions, rate of consumption, or changes in the profile of the risk distribution.

Other questions are important to consider as the risk appetite statement is constructed. Consider these in the process of reviewing or establishing the risk appetite statement:

- **How does your risk-taking compare to your competitors'?** How does the firm position itself? Make sure that wherever the company is posi-tioned across the risk spectrum, it is leading in returns. Remember that the riskier the firm, the more profits that will be expected.
- **Are there specific types of risk that you won't take?** This is a core ques-tion whose answer must be collectively clear. What things do we want to avoid and why? This is the key opportunity to send the organization a very clear message about the types of things we will and won't do as a firm.
- **Are there specific external expectations from regulators or other stake-holders that must be factored in?** Let's not forget that in many, if not

most, jurisdictions, regulators very likely will request this statement. What must we ensure is included? Are there any undertakings, limitations on activities, or general expectations or agreements that must be factored in?

■ **What strategic challenges are facing the institution? Do any of these hold specific capital implications?** A major strategic shift or investment almost certainly will change the capital base. This must be figured in as well as the knock on implications to the rest of the firm.

■ **What signals will the capital position send to external parties or investors?** For publicly traded firms, the capital position is clearly disclosed. In this age of expanded notes and explanations in the financial statements, marketing wrappers, and analyst briefings, you must ensure that the information on the risk and capital position is disclosed one way or another. For some, local disclosures for Basel II and Solvency II will satisfy that. Let's make it to our advantage.

■ **What is the maximum sustainable loss?** This is the drop-dead point. Don't forget liquidity risk in this estimation because in a real crisis, the ability to convert assets to cash capital rapidly will be challenged. The value of some assets will diminish rapidly. A natural loss with this must be figured in.

■ **What does the forecast suggest the risk profile will be in one year, in three years?** It's not just about sorting out the current year. Although the teams may be great at manipulating the capital basis, doing it right is a multi-year process. If capital is limited or if the rate of growth discovers a limiting capital supply over time, then this should figure into planning now. This goes not only for capital-raising and general capital management but also for portfolio management.

■ **What is the level of core capital generation? What are its implications?** In line with the previous statement, is the rate of growth and cash generation sufficient to support the capital requirements? Some institutions strive for a net neutral position. This can be tricky, and if the firm is not there, it will take some time to construct. This requires a careful understanding of the balance between risk, return, and real cash flows. Go back to the multi-year economic profit calculations for help.

All of these questions should be considered. The specific answers may or may not find their way into the risk appetite statement explicitly. But likely will form the basis of what does. The typical risk appetite statement is a fairly concise statement of capital expectations and key concepts in the consideration of risks throughout the organization. The value of the document often is less in the specifics of the outcome as it is in the *process* of asking and answering the questions posed. It's often the debate around what is and isn't important, the direction of organization, and the implications on capital consumption and return that provides the true value. Thereafter, the document provides a reference point from which the organization can manage (see Figure 6.3).

Part I. Summary Risk Appetite Statement:

XYZ Financial Group will operate within a _____ (e.g. low, medium, high) tolerance for risk. As such, we will utilize a target credit rating of _____ (e.g. AAA, AA, A, BBB) as our benchmark solvency standard, and in line with that a confidence interval of _____(e.g. 99.9%, 99.95%, 99.97%) as our target threshold applied to our risk models. Commensurate to these levels, we will not risk more than _____% of economic capital/equity and _____% of earnings.

This will be reflected in our willingness to focus on the following core activities and risks:_____.

Further, we will specifically refrain from pursuing the following activities and risks:_____.

Part II: Statement of Key Risk Taking:

XYZ Financial Group will operate under the following considerations for our key risks and other factors:

Financial Risks: Our core financial risks are _____ (liquidity, interest rate, credit, market). We will operate within the following expectations for each:

- e.g. Liquidity Risk: XYZ Inc expects an aggressive posture on liquidity risk over the next year and plans to consider _____ % of free cash flow at risk.

Operational Risks: Our core operational risks are _____ (people, systems, process, etc.). We will operate within the following expectations for each:

- e.g. Our people are key to our strategy and reputation. We will ensure that our key indicators are all rated medium to high and all people-related scenarios will be managed to ensure lowest probability.

Strategic Risks: Our core strategic risks are _____. We will operate within the following expectations for each:

- e.g. Reputation Risk: We consider our reputation to be our greatest strength and commercial asset. We will take a conservative position regarding the protection of our reputation. All new undertakings must be reviewed at senior management committee. Any emerging issues with customers or the community must be escalated immediately.

FIGURE 6.3   Risk Appetite Statement—XYZ Financial Group

Part III: Risk vs. Return:

We will target _____% risk adjusted return on capital (RAROC) and apply that as our minimum hurdle rate for new projects and other transactions. We expect that each department will generate a return that meets or exceeds that level. A forecast for the company return and risk composition is attached as an appendix.

Part IV: Thresholds:

Each risk will be monitored in line with the operating policies in place and a quarterly report will be provided monitoring the level of risk taking against thresholds as set out below in total and for each of our departments. A buffer of 15% will be set for each risk. A trigger monitoring framework will be used in order to signal activities in advance of a limit breach.

	Department A		Department B		Total Company	
Risk	Warning	Max	Warning	Max	Warning	Max
Credit Risk	$____	$____	$____	$____	$____	$____
Market Risk	$____	$____	$____	$____	$____	$____
Operational Risk	$____	$____	$____	$____	$____	$____

FIGURE 6.3 (*Continued*)

MANAGING THE RISK APPETITE (PROCESS)

The risk appetite process is not just one of establishing the risk appetite statement. Although that is an important and critical process in and of itself, once in place, it becomes a living document that effectively drives the institution's risk taking throughout the year. It doesn't end with board ratification of the statement

There's more. A big part of establishing a risk appetite is how the organization will monitor adherence to it.

For most firms, this means it's critical to establish limits, triggers, and a process for addressing a breach. We've briefly discussed the idea of putting limits in place. Typically, we think about limits in two levels: those at the top of the house and those at the business-unit level. Most of the day-to-day management of risk appetite is at the business-unit level, but the top-of-the house position is where it starts.

Determine how much buffer is required at the top. That is the degree of difference between the limit and the amount of capital that is the institution's ultimate-loss position. For most, this ultimate-loss position is not the maximum sustainable loss, it is something shy of that or may even be something shy of the regulatory or economic capital minimum. Many institutions start with a hard-core policy around maintaining this position, and then back off to create a limit that supports the ability to make notifications and/ or raise funds in accordance with the support of that position. That's the top-of-the house limit. The business-line positions are allocated from there.

The business-line limits themselves reflect the process of establishing a balance between the business lines' need to support their budgeted growth and risk profiles and need to support other strategic interests. Don't underestimate the challenge of this process. For most business lines, it's not a simple process to establish a reliable estimate of growth, let alone a sufficient understanding of business mix to produce a reasonable capital estimate. It generally involves an iterative process that supports bottom-up estimates from core product lines. These estimates are typically generated as volume estimates and may challenge the business's ability to establish a view of potential mix sufficient for modelers to generate capital forecasts. Many organizations fall back on simple growth estimates. If this is your plan, it's probably a fair place to start. But recognize that the variability during the business year can be enormous.

Some organizations construct a "bid" process whereby business lines establish their individual expectations for capital, the commensurate revenue and growth projections that support those, and then establish risk-adjusted return estimates. These, in turn, are stacked up against other business lines to ensure that each business line is pulling its weight. Capital is allocated as a "zero-sum" game, a pie that is fully allocated. If during the year the business line is not supporting its promised return commitment, the capital can be withdrawn and reallocated elsewhere.

That is only one model and it is best applied where organizations are larger or have constructed separate balance sheets for each major business line or geographical center. It transfers the responsibility of tracking and management strictly to the business line. There are many variants on this technique, but the idea is simple: Establish performance expectations and limits and make sure business lines understand that they need to deliver to both of those or they will lose their resources.

Taking the process further, it is useful to also establish triggers that warn when limits are approached. Some organizations manage this by establishing large buffers on the limits themselves, and then worry less about the underlying mechanics of how those occur. However, for dynamically growing organizations, it is wise to manage with greater forethought. Trigger processes often are constructed with two sets of triggers: a maximum "warning" threshold which signals the approach of a limit; and triggers that describe the portfolio's pattern or behavior before a meaningful change in the actual capital position.

The maximum warning threshold is usually a simple trigger that may be established as a percent of the total limit. It is set up to raise a flag when the limit is being approached. It usually will trigger a process of closer review of the capital and portfolio positions and generate internal discussions within business lines. Key questions to be considered include how fast the pace of the current business will bring on a full breach, whether this is a sustainable position given the timing within the fiscal year, and whether the business can be sensibly paired back to manage through to the end of the year. Bigger decisions may involve reallocating capital within the business line or even constraining the growth of business. Depending on the reason for the breach, this may invoke a wholesale shutdown of certain business activities.

These sorts of breaches often are reasonable and almost expected within a normal and strong business environment. It is important then to provide a process for business lines to appeal for more capital from the group risk and capital committee, perhaps even the board. The breach may be resolved by establishing a short business case and appealing for an increase in the limit.

Other triggers also may be useful, including limits that describe the shape of the loss curve. Limits or triggers may be established on expectations around the mean (provisions), two, and three standard deviations. These provide an excellent means of monitoring any meaningful increase in risk within the portfolio. They also provide a trigger for deeper analysis and potentially for portfolio reallocation, hedging, asset sales, perhaps even a pullback of certain position-taking (see Figure 6.4).

This is another area where stress testing can come in handy. Stress tests can help to discern what these limits or triggers should be and how the institution might respond. Stress tests can identify both the magnitude of a

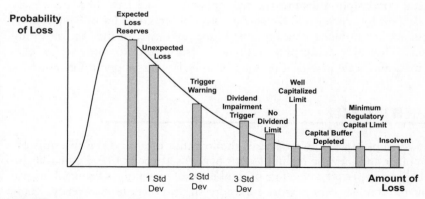

FIGURE 6.4 Example Economic Capital Trigger Framework

meaningful shift in the risk profile and what changes in the portfolio are likely to generate these types of shifts.

GOVERNANCE AND RISK APPETITE

Ultimately, the risk appetite statement must be ratified by senior management, the risk and capital committee, and the board. Many institutions include this as part of the main board proceedings and not just an activity of the board's risk committee. That's because the risk appetite statement is a critical declaration that defines not only the activities of the risk and finance teams but also defines the broader operations of the institution, its strategies, and general business dealings. It also defines the ultimate performance profile targeted for the coming year.

To this end, the oversight of risk appetite becomes a major feature in standard committee meetings at each level of the organization. Performance versus limits should be built into routine reporting, and a regular forecast also should be managed. Forecasting can be a tricky process, but it's not unreasonable for most analytics teams to establish a view for the rate of growth of capital relative to portfolio growth and mix of risk within the portfolio. Loss events can be monitored and set against this forecast as well. In many dealing rooms, it's common practice to manage a stop-loss position that tallies total losses against a total allowable loss position and expected loss position. The concept is the same for the broader organization and its risk-monitoring position. A breach of limits should rarely come as a surprise. For most types of day-to-day business management, it should be well forecasted and managed.

A formal process must be put in place for trigger and limit breaches. This process cannot be one of "shoot the messenger." The analytics team that tracks capital consumption against the risk appetite should have in place a clear process for forecasting and flagging a potential breach and a well-understood approach for bringing issues to committee. Likewise, in the case of an unexpected loss event, clear processes must be put in place to notify senior management and begin investigating and triggering liquidity support if necessary.

THE LIVING WILL

The concept of a *living will* takes the institution beyond the risk appetite statement and into the realm of what happens afterward. The global financial crisis has set off a new line of thinking that encourages financial institutions to establish a framework for addressing a potential insolvency. Many regulators are putting this concept into requirements for what they call *systemically important financial intermediaries* (SIFIs), but even smaller institutions are not beyond this level of thinking.

The general idea is that a bank must prepare for its potential demise and do so with the approval of regulators and central banks—not only in its home country but also in other major centers of operations. This is obviously a big deal for big, complex banks. But it's not such a hardship for small banks with little overseas operations. The concept is to provide for the orderly management of a financial institution through its demise, particularly ensuring the protection of depositors. This is an issue especially for banks domiciled in countries with little or no deposit insurance. At this stage, living wills likely will be required of all major banks in most countries. But they also are likely to become a major feature for other financial institutions, big and small, as a standard component of good corporate governance and a signal to shareholders, bond holders, and rating agencies that they are well managed and "in control."

The typical Living Will includes several key components:

- **Financial structure and mapping of assets.** It establishes a clear statement of the institution's financial structure and assets and the mechanism to unwind or elucidate complex tax structures. For larger financial institutions, many regulators are strongly encouraging that this be done in advance with even a potential unwinding of complex structures and the establishment of independent balance sheets for each overseas entity.
- **Plans to keep the institution alive, as needed, and plans for the orderly management of assets and arrangements.** These involve fast liquidation of assets, central bank support, attention to the settlement, delivery and netting of financial market contracts, management of credit default swap (CDS) guarantees, reallocation of positions taken on behalf of other entities, and arrangements for client asset protection.
- **Burden sharing for central banks.** This provides that central banks in each major center of operation agree to provide liquidity support. For larger institutions, this may involve bi-lateral agreements.
- **Contingent funding and de-risking plans.** These should include which businesses and assets should be sold and in what order, plus plans to stabilize funding and liquidity.
- **Deposit guarantee schemes.** These also involve central bank support, including regulators and central banks in countries that are not home jurisdiction.
- **Lists of information.** These include all of the lists of information that may be required by authorities in the event of a crisis—lists of counterparties; inventory and locations of assets, including physical assets;

details on client assets; locations of custodians; details of information storage and IT systems (including the place and form in which data are retained and back up plans); locations of titles and other collateral.

The plans should be split into three segments:

1. Pre-resolution to allow banks to restructure their operations before they get into difficulty
2. In resolution, so when problems arise, the blue prints for break up can help the authorities
3. Post-resolution to smooth out problems in the aftermath of a bank or financial institution failing

In some jurisdictions, central banks may require SIFIs to hold more capital to support depositors, particularly where deposit guarantees are limited.

At this stage, this concept is relatively new and is being put in place for the first time. There are obvious issues and complications particularly where bi-lateral agreements are required—no one entity wants to wear any more risk than it can get away with and no one entity wants to let go of any assets that it may be able to sweep up within its sovereign rights. Nevertheless, much of the development of a living will yields a helpful tool set which can bring transparency and value to current operations as well as that which is intended in the event of a crisis.

CHAPTER 7

Integrating Risk Management into Your Organization

EXECUTIVE SUMMARY

Even the most holistic and comprehensive risk management strategy won't help you if it just lives in the board room. The strategy has to permeate and infuse every level of the organization—it must be enterprise wide; it must be integrated into the daily life of everyone in the company. Risk management must become part of the culture; it must be embedded in routine processes. Everyone must see risk management as part of their responsibility. This chapter makes the case for establishing a culture that is aware of risk—and finds a balance between being overly cautious and overly exposed.

EMBEDDING RISK MANAGEMENT

Time and time again, we've found that the best way to manage risk is to make it the mandate of the entire organization. It must be a core part of the way everyone throughout the organization thinks and approaches problems and decisions. This involves integrating risk-management thinking into daily life. It must seep into the culture, the approach to risk taking, the way people analyze and make decisions, and the language used around risk-taking. At the end of the day, the objective of all of this activity is to achieve a balance between risk-taking and the actual losses incurred so that risk is relatively manageable, predictable, and well understood.

So risk management must be integrated into the fiber of the organization. People at all levels need to understand the language around risk, the concepts and what is expected of them. Not everyone needs to be a risk expert, but they do need to be educated in basic terms and know how the concepts apply to their roles and responsibilities. Risk concepts must be utilized at all levels and in most, if not all, activities. The concepts imparted need not be complicated or sophisticated. In fact, some of the most successful institutions have achieved a strong risk-management capability exactly by simplifying the framework they establish, including the relative simplicity around measures and reporting. Think of it as an elegant simplicity.

In this area, we frequently use the concept of *enterprise risk management* (ERM) to establish an institution-wide framework for risk management. This is the goal. Blazing the path to achieving it, however, is one of the most complex projects a financial institution can undertake—mainly because there is no clear definition of ERM.

WHAT IS ENTERPRISE RISK MANAGEMENT?

ERM has received a lot of attention recently. Ask a group of people about ERM, and you're likely to get a variety of responses. Personal opinions about ERM can be shaped by training, experience, and frame of reference. There seems to be two schools of thought on the subject: Some people see ERM as a set of tactics, and others see ERM as a strategy. This divergence of view explains why you can find people in the same firm disagreeing vehemently about ERM.

The term itself can be defined narrowly: Simply ensuring that all key risks are measured and consolidated in a single economic capital measure and managed accordingly.

Or it can be defined broadly: A holistic view of strategic management leveraged through the ability to capture, manage, measure, and forecast in an integrated framework that captures interrelated dependencies of risk, return, and growth across all conceivable risks. That management is done through an equally integrated framework of organization and governance that supports all those elements—kind of a "holy grail" approach.

Ten things that most people can agree on are that ERM:

1. Is not about measurement alone
2. Goes beyond just the core headline risk classes
3. Must include some leverage into the strategic thinking of the organization
4. Establishes a comprehensive performance-management approach rooted in risk-adjusted return metrics
5. Includes a well-defined governance framework reaching all the way to board level

6. Features a deep understanding and use of economic capital
7. Includes the development of a strong risk culture
8. Requires a supporting infrastructure of systems and data
9. Relies on a well-developed organization with clear risk-management roles and responsibilities
10. Is best leveraged when risk concepts are well understood and the organization has developed a common language around risk

It's no coincidence that these general observations about ERM are similar to the risk-management principles laid out earlier in this book. The whole idea of ERM is ensuring sufficient coverage of risks in the organization's management, measurement, and governance frameworks.

In an effective ERM framework, awareness of risk is elevated above and out of the traditional business silos and made visible to the organization's senior management.

Integration is the key word that sets ERM apart from simpler forms of risk management. ERM is about integrating risk classes, measurements, management, systems, processes, organization, and governance—and ideally, striking a balanced approach. It's about achieving a consolidated approach that is complete, comprehensive, and embedded. This is why it is at once both simple and challenging and why it requires continuous improvement.

We've taken the risk-management principles discussed earlier and put them on steroids.

There are key factors to success. Organizations that are the best at achieving some semblance of ERM have these five things in common:

1. Clear articulation and buy-in of the role and capabilities of the risk-management function as it pertains to business activities, including a clear understanding of current and target culture, business priorities, and participation
2. A well-understood framework for governance and control, taking into consideration the balance between business influence, central control, transparency, and efficiency
3. Fully risk-adjusted performance management based on risk-adjusted profitability metrics using risk and economic capital measures:
   ■ Integrated into all levels of business analytics and decision-making
   ■ A core component of remuneration at all levels
4. An integrated IT architecture that supports efficient and reliable data queries, management and information system (MIS) and reporting needs, and forward thinking analytics requirements
5. Focus on developing business-centric analytical support at every level of decision-making and a simple but efficient core reporting and monitoring framework

The tricky bit is that, although this all seems sensible and like a good idea, it's fairly hard to quantify the benefit. The "vision" if taken in its entirety is an expensive proposition relying upon enormous organizational commitment over a number of years. The reality is that there will be losses anyway—they are a natural part of life in most financial institutions—and it's pretty hard to calculate losses avoided. In the end, it's more about how well decisions can be made, how to leverage information into better management, improved propositions, precision pricing, enhanced customer management, and a more efficient portfolio position overall. This is where the big value comes from.

That's why it's best to consider the approach as a journey. It's a process of developing organizational change that will require patience and persistence in many cases. And at the very least, it's usually an investment in education. If the organization does not have a strong risk-management capability or culture, it will involve a bigger effort. The best approach is to start with a mandate from the top and a line of reasoning that is driven from a basis of need for improved transparency around risks and decision-making.

Develop a framework that describes the component parts of the vision and the process that the firm will take to get there. Roll it out alongside education on basic risk-management concepts and terms.

The most powerful aspects of ERM are in its uses in day-to-day business management—both in back-office activities and in front-office business-line and customer-management activities.

CULTURE

Developing a risk culture is one of the most important things you can do to support and manage your organization's risk. The way in which key decision-makers view the relationship between risk and the company defines the tone and spirit of the culture. Like any culture, however, it thrives only to the degree to which everyone contributes to its success. And when it comes to risk, every company has its own nuances. Some organizations do very well with high-risk cultures and activities such as hedge funds or proprietary trading desks. This can be fine as long as you and your workforce are critically aware of the consequences and what it means to your investment in risk management. Everyone must understand it and have a stake in it. Other companies are inherently risk averse, and it is reflected in the way they manage their day-to-day activities and decision-making. They make measured, careful decisions and typically support them with careful analysis, including risk exposure analysis that makes a careful assessment of probabilities, their impact, and their effect on liquidity and capital.

You can go a long way by simply making people aware of risk and the issues it presents. This alone can be one of the best risk-mitigation methods. Many studies have shown that most people don't perceive risk in a rational sense, nor do they understand their own contribution to creating risk. For example, most people rate themselves as better-than-average drivers, yet statistics suggest 90% of all accidents are caused by human error.

Ten factors have been studied and proven to matter when thinking about a risk culture. The level of urgency with which people take risk and manage it depends upon their views of these factors:

1. Randomness or intent of risk
2. Immediacy of effect
3. Risk knowledge by the person(s) exposed to the risk source
4. Technical knowledge
5. Control over the risk
6. Newness of risks
7. Style in which it occurs—whether it is chronic or catastrophic. Do your risks occur one at a time or can they occur in large numbers?
8. Commonness of risk. Have people become accustomed to the risk and learned to live with it? Can they think about it reasonably and calmly, or do people dread it?
9. Severity of consequences
10. Trust in the agency, persons, or approaches that manage the risk

The art in addressing the issue is obtaining a clear understanding of what is meant by "risk culture." It can be defined as the system of values and behaviors present throughout an organization that shape risk decisions. Risk culture influences the decisions of management and employees, even if they are not consciously weighing risks and benefits.

One element of risk culture is the degree to which individuals understand that risk and compliance rules apply to everyone as they conduct business. To start, that requires a common understanding of the organization and its business purpose. Some today seem to have lost sight of those business goals, forgetting that they serve the company and shareholders, not the other way around.

In a recent survey of nearly 500 bank executives, nearly half (48 percent) of respondents cited risk culture as a leading contributor to the recent credit crisis. Clearly, those financial institutions with histories of strong risk culture have weathered the storm best. This is frequently the case of institutions that have taken large losses of any kind. In post-mortem evaluations of cases involving large events, risk culture frequently was a major contributor. The problems in those cases usually were a lack of concern—even disregard—for consequences, and it usually followed big profit taking, particularly in dealing-room scenarios.

One very large and well publicized dealing-room loss was followed by a comprehensive review of processes and practices in the organization. Although the loss was specifically caused by a trader perpetrating a fraud, the review discovered that the overall attitude toward risk and risk-management was severely lax. Risk management was ignored and met with disdain and even derision. It was difficult for risk managers to exert any control over the organization, whether contributing to decisions about specific risk-taking or trying to develop better processes for monitoring and managing risks.

Short of a near-fatal loss—which nearly always causes a rapid culture change—there are two key levers for affecting change around risk culture: one is driving a "tone from the top"; the other is developing a robust, company-wide education program to ensure that everyone understands risk concepts, their role in risk management, and the consequences of non-compliance.

The first step to asserting the importance of risk culture is starting a dialogue on the topic with management. This must begin with board, whose members have to embrace the tone and drive expectations downward. Likewise, the best way to convey expectations is to walk the walk and talk the talk. The board and senior management must demonstrate to employees that they embrace the risk culture, make decisions using risk information, and care about the quality of measures and their implications.

A management team that places importance on risk culture is essential to creating the right risk-management tone throughout the enterprise. While the phrase "tone at the top" may be over-used, there is simple truth in the idea that when leadership sets the example, others will follow. Risk culture can't be changed if the charge is coming from the risk-management function alone; leadership must be the real driver of change. It must not only come from the management team but be rapidly driven down to the supervisory level. Employees tend to look to their immediate supervisors as role models, so even lower levels of the organization must be in line with the themes, concepts, and expectations.

Setting the appropriate tone at the top requires good communication. Leadership must send a message that is heard throughout all levels of the organization—not just in the boardroom. Risk culture is not something that can be changed overnight. It requires constant, consistent messages to employees that managing risk is a part of their daily responsibilities and that it is not only valued but critical to the company's success and survival.

Communications and training is a key lever for achieving ERM. Although risk culture has become a fundamental building block of good ERM practices, many companies show evidence of deficiencies in this area. For instance, more than half (58 percent) of companies surveyed said their employees had little or no understanding of how risk exposures should be assessed for likelihood and impact. One-third of those same respondents also said that key leaders in their organization had no formal risk-management training or guidance.

Building an ERM capability requires understanding and a strong culture to support it. Otherwise the program likely will fail to prevent poor decision-making. Employees must understand how to make educated risk-related decisions to ensure consistent risk behavior throughout the organization. But without training, there is no basis for critical thinking and judgment around risk decision-making. This is why it's essential that a well-constructed communication and education program be a key component of any ERM program. Those that don't include one are destined to fail.

INCENTIVES AND COMPENSATION

Recent discussions of financial-services companies' failings have brought the issue of incentives into the spotlight. Recent publicity on the topic has prompted many companies to question whether their own incentive programs properly reward employees for performance consistent with the firm's values and risk appetite.

When companies reward reckless conduct or results gained through any means, the risk-management message is diluted. Rewards for all employees at all levels—from the shop floor to the CEO—should depend on whether their actions comply with the organization's strategy and risk appetite. Further, the evaluations of chief executive officers (CEOs), chief financial officers (CFOs), and other senior managers must include their ability to promote appropriate risk behavior throughout the organization and make appropriate risk-based decisions.

Rewarding inappropriate risk conduct sets a bad example for how employees should conduct themselves. It also sends the message that the company does not value risk management, and that may discourage employees from reporting unethical or unwise conduct. In addition to setting appropriate standards, organizations must create formal working channels and procedures for reporting incidents and ensure that confidentiality is upheld.

Some of the best practices are found with companies that have woven risk-adjusted performance measures directly into the compensation scheme. This approach is not to be taken lightly; it can be a tough transition. It involves ensuring that everyone understands the measures, that measures are well thought out and don't generate undesirable behavior, and that they are sufficiently straight-forward that managers understand how they will achieve their goals.

A key example of this is in the use of risk-adjusted return on capital (RAROC). We've talked about some of its characteristics previously, but as a compensation tool, these can be accentuated. It's generally a simple measure that is readily obtained and easily understood. But even this can go wrong in some institutions. It doesn't include a dimension of overall size and growth. Using it on its own can sometimes yield the wrong results. Imagine that in an organization's hunt for improved returns, it is feasible to winnow down the portfolio, successively shrinking the business in the pursuit of the best returns.

Other organizations have placed an over-emphasis on the numerator, sometimes referred to as cash earnings or risk-adjusted profit. This may seem like an easy transition step or a good way to manage intra-period benchmarks. But it can drive an overemphasis on the capital benefit line. Remember that as risks increase, so does the capital benefit. This is typically well offset by reserves and capital, but timing differences or movement against very low-risk portfolios can drive short-term outcomes past this seemingly minor term.

RAROC also tends to be more volatile. It may easily swing from one period to the next and be quite dependent on movements in the capital measure, which can stir great controversy, particularly when it is newly installed. This tendency can drive discussions away from meaningful behavioral change and revert to unnecessary quibbling.

More often, organizations have greater long-term success with either a combination of measures, such as RAROC + growth, or more likely with measures such as economic profit (EP). The challenge here is that, although the measure is really no more complex than RAROC, it often is perceived as more complex. So its implementation requires more education or a more step-wise approach.

It's important to establish a balance between growth, return, and risk. I call this the three-legged stool of performance management. It's also important to start simply, then build as the organization gains acceptance and confidence. This may mean starting with a shadow tracking of measures while creating a stoplight approach to serious non-compliance issues. This requires establishing the view that infractions simply are not tolerated and serving up severe consequences for breaches. Poor attitude or more minor infractions may be noted on a sliding scale whereby warnings are issued for "amber behavior," and "red behavior" has more serious consequences. The measures themselves and the approach to their use can be phased in over time to ultimately become a strong link among performance, behavior, and outcomes.

YOUR ORGANIZATION

Risk management is everyone's business. Firmly establishing that concept is one of the first and most important steps toward integrating risk-management into your organization. Everyone in the company must be aware of risk and hold a basic understanding of the risks associated with the company and their jobs. One of the keys to this is to make sure risk management is an explicit part of each person's job description. Employees should be aware of the risks prevalent in the lines of business they serve, how they may relate to their jobs, and how they may manifest.

This often starts with the hiring process. Organizations that make sure new employees exemplify the desired risk culture can more readily shape the behaviors of the broader employee base. They build it in by hiring people who share similar values and ethics. It also allows the company to set expectations from the start.

This is where a structured education program that updates regularly is crucial. Some organizations even establish certification programs for role descriptions. Such programs have become even more important since the advent of Basel II, in which demonstrating deep knowledge and use of risk approaches is a mantra. In some jurisdictions, regulators conduct random interviews of various employees, some who have relatively little direct touch points on regulatory risk-management issues.

Some specific roles can function as backstops to risk management. Many staff functions are, in effect, an extension of the risk-management team. All have supporting roles in designing and shaping effective risk-management capabilities.

Human Resources

The human resource function carries a two-fold role in risk management:

1. Implement and manage initiatives that relate to the broader culture and capabilities of the organization
2. Support the specific hiring of personnel

The human resources department implements training and cultural-awareness programs and change-management. The department also designs and implements the company's code of conduct and addresses many related broad policy issues.

The department also is integral in identifying and developing the business's leadership, including succession planning. The criteria for the company's future leaders should be shaped by their personal values and how they utilize those values in their jobs. This includes their attitudes about risk management and taking risk relative to return.

Legal

The legal function ensures that contracts are made and followed, the company is kept abreast of new laws and regulations that may affect operating policies, customer disclosure requirements are followed, and more. The legal folks often interact with (or are) the compliance officers that provide critical information on whether planned transactions or protocols conform to legal and ethical requirements. They also track the adherence to those requirements.

The legal team often is set aside from many formal risk-management activities yet may be the risk manager's greatest ally. It is important to include the legal department in communication, education, and even the development of compliance management and other aspects of operational risk management. The legal team may become a key part of the risk process in identifying risks and managing risk mitigation. Consider how to include legal in your risk-management reporting and monitoring framework.

Strategic Planning

We've already touched on the importance of the link between risk-management, the risk appetite, and strategic planning. So it goes to reason that the strategic planning team members need to be included in the sphere of influence of risk management. They need to understand the basics but also know how to work with the risk-management team to pull risk insights and metrics into the strategic planning process and specific strategic decisions.

Finance and Accounting

Here again, risk management must be deeply woven into the finance and accounting processes. This takes on a number of different dimensions:

- Their broad, company-wide reach often makes them aware of the plans of all different functions.
- Their lead role in budgeting and planning.

- Their role in tracking and analyzing performance; it's usually finance that administers and reports on any risk-adjusted performance metrics and sets some of the underlying components of the calculations, such as the funds transfer rate.
- They are responsible for the company's balance sheet hedging and markets activities. So in this role are potential sources or direct managers of risk.
- They are responsible for the company's funding, including securitization and capital raising activities.
- They often interface with investors and the board.
- They interface with equity and credit analysts and often are one of the key conduits to the company's regulators.
- They are responsible for the company's financial reporting and for designing, implementing, and monitoring the company's external financial reporting requirements.
- They often are critical for setting the company tone regarding ethical conduct.

The CFO is typically at the table when objectives are established, strategies decided, risks analyzed, and decisions made. More broadly, the CFO is also strongly influential with investors. In addition, he often drives the strategy regarding how reserves, capital, and buffers around them are implemented.

Many organizations have traditionally set the responsibilities of the chief risk officer (CRO) with the CFO as a dual role or with the CRO reporting to the CFO. In recent years, this has been frowned upon by regulatory agencies, which greatly prefer separation of risk management and risk-taking activities. Nevertheless, many of the requirements of Basel II (and Basel III) push the two groups closer together than ever, interweaving them in the development of the risk appetite, integration of risk-adjusted performance metrics, and management of capital. This is one of the great challenges in adopting Basel II.

It is important to make the CFO an integral player in risk-management activities. Develop a specific and well-articulated view of risk-management roles and the finance function and how they will work together.

Many other roles within the organization are also important to risk-management. In some cases, it may even be appropriate to extend beyond the organization's boundaries to include strategic partners, vendors, and service providers. While it may not be reasonable to expect outside service providers to have the same risk culture as your organization, a company may set service levels and metrics to ensure that providers manage risks within your company's guidelines. Companies must take oversight of these outside support organizations to ensure they meet their own risk standards.

Risks and controls should be a consideration when choosing new partners, and they should be reevaluated on a regular basis to help avoid the potential of vicarious liability by the poor decisions of a partner.

LINES OF DEFENSE

The "four lines of defense" is a common organizational model in risk-management. Some may refer to it as the "three lines of defense," but I subscribe to the philosophy that senior management and the board—the fourth line—are critical backstops for the firm's activities.

The "four lines of defense" model describes the basic roles within the company for managing risk. It presumes that risk is everyone's business. Each person assumes a slightly different function that depends on his or her role in the organization. The four lines include: business management (front line); risk and compliance management; audit; and senior management/board.

Part of the premise associated with this model is that companies cannot effectively manage risk by compartmentalizing. It takes a whole company working together to manage risks in a successful, cost-efficient manner and to maintain a desirable risk culture. This takes on greater significance in light of the ever-soaring cost of compliance with varying regulations and other requirements.

Also, by including a total company view of organizational roles and responsibilities, risk approaches become better embedded in a company's operations and culture. This begins at the early stages of strategy formulation and product development and continues through the product and customer lifecycles. This enables the formal risk organization to serve an advisory role in deepening capabilities, particularly where risks are most prevalent.

The First Line of Defense: Front-Line Business Management

Front-line managers form the first line of defense. This consists of business management functions, particularly those dealing with developing, producing, and selling products. The people handling these duties drive many of the firm's day-to-day risks. They are best positioned to keep an eye on risks, understand what decisions to make (and not make), which customers and products to focus on, terms and conditions, and how to maintain production and systems.

The front line must work within the guidelines set by the risk-management team—that is, controls and limits. To that end, the risk-management department must remain independent to ensure it has no direct stake or conflict of interest in decisions.

Senior managers are integral components to any front line. Since they oversee key functions and business lines, it makes common sense to give them the day-to-day responsibility for managing risks. They convert strategy into actions, which creates an intrinsic need to ensure they are identifying and assessing risks and risk responses. The process works when they guide the implementation of the risk-management process within their spheres of responsibility. They also strive to make their approach consistent with the company's risk tolerances.

The Second Line of Defense:
The Risk Management Team

The team requires a clear mandate and authority to make risk-management decisions. It runs the risk-management process. Team members provide other groups in the company, support and guidance for identification of and day-to-day management of risks. They also may offer focused special support in the analyzing of strategic initiatives.

Sometimes, the role of the risk and compliance team may extend beyond the specific risk measures and mitigation approaches. This happens when the support the team provides to the business lines also involves optimizing and improving processes and pricing, for example. For many organizations, this level of partnership with business lines may be a goal. The risk-management organization often starts as little more than an internal policing activity. But in most cases, for risk management to become truly successful and integrated into the fiber of the company, it is necessary to evolve the risk-management team to a role more similar to a business line partner or advisor. Recall the evolution of the risk function's role that we introduced in Chapter 3.

A *partnership model* allows organizations to better understand their risks and to join planning and management together. It allows the risk-compliance team to not only safeguard the organization but also work with various divisions or departments to optimize their capabilities. Most companies find that partnering is the best approach for building overall organizational awareness, efficiency, and compliance.

Nevertheless, it remains critical to maintain a semblance of independence and have both the organizational mandate and the gravitas to say "no" when it's warranted. Conversely, part of the having the appropriate level of organizational maturity is being able to wield influence without having to force the issue. These characteristics are among those most critical to creating an effective risk-management team—one that will drive development of the culture and capabilities desired by the Board.

The CRO role recently has become more prominent in most financial-services firms. For banks, it has become a virtual mandate in most jurisdictions. Even in insurance groups, more and more have adopted a chief risk officer role—more than 70% now have them. The role itself has morphed to gain greater importance. In many companies, the CRO no longer reports to a CFO or chief operating officer (COO). It now stands alone and reports to the CEO and sometimes even has a reporting line to the board. This sends a signal of seriousness to the organization and to external parties alike. Many regulatory authorities eschew a subordinate reporting line. To maintain independence, it is critical that the CRO remains separate.

As regulatory requirements expand, so does the role of the CRO. Ultimately, the CRO is responsible for day-to-day risk management. That includes identifying risks, ensuring that they are assessed and monitored, and monitoring progress in the implementation of risk mitigation. He or she makes sure information about risks is reported throughout the organization and ensures that the organization's risk appetite is defined and maintained. The CRO coordinates and facilitates the risk management process, working with other managers to establish an effective risk-management framework and approach. Full duties include:

- Establishing risk-management policies, defining roles and responsibilities, and participating in setting goals for implementation of risk-management capabilities
- Framing accountability and authority for risk management in the business units or departments
- Ensuring that the company develops a basis of risk-management competence and knowledge. This includes an appropriate level of related technical expertise
- Aligning risk-management responses with the company's risk tolerance
- Ensuring the integration of risk management into business planning and other management activities
- Ensuring a common risk-management language that includes common measures around likelihood, impact, expected loss, and unexpected loss
- Overseeing the development of specific risk tolerances and controls for different business activities
- Establishing (or ensuring the establishment) of reporting approaches, including quantitative and qualitative information and thresholds
- Overseeing the monitoring of the process
- Ensuring that there is appropriate reporting to senior management, the CEO, and the board, and recommending actions as needed

This role comes with a big challenge. Although the CRO takes responsibility and authority for risk-management implementation and decisions, line managers still must take primary responsibility and accountability for managing risk within their respective areas. After all, they usually generate most of the risk.

The Third Line of Defense: Audit

The internal audit department plays a key role in evaluating the effectiveness of the risk-management process. Auditors consider the risk-management process and control review to be a natural part of their role. It is explicitly stated by all of the bodies that govern auditing standards.

It is important to note that auditors do not—and should not—hold primary responsibility for establishing and maintaining risk-management framework. That is the responsibility of the CEO and CRO.

Auditors focus on the quality of the financial statements. The information presented within those statements should provide a fair view of the company's financial position. While poor risk management may not affect the statement of today's financial position, it can make an audit more expensive and the auditor's job of verifying the information more difficult. In all likelihood, that next financial statement won't look so rosy.

In recent years, greater requirements for validation of risk-management processes and models have taxed the auditors' traditional approaches and scope. To respond, many audit teams have had to beef up their skill sets and understanding of risk management—particularly technical aspects. For many organizations, the concept of independent model validation has created enormous debate over who should do it. On the surface, it may seem like a natural role for audit, but it often requires more detailed technical competence than an auditor would have. Regardless of which approach is used, the audit role must expand to encompass a role in the review— whether it be to actually perform the technical review or to review it. The independence of the auditors' role and the viewpoint they bring is a critical contributing factor.

The Fourth Line of Defense: Senior Management and the Board

Realistically, they must set the tone, lead the charge, and assume ultimate responsibility for the process. Both the board and senior management hold dual roles in ensuring that the risk-management process is implemented and conducted in line with the firm's values and requirements. They ensure that the companywide implementation of risk management is effective.

They also have a critical oversight role in risk management. It includes:

- Deciding and ensuring the extent to which risk management is implemented across and down the organization
- Setting the company's risk appetite
- Reviewing the company's risk portfolio and comparing it against the risk appetite
- Determining how the company will respond to its most significant risks

The board and senior management lead and participate in many key decisions and adjunct activities that create and/or utilize risk and the risk-management thought processes. They set strategy, create high-level objectives, and determine resource allocation in the broader sense. However, there are some subtle differences between board and senior management responsibilities. Management is directly responsible for all of the activities, while the board provides the oversight.

But the buck stops with the CEO. The regulator's knuckles will rap loudly on the CEO's door first. The CEO has ultimate responsibility to appropriately manage risk. That includes ensuring the right culture and environment exists for managing risk. The tone is set from the top.

The CEO's specific responsibilities regarding risk management are:

- Providing leadership and direction to senior managers
- Meeting periodically with senior managers responsible for the key functions and business lines to review how they are managing risk
- Understanding the risks inherent in the operations
- Understanding the risk-measurement, monitoring, and mitigation put in place, as well as the status of any on-going efforts.

Together, the CEO and senior management establish the principles, values, and major operating policies that form the basis of the risk-management framework. They also establish the risk appetite and culture and ensure that key policies are appropriately communicated.

REPORTING, MONITORING, AND DECISION-MAKING

The ability to develop and manage an effective reporting and monitoring capability is an anathema for many organizations. We often hear about the use of the "risk dashboard" or similar forms of reporting and monitoring mechanisms, but the truth is that few organizations have such things and fewer yet even have a reporting framework that works particularly well.

Reporting on risks probably seems like one of the most boring things you could do. It ranks right up there with watching grass grow. This may be one reason why it rarely gets its due attention. But a well-constructed reporting approach is a beautiful thing. Think of it as "turning on the lights while driving at night." It's possible to manage without them, but it's a whole lot easier with them. A reporting approach gives people confidence in where the organization stands, and if well constructed, allows for clear decision-making.

The flip side is also true. A poorly-designed report can often wind up in the circular file, making the exercise a waste of time and money. So given that most companies are in the minority on this point, what to do? It's important to be clear and ruthless about what must to be reported, who receives it, how to array high-impact information, and how often should reports be issued.

Here's a start.

How to Report

Start your reporting by focusing on the summary statement. What are the key messages from last period to this period that must be put forward to the target audience? There are four major things to build into a risk report: the key risks; why they are critical; how they are changing over time; and what you are doing to stop or mitigate them. Try to limit your key risks to those that are truly vital. Can you tell a full story by talking about only the top ten risks? Can you tell it with the top five?

Keep the report physically small. Even many large organizations have ordered report writers to keep this statement to *two pages*. Nobody has enough time to review an exhaustive manuscript; they don't want 60-page reports on risk. What are your risks? How have they changed? What do you need to act on—now? That's the report.

Who will read it? Consider your audience. Think carefully about who needs to know specific types of information and at what level. As a rule of thumb, the higher you climb in an organization, the more important it is to communicate using the "rule of less than seven" and odd clusters. This becomes more challenging, because more risks usually appear as your reporting "rolls up" toward the top.

What's the "rule of less than seven?" The human mind can remember fewer than seven items simultaneously. (That's why phone numbers originally were built on seven digits!). The mind also responds to items in odd number clusters. When reporting risks processes, aim for three or five key points. That way, recipients are more likely to retain—and hopefully act upon—the key messages.

Always keep your focus on the top risks. The CEO most likely cares only about the top five to ten for the entire organization. In one case, the CEO focused strictly on the top five, realizing he could only address the top five issues at any given time. Once those were eliminated, he'd always have at least five more waiting. The lower-ranking risks would have percolated upward or "vanished" in one way or another.

Also, remember that in risk management, you want to engender interest and understanding by many people—several of whom are particularly important in the firm-wide management of risk. You want to help them help you.

How to Create an Impact

Besides keeping it focused and tight, be sure the report spotlights not only pure risks but also risks versus returns. That way, you can gain perspective over the entire view of the key risks' relationship to your business. Don't forget to build in some good news as well—like successfully implemented risk mitigation or an averted risk event. Make sure that risk and risk management can be viewed positively, especially when you're building toward a change in the company's culture and attitude toward risk.

How Often to Report

Consider the type of business you're in, and go from there. If transactions are few and lumpy, it may not be necessary to report too frequently. If it's a fast-paced business where the portfolio turns over daily, then daily may be appropriate. Most organizations ultimately are driven by monthly and quarterly business cycles, which would answer at least some of these issues.

Decision-Making

One of the most critical points is to ensure that the information can be used for decision-making—and is. This in itself may be a cultural transition, but it's important to facilitate that move rather than hinder it.

Most organizations say they consider risk when making decisions, but the reality is that it's often done informally. They rely on individuals' understanding, experience, and skills in risk management and may not even consult their risk-management team. Often there are unintended consequences that are not considered, such as brand, reputation, and regulatory noncompliance—particularly if considering a decision that is being acted out over multiple jurisdictions.

Organizations with a strong risk culture have a consistent, repeatable approach to risk when making key business decisions—including discussion of risk and a review of risk scenarios that help management and the board understand the interrelationship and impacts of risks. A discussion of risk in the formal decision-making process can help executives feel comfortable with their decisions, allowing them to pursue the interests of the company more assertively.

LEVERAGING YOUR BUSINESS RHYTHM

Most companies run on some sort of yearly cycle. It is often finance-driven, beginning just before the start of the financial year with the development of strategic planning and budgeting. There may be hard checks when interim financial statements are due or an investor or board review is pending. These reviews often take place quarterly. The whole cycle ends with consolidating the financial position and developing the yearly financial statements.

The cycle of activities that revolve around strategic and financial management define the *business rhythm*. Much of the company falls in line with plans, budgets, and reporting targets in some form or another. The company should do the same with risk. Embed risk into each of these activities and they should integrate with the existing cycles. This also helps to embed a routine framework of risk activities and ensure that risk is a key component in how people think. It also helps drive the process around *both* the strategic plan and the risk appetite (see Figure 7.1).

Planning, Budgeting, and Forecasting

Business rhythm starts with the annual business plan. The business plan creates a broad, and hopefully specific, view of what the balance sheet and profit and loss (P&L) should look like at the end of the year. It also spells out financial activities that must occur to support it, and in turn, the risk-management implications.

When you build risk into your business plan, include answers to the following questions:

- Is risk information included in the company's strategic planning?
- Have you considered how your plans affect risk?
- Will new initiatives carry different or more risks?
- Could they reduce risk?

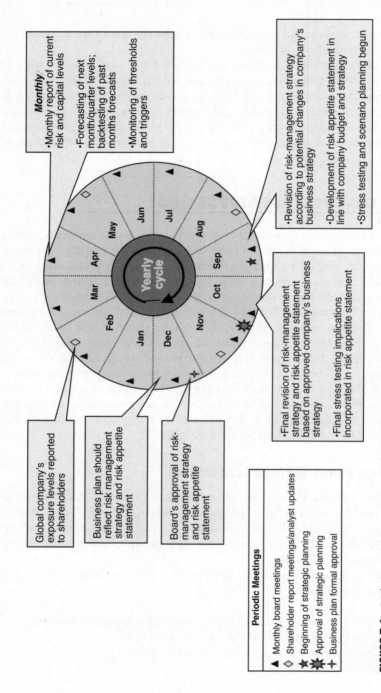

Monthly
- Monthly report of current risk and capital levels
- Forecasting of next month/quarter levels; backtesting of past months forecasts
- Monitoring of thresholds and triggers

- Revision of risk-management strategy according to potential changes in company's business strategy
- Development of risk appetite statement in line with company budget and strategy
- Stress testing and scenario planning begun

- Final revision of risk-management strategy and risk appetite statement based on approved company's business strategy
- Final stress testing implications incorporated in risk appetite statement

Global company's exposure levels reported to shareholders

Business plan should reflect risk management strategy and risk appetite statement

Board's approval of risk-management strategy and risk appetite statement

Yearly cycle

Jan Feb Mar Apr May Jun Jul Aug Sep Oct Nov Dec

Periodic Meetings
◄ Monthly board meetings
◇ Shareholder report meetings/analyst updates
★ Beginning of strategic planning
✸ Approval of strategic planning
✛ Business plan formal approval

FIGURE 7.1 Risk Appetite Integration with The Business Rhythm

- How do the new initiatives measure up on a risk versus return basis?
- Will any of the plans require new or additional mitigation?
- How will you monitor risks as you implement the new plan?
- Will you require specifically new investment to support this?
- Will you require more capital for buffers or reserves?
- Have you discussed this topic at senior management and board meetings?

When integrating risk into the business plan, make sure to review the risk appetite. This should be considered yearly as part of the process. As you look at the issue, ask:

- Has your risk appetite changed since last year?
- Will any plans or initiatives require you to reconsider your risk appetite?
- How will the thresholds identified in the risk appetite be affected?
- Should these thresholds change to reflect company growth or changes in the inherent risk profile?
- Who needs to participate in decisions that may arise from this process?

The best organizations project the growth and mix of their business, and then apply risk measures. They do so to understand changes in expected loss, unexpected loss, and how diversification can affect the overall risks. These steps enable the company to estimate what sort of reserves, capital, and liquidity considerations and other forms of mitigation will be required—all of which falls into the budgeting process.

Have you developed an explicit budget for risk management? Does it allow for continuous improvement? Does it consider the changing profile of company risks and growth? The core risk budget usually needs to increase if the company is growing.

For many companies, it can be a daunting affair to establish a sufficient forecast of expected losses and capital. It's surprising how few actually attempt to develop the capability. Capital forecasting, in particular, is rarely more developed than the "thumb in the air" approach.

Yet it is absolutely possible to project capital requirements with simple models based on the economic capital models that support analysis of growth, mix, and even diversification These models also can project other key factors such as core capital generation and risk-adjusted return implications. The process of working with the business lines to establish their view and expectation can, once again, become a valuable component of instilling awareness of their actions and their affect on the risk profile of the firm.

ERM AND COSO

As a final point to this theme, I'd be remiss in overlooking the groundbreaking work some years ago by the Committee of Sponsoring Organizations to the Treadway Commission (COSO). The body of work attempted to set a standard for ERM. The committee's standard is rooted in sound approaches for organizational compliance management and establishes a framework described as three dimensional.

These start with the *internal control objectives*, the organization's means of achieving its objectives. They include:

- Strategic: high-level goals, aligned with and supporting its mission
- Operations: effective and efficient use of its resources
- Reporting: reliability of reporting
- Compliance: compliance with applicable laws and regulations

The second concept is the *components of enterprise risk management*. They include:

- **Internal environment.** The internal environment encompasses the tone of an organization, and sets the basis for how risk is viewed and addressed by an organization's people, including risk-management philosophy and risk appetite, integrity and ethical values, and the environment in which they operate.
- **Objective setting.** Objectives must exist before management can identify potential events affecting their achievement. Enterprise risk management ensures that management has in place a process to set objectives and that the chosen objectives support and align with the organization's mission and are consistent with its risk appetite.
- **Event identification.** Internal and external events affecting achievement of an entity's objectives must be identified, distinguishing between risks and opportunities. Opportunities are channeled back to management's strategy or objective-setting processes.
- **Risk assessment.** Risks are analyzed, considering likelihood and impact, as a basis for determining how they should be managed. Risks are assessed on an inherent and a residual basis.
- **Risk response.** Management selects risk responses—avoiding, accepting, reducing, or sharing risk—developing a set of actions to align risks with the entity's risk tolerances and risk appetite.
- **Control activities.** Policies and procedures are established and implemented to help ensure the risk responses are effectively carried out.
- **Information and communication.** Relevant information is identified, captured, and communicated in a form and time frame that enable

people to carry out their responsibilities. Effective communication also occurs in a broader sense, flowing down, across, and up the entity.

- **Monitoring.** The entirety of enterprise risk management is monitored and modifications made as necessary. Monitoring is accomplished through ongoing management activities, separate evaluations, or both.

The requirements of each of these two dimensions may be further defined on each level of the enterprise, the third dimension, defined as:

- Subsidiary
- Business-unit
- Division
- Entity-level

It is a superb framework for identifying and managing risk and for compliance in a generalized framework—especially in a formal audit review framework. It applies to all types of institutions, not only financial-services firms. However, it has frequently caused confusion with senior management. Particularly at the onset of many Basel II programs or other similar sorts of transformational enterprise-wide risk-management programs, the inevitable question comes up, "Haven't we already done that?" The short answer is that it is absolutely supportive of the concepts put forth in Basel II, particularly in the Pillar II framework where the organization is asked to evaluate its risks more holistically and ensure appropriate process, monitoring and governance, in addition to measurement.

However, although unintended as such, the typical implementations of COSO tend to be more limited to the audit and compliance community and fairly tactical in nature. On this level, they will not sufficiently address many of the requirements of a financial-services firm. The requirements for specific forms of risk measurement and management, tied with the financial obligations of reserves and capital that are coupled with that, go beyond the more general guidelines of COSO. Equally, the level and degree to which risk culture plays a part in the success or failure of a financial-services entity tends to be underplayed in COSO although it is mentioned as a critical component.

Nevertheless the framework is often a helpful place to start, and by all accounts should be raised in its importance as a useful guideline to extend beyond the audit community. It speaks to a broader audience and broader use within a firm, particularly one that is embarking anew on an approach to risk-management thinking across the organization.

CHAPTER 8

Leveraging Risk for Business Excellence

EXECUTIVE SUMMARY

Congratulations! You've made it to the pot of gold, at least figuratively speaking. This chapter is the payoff—here is where we discuss the mechanisms for leveraging risk management to grow your business and make more money. We look at all the various tools and tactics available for turning risk into real profit—without throwing safety overboard. We look at targeting, segmentation, product selection, pricing, cost management, asset allocation, optimization, and a host of other business processes that can be cranked up and significantly improved with the addition of metrics and knowledge generated from managing risk. We look at how risk management can be integrated into business planning to create sustainable long-term strategies that will carry you far beyond the competition.

MORE THAN COMPLIANCE

Many if not most people think about risk management as a back-office activity that is part of compliance. It's that annoying piece of overhead that regulators say we have to do and that management reluctantly drags itself through—like taking bad tasting medicine.

The irony is that your risk-management capabilities may be one of your greatest strategic assets—or detriments, as the case may be. We have frequently discussed it in this book as something that should be integrated into decision-making—and not only because it builds better risk management. It also builds better portfolios, adds laser precision to your strategies, and raises profitability. It's also how we more effectively manage when things do go wrong in down markets or when a risk event occurs. Being the best at managing downside risk often means being the last one standing—or the least injured.

Having good risk management doesn't mean you have to be conservative. It means you're being smart. There are a few notable "high risk" players who have demonstrated repeatedly that they can be high risk and not crash and burn every time they hit turbulent weather. That's because they're good at risk management. Their high risk strategy is not taken out of ignorance and an overly aggressive growth stance. They target high risk and manage it accordingly.

When I think about risk measures and management, I think of what I can do with the information to run the business better. I want to know that the investment in risk capabilities will give me a return in the business. It's not an uncommon bias, but it is one that risk folks often have difficulty embracing because many don't come from a business background or because it's not their first objective. This is the reason I ultimately gravitated to risk management as a discipline—because I could see the myriad of uses for the information in improving business decisions—making better decisions faster, executing strategies with greater insight, and structuring portfolios better, smarter, and faster.

It's also why I have extreme biases on the specific forms of measurement employed and the investment in those measures. I'm acutely aware of the 80/20 principal, which we discussed early in this book. There are times when risk measures are simply "good enough" for their application, and 80% to 90% implementation is more than adequate for sound monitoring and management. But sometimes more is needed—either because of the types of risks or the types of applications for the information. It's important to be clear about these points because it's easy to invest a lot of money and effort in something that goes unused. And that could just as easily disquiet an organization, particularly when that oh-so-precious risk culture is not yet fully developed. Be clear about the intended application and reasons behind the level of capability chosen.

So here's where we give you something to put that investment toward. The real reason why you make a risk-management investment is to see a real return. I think of these capabilities in three broad classes: managing the downside; leveraging the upside; and optimization. These can be done in any order. Depending on the condition of the market and the institution, I can make a case for any starting point. The important thing is to *start*. Building risk intuition into business management is probably the most important thing an organization can do. Not only because it gets us that all-important return on investment, but also because it often is the catalyst for getting the business lines on board and drawing them into the risk culture.

I always can spot the point of arrival for an organization that has been on the road to building good risk management: It's when the business lines start to "poach," or bring on board their own risk people. That might seem like a wholesale anarchistic nightmare, but it's actually a good sign. It means the businesses now are valuing the capabilities the risk team brings to them and they want to capture the team for themselves. They are now believers. Of course, unwinding the mess this somewhat bad behavior can produce is a bit of a problem to overcome. You can do so with pride.

INTRODUCING THE CUSTOMER LIFECYCLE

Managing the customer lifecycle is often the first port of call when considering what we can do with risk-management applications. Think about each potential customer as an opportunity. It would be financial services nirvana if we simply could identify the customers who fit our risk profile, need the product set that also suits our risk appetite, get them to buy at the price that accounts for their risk profile, keep them performing indefinitely without defaulting or making a claim, ticking over year in and year out and buying more products.

Well, it's largely doable. The tools are out there to aid the process and they all take risk measures and analytics as a core input.

Think about managing the customer lifecycle on two dimensions. The first is the product lifecycle. It's how we acquire customers within a product line and manage them through their use of the product. The second dimension is a broader view of the customer-need profiles. It's more broadly identifying customers' product preferences and requirements at each stage of their lives—if we're lucky, from their early needs to the end.

Clearly, both of these concepts intertwine as we work with customers over time. Each process can be heavily leveraged and enhanced through the use of risk metrics and related analytics. More than a decade ago, we called this concept *customer relationship management* or *CRM*. The idea got quite a bit of play at the dawn of the Internet era, when new systems were being conceived to assist this capability. It's safe to say that few companies had good experiences with this. The programs had unwieldy data requirements and messy systems-implementations, making them very expensive and not so useful in the end.

Since then, two things have happened: We've gotten smarter about how we bite off these sorts of projects, and database- and systems-capabilities have improved. The all-singing, all-dancing CRM system may still be a ways off, but it's now pretty easy to bite off specific problem segments of the lifecycle, apply risk analytics, and get insights about our customers that we can use in specific business decisions at each stage of customer interaction.

Think of the customer-management lifecycle as a continuous set of interactions, from first contact to the point of exit, with numerous touch points in between. We typically start with the idea that we can identify and target customers that we want—the right customers for our products, our funding profile, and our risk appetite. This is the acquisition stage. It includes obtaining knowledge of customer's risk-adjusted profitability, segmentation and targeting, product development, soliciting and pricing. All of these can be driven with analytics rooted in risk and risk-adjusted profitability measures.

The middle phases of the customer-management lifecycle involve monitoring customer behavior to ensure it continues to perform as intended and managing cross-sell and new product opportunities. This may be immediate or across the stages of a customer's life but ideally both. We use the information on how the customer performs to understand what else may be needed, armed with even greater precision on the customer's risk and profitability profile. We also can track customer payment and utilization to identify trouble before a major problem develops. This way, we can manage rapid intervention.

The last stage of the lifecycle is the management of customer delinquency—or lapses in payment. How we manage it can become uniquely important and differentiating, both in our ability to reduce loss to the institution and our ability to garner customer loyalty—maybe even good publicity.

These approaches, in part or in whole, frequently are applied to credit-risk management, particularly the fine art of credit-card management. But they are fully applicable to most risks and most products, whether other lending products, insurance products, deposit products, or even items outside of traditional financial services products. These approaches apply to almost anything when there are repeated interactions with customers, particularly payments-related ones (see Figure 8.1).

LEVERAGING THE UPSIDE

Taking a closer look at the individual concepts of customer lifecycle, let's start with techniques that directly—and rapidly—add to the bottom line. Many forget that this is one of the first and best ways to apply risk measures and capabilities. We set up capabilities to ensure we have the right customers with the right products for our risk profile. Sounds like the job of product managers or marketing, right? The risk-management person should be

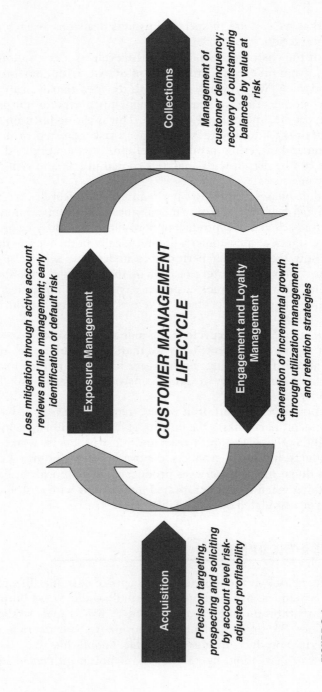

FIGURE 8.1 Customer Management Lifecycle

CUSTOMER MANAGEMENT LIFECYCLE

Collections

Management of customer delinquency; recovery of outstanding balances by value at risk

Exposure Management

Loss mitigation through active account reviews and line management; early identification of default risk

Engagement and Loyalty Management

Generation of incremental growth through utilization management and retention strategies

Acquisition

Precision targeting, prospecting and soliciting by account level risk-adjusted profitability

168

the marketing or product person's best friend. Alas, these two often speak such dramatically different languages that it doesn't always happen. But why not? It only requires harnessing those analytic skills and putting them to work growing our business—the right way.

Two of the very best applications involve how we target customers and how we price them. It's incredibly simple: If we want to attract and acquire a customer, we must understand that customer's profile and how to offer a price that wins its business while maximizing our profitability.

Segmentation and Targeting

Using risk analytics to support segmentation and targeting of customers melds several market-segmentation techniques—this is why it becomes so powerful. There are four common ways to segment customers:

1. **Behavioral segmentation.** The way customers and prospects behave in their use of a product
2. **Demographic, or life-phase, segmentation.** Customers' needs based on identifiable attributes
3. **Profitability, or current value, segmentation.** How much worth customers potentially hold for the organization
4. **Attitudinal, or psychographic, segmentation.** Attitudes and beliefs, often incorporating motivations and lifestyle

These can be constructed a priori or post hoc. That is, we can more or less take an educated guess at the segments, or we can analyze them using data and statistical techniques.

In any of these types of approaches, we'd want to identify segments that are significant, uniform, actionable, and finite. Each segment defines significant differences in the purchase decision or profitability of a product. Within each segment, the population is relatively uniform. The segment can be identified in a way that we can base decisions on it. In a financial services context, this usually means we can distinguish someone in the segment before a product is purchased, and we can solicit them through various channels. Finally, the segmentation scheme should be finite. That is, not too many segments are constructed; build only an actionable few.

In a risk-driven analysis, we would combine behavioral elements with our old friend the risk-adjusted profitability analysis. This identifies the characteristics of customers who will provide the best risk-adjusted profitability. This may be constructed over a defined horizon time, or in a customer-lifetime value analysis, it may be built over a longer period when loyalty and service dimensions also are considered.

Customer behavioral patterns around risk (such as delinquency), product usage, payment life, cost to serve, and other factors can be loaded into a profitability calculation like those previously described. Then, profitability can be analyzed against numerous other attributes to derive a breakdown of attributes that lead to specific profitability profiles. The analysis generally involves some form of clustering or decision-tree method (such as a chi-squared automatic interaction detector CHAID). Thus, we can identify specific, actionable attributes to identify customers—as they walk in the door—who would yield the most-desired risk and profitability profile.

These factors often can be combined with life-phase segmentation, and sometimes certain attitudinal identifiers, to further sharpen the ability to market and target specific products to new and existing customers. These exercises often lead to millions of dollars of improvements in the overall customer and profitability profile. Returns typically raise long-term profitability 10% to 20% and often provide cost savings of similar percentages or more. That's because marketing campaigns are more selective and can be combined with solicitation channel preferences.

One large North American financial institution that I worked with did just this. They wanted to fine-tune their portfolio and were concerned about increases in delinquencies and decreases in growth. They were aware that their portfolio was highly pocketed, both by geography and customer profile. As a result, they decided to start the process by rethinking—understanding how they viewed customer segments. Their rationale was that if they could understand their segments better they could more proactively tailor strategies to yield the risk-adjusted return profile that they desired. It sounds pretty straight forward.

We were able to conduct an analysis that first understood the profile of customers that were yielding the best risk/return profile and the drivers of that profile. In doing so, we were able to construct over sixty micro segments and twelve broad segment groupings. We then were able to link these to the specific drivers of risk-adjusted return over time. Thus, identifying the best customers on a long-term performance basis and how we could spot them when they walked in the door, whether they were current customers or new customers. Armed with this information, we could devise targeting strategies, cross-sell strategies, retention strategies, and customer exposure strategies to address different profiles and different issues within the portfolio.

The capability becomes an exceedingly powerful tool which has further evolved and is still used for managing a large national portfolio.

So what really matters? There are a few factors that significantly affect our segments—and it doesn't much matter which specific product we're dealing with. Of course, the deep dark specifics are in the factors particular to the analysis: your reputation and competitive position, the product in question, market in which it competes, and other such factors.

Two important concepts in holding on to customers are *time on book* and *horizon time*.

Not surprisingly, one of the biggest drivers of customer profitability is how long a customer stays with you in the product at hand—time on book. Many financial services products involve payment streams or other related factors, such as duration, which has real value both in providing stability of cash flows and in providing real long-term profit. Depending on the product, this can be a challenge—consider mortgage products which might routinely renew or be subject to prepayment. So it's important to find ways to keep the customer on your book, despite macro-economic cycles and routine events.

Two key considerations are:

1. **Risk.** You guessed it; the risk of an individual customer can be a big factor. It is important to segment for these for two reasons. Firstly, it allows us to identify these customers and set prices for them that minimize negative impact on profitability. Secondly, we may want to manage them differently. The importance of risk is no surprise. Customers who default on their obligations not only end those precious payment streams but also owe us money. We incur expenses in the process of recovery, and even if most of the money comes back, we've spent time and some form of investment to collect it.
2. **Relationship.** Yes, relationship matters. It matters in two very meaningful ways: Customers who have relationships with us tend to stick around longer (increased *horizon time*) and often take more of our products; they also tend to have lower risk, paying obligations to an institution where they have a relationship before paying others. These are very direct economic outcomes, but these customers provide an indirect benefit: they provide us greater information value. The data they provide allows us to better manage both them and similarly profiled customers.

The difficulty with relationships is how to define them. What exactly constitutes a relationship? Is it a customer who has been with us a long time? One who has a lot of money with us? Or one who has many of our products? The answer may be all of these, but the specifics can vary. Customers with many products may, in fact, cost us more because they may have multiple channel preferences. They may be "shoppers" of products, particularly when they are low-cost options, or a customer who needs sources of credit and therefore may become a higher risk. The key is to find the signal that may denote the primary financial institution with which the customer does business. In highly competitive markets, this can be very tricky. Any market that is overbanked, for example, can face big challenges in identifying this trait. Identifying it, however, will pay dividends.

Other factors can "pop" as key contributors to the profitability equation. Product choices, such as balance tier and term in a lending scenario, are big ones. These characteristics often are secondary indicators of risk. Also, they often relate to narrow thresholds where cost to serve may tick up over the value of the transaction in certain segments. For these reasons, it can be extremely important to understand the break-even points across the portfolio and use the segmentation analysis to identify these.

Pricing

Pricing is another key area where risk techniques can be turned outward to make us money. Pricing in some ways is the simplest of all applications but, strangely, is the one that more institutions seem to get materially wrong. Some can get it so wrong that it has dire consequences for a portfolio, particularly in a downturn. That's because there can be lots of moving parts in a pricing equation, and although each one is seemingly simple, each opens an opportunity to get it wrong.

EXAMPLE

Here's an example of an instance in which a bank's pricing blunder resulted in regulatory intervention and takeover. One of the bank's many problems was extremely poor margins, particularly relative to the risk of its portfolio. This was less apparent when times were good and the bank was growing portfolio volume. But the risk became very apparent when the credit downturn occurred and its accounts rapidly began to default.

The bank had pricing models in place, but critical material errors in the models caused it to price too low—particularly relative to risk. As you might imagine, low price made the bank very successful at attracting large volumes of customers—but not always the right ones at the right price. Management made matters worse with a strategy to attract somewhat riskier customers. The bank did have a degree of risk-based pricing that provided better gross returns on these customers, so they chose to attract those risky customers in the hope that they would never fail. But management did not realize the assumptions in the pricing models did not *adequately* price for risk. When times turned tough, the portfolio began to rapidly decline and the pricing they were receiving wasn't enough.

As in many other examples we've reviewed, management had lost track of what was actually in their pricing models. The models had become black boxes. The bank had numerous problems with their pricing models. Poor assumptions loaded into the models at numerous locations resulted in a compounding of effects. Critical faults included horizon times, loss assumptions, cost assumptions, and capital assumptions. Their models were not a little off; they were way off. Ultimately, the bank collapsed.

They may have avoided this major contributor to the failure by challenging their assumptions, using a third party to help them consider options to the assumptions built into the models and the models' overall structures. These specifics, we've learned, must be documented and reviewed routinely, including inputs to the models to ensure they reflect the current and near future economic environment. A governance process for the models should ensure the process is working, to resolve issues, challenge the assumptions, and ensure alignment with the organization's risk appetite.

The pricing equation basically is the profitability equation inverted. We're entering our hurdle rate—our expected return—and extracting the price we need to get it. We're doing nothing more than employing the methods we discussed earlier in risk-adjusted profitability. There are a few nuances, of course. And as you may have guessed, the devil is in the details.

There are a few initial considerations when confronting a pricing model for the first time:

RAROC versus Economic Profit versus NPV This is the first question that must be answered when using the pricing equation. Which profitability metric do we use? There are numerous options, even more than the three proposed here. We could also consider return on assets (ROA) and return on equity (ROE). But for most organizations that want a reasonable bead on pricing for the risk of their customers or portfolio, some variant of our basic three are where to start.

When we use the term *risk-adjusted return on capital* (RAROC), we're referring to risk-adjusted return divided by economic capital. This is where most organizations start because the term RAROC resonates with people. As described in previous chapters, it suffers from two shortcomings:

1. **It doesn't support a view of a transaction's absolute contribution.** So a large transaction that is somewhat riskier than a small transaction would be less attractive on this basis. Unless married with other measures and goals, this profitability metric often whittles the portfolio down to nothingness in the interest of getting higher RAROCs for each transaction. However, in a single pricing scenario where a hurdle rate is the expected outcome, RAROC may work well.
2. **RAROC tends to be highly variable.** Relatively small changes in capital can cause surprisingly large swings in the outcome. So it can become unwieldy to work with.

Moreover, RAROC can be a problem in multi-period methods. Let's just say, I haven't yet seen a pricing analyst get this right. Organizations often impose group-level-averaging conventions meant not for pricing but year-on-year portfolio analysis. When applied at a single transaction level, huge distortions can occur, which trickle out into the market.

Having said all this, RAROC nonetheless can be a good place to start. It's often conceptually easier to implement and will get the ball rolling. Just keep in mind some of these downsides.

Economic profit (EP) is constructed with the same set of inputs as RAROC yet doesn't have its downsides, making it a better metric for most situations. Economic profit's only major flaw is that it yields an absolute number, which many people find disquieting. Some say, a percent return "feels" better than an absolute number. The simple fact is that, like net present value (NPV), if the number is positive, we're good. In fact, the more positive, the better.

NPV is a variant we often find in pricing applications. As a reminder from Chapter 5, it's also constructed from the same inputs and is really a variant on EP, and a slight variant at that. If NPV and EP are both calculated correctly, in a financial services situation where hurdle rates and cost of capital converge and capital investment is clear, then NPV and EP should be identical. EP has a small advantage in these situations because capital is deducted as a percent charge in every period, not deducted in a large whack at the beginning then added back slowly over time as in NPV. The mathematical result is the same, but in the event that the horizon is incorrect, then EP tends to provide a better approximation than NPV and causes less trouble in the long term. We've seen an example of this already.

Single Period versus Multi-period   This line of discussion rapidly brings us to another conundrum: whether to make the pricing model single-period model or multi-period. The simple answer is that multi-period models are almost always better than single-period models. BUT they are far more complex and subject to many more errors and problems. So if risk-based pricing is a new concept and your organization wants to step into it slowly, start with a single-period (usually one-year horizon) model and work out from there.

The key issue to tackle with the multi-period model is the horizon time. If you're pricing a product that has a relatively short maturity, let's say less than three years, then horizon time is not a big issue. But for products that could go on seemingly indefinitely, horizon time is a major issue.

In these circumstances, the multi-period approach is generally the way to go, but don't go overboard with the horizon time. This is often where folks run into serious problems. Almost every hard core analyst I've ever met wants to be specific. They want to model exactly how long any single transaction may be on the books. What they tend to forget is that we're pricing. In pricing, we want to ensure that we price for the lowest common denominator, not the highest. If we know a product lasts on our portfolio for an average of six years, but some customers may stay with us for fifteen years, where do we want to be pricing? Certainly closer to six years than to fifteen.

Strike an Investment Horizon; Think like an Investor   Horizon time is no different than any other risk equation. There will be volatility around it, and since that makes a big difference in our pricing, it's important to analyze it. You need to understand average and standard deviation, and you must understand the factors that might affect them: Is it interest rates, as in many financial-services products, or is it something else? This analysis may not have to be exhaustive, but it is important to establish a view.

Interestingly, I've found that more companies get it wrong by trying to extend the horizon time, thinking they're getting more precise. Many of the companies that are winners take a simple view of an investment horizon. Most firms have some idea of how many years they expect to achieve a positive return on various forms of investment. Pricing financial products does not have to be different: Is it three years? Five years? This is by far the easiest way to think about horizon time and usually the most successful strategy. It's simple, easy, and effective.

I worked with a client that built a beautifully sophisticated pricing model but erred badly by trying to model the horizon time to a precise measure. The firm baked into their models a very long horizon time because it had a few customers who had very good relationships and stayed around for long periods. What the company had badly missed in its calculations was that most of the portfolio did not become profitable until seven years into the life of the product—three years after the average life of the portfolio. They were relying on a few good customers to carry their portfolio and were effectively losing money on the rest.

Multi-period measures can get you in other ways. Their ability to model cash flows at a fairly discrete level over many periods raise issues involving resources, skills, and refresh rates.

But don't be discouraged. The benefits usually outweigh the downsides, particularly in highly competitive markets. Understanding the nuances of multiple years and being able to break down multiple years to months can improve accuracy of spreads by multiples. It effectively allows you to set prices and attract customers that you likely would have had to turn away with a less refined approach.

Pricing Segmentation Segmentation is a major factor in pricing, especially in large retail markets. But which segments? How many sub-segments? Most financial services products have some framework of product options, so that's a good place to start. Begin with the key drivers of risk—things that can be discerned at the point of sale. For a loan, it might be credit rating and loan-to-value (LTV), with product differentiators of balance tier and term. From there, consider relationship factors and whether they matter for attracting or retaining customers.

In competitive markets, pricing segmentation is often an important differentiator and helps define where an institution wants to compete—who precisely they want to attract or discourage. Like many of our other benefits, however, there are downsides. Just as having multi-periods helped us become more precise, so does segmentation. But it carries some of the same analytical burdens. We have to find differentiating pricing elements for each of the line items in our profitability/pricing equation. These now must be modeled across multiple periods. It adds to the burden, but adds to the payoff.

Adverse Selection Adverse selection casts another vote for segmentation, particularly for risk. Adverse selection occurs when we price outside of market for any given level of risk. High-risk customers will pay higher prices because they have fewer options or will more aggressively seek good deals where risks are poorly assessed. Competitors learn to differentiate for risk and either reject higher risks or price for them. We run into real problems if we don't realize when we're over-pricing. We may be losing good customers who want lower prices and attracting customers who are riskier. This may not even become apparent in some products for many years or until a downturn occurs (see Figure 8.2).

Credit-rating analysis and more granular segmentation can frequently help us avoid adverse selection at its onset. Better customer rating models and more granular segmentation can typically avoid or even completely

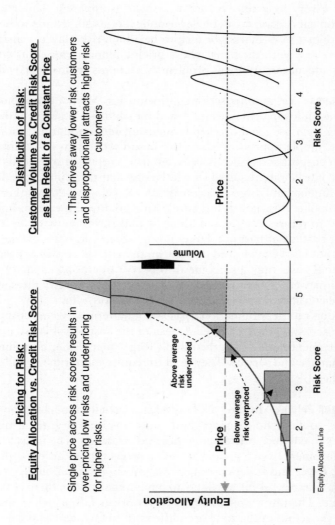

Pricing for Risk:
Equity Allocation vs. Credit Risk Score

Single price across risk scores results in over-pricing low risks and underpricing for higher risks...

Distribution of Risk:
Customer Volume vs. Credit Risk Score
as the Result of a Constant Price

...This drives away lower risk customers and disproportionally attracts higher risk customers

Above average risk under-priced

Below average risk overpriced

Risk Score

Price

Equity Allocation

Volume

Equity Allocation Line

Risk Score

Price

FIGURE 8.2 Mechanics of Adverse Selection

eliminate adverse selection. This is particularly true where credit risks are narrowly differentiated.

However, it's important to monitor the long-term effects of pricing. Adverse selection may not show up for years, and lapsed models may appear to suffice for a very long time before a problem is apparent. Unfortunately, when a problem occurs, it can be devastating. So it's something to be aware of. If you're in a risky market or seek to be a high-risk player, consider this issue. As we saw with the bank whose pricing blunder caused its collapse, any pricing model can cause this problem if the inputs are incorrectly defined.

Cost Measures   Yet another set of considerations. Many institutions struggle with the philosophical question—and the ability—to generate marginal costs rather than use fixed overheads allocated across the transaction basis. Consider a simple approach. There are broadly two ways to think about costs: with corporate overheads or without. If corporate overheads are included, the hurdle rate required should be one that takes into consideration corporate funding and diversification abilities as being part of a larger group. So above-the-line costs go up, but hurdle rates go down. If each business line is expected to return as if "stand alone"—that is, in line with an industry competitor that is not part of a larger group—then corporate overheads are irrelevant, but hurdle rates need to come up to match pure play expectations.

Marginal costs may also come into play if operating capacity is constrained. If new equipment is required over a certain capacity threshold this needs to be considered and amortized across the portfolio.

Also, don't forget origination costs and long-term servicing costs. These may differ across segments as well. Consider the cost of risk as an example. If you're segmenting for risk, then don't forget that riskier customers cost more to manage and service. They tend to require more time in call centers and elsewhere.

Elasticity and Pricing   In the past few years, elasticity modeling for pricing has begun to take hold. More and more institutions are using these approaches to enhance pricing analytics and strategies. The ideas are fairly simple. Customers have a greater or lesser propensity to accept a price. As prices rise, fewer and fewer customers are willing to buy. Equally, as prices fall, more and more people are likely to buy. In the middle, there is a zone of indifference. The important question is: As prices fall, at what point will customers move out of the zone of indifference to buy, and as prices rise, at what point do customers walk away? (See Figure 8.3.)

Knowing and understanding the nuances of this profile are critical to understanding customer buying-behavior. Consider that if we know the shape of this curve, we also can understand how price impacts volume and

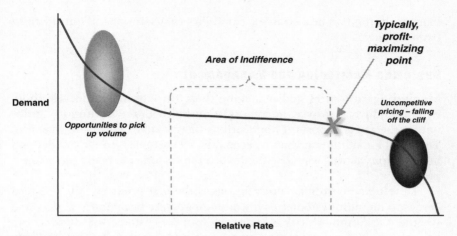

FIGURE 8.3   Typical Price Elasticity of Loan Demand Curve

profit. Now, consider that each segment will have specifically different price-response profiles. So if we can determine these for each segment, we can optimize our objective function—that is, grow volume or grow profit—and do so at the most optimum price point, without giving away too much money or turning away too many customers.

Now, one final step. Where risk is a key consideration, the risk-based price still matters. We can still use it to construct a "floor" price. This is the price we can't move below and still maintain minimum hurdle profitability. So in a volume-maximizing scenario, elasticity models will drive prices down, but the floor model ensures we don't go too low. The same equation allows us to evaluate our consolidated profit and volume decisions across segments, arriving at an optimum price to achieve the best attainable profit for all pricing strategies across a portfolio. If you're in a market where a single price point is used and segmentation of pricing is uncommon, this is particularly important for understanding how that single price point will play out across the whole portfolio. If your market applies multiple prices by segment, or if you want to introduce it, this approach allows you to manage these prices over what can become a complex grid of options.

MANAGING THE DOWNSIDE

Managing the downside is much what it sounds like. It requires setting up capabilities to ensure we have the right customers with the right products for our profile of risk and that we can spot them before they go bad.

Done well, this can be a strategic capability that sets one institution apart from another.

Customer Monitoring and Management

Monitoring customers and managing them through their lifecycle, both within products and over the long relationship with the institution, can be one of the most important applications of risk management to business. This is all about finding ways to keep tabs on customers so we can develop interventions as well as understand when the customer is ready for the next product.

Developing customer interventions is the first point of call. The idea here is to monitor customer payment and purchase behavior to understand whether the customer's risk is increasing or if the customer-need profile can be serviced without taking on significant additional risk. This is where scorecards can come into play. Remember the behavioral scorecard from previous chapters? This can be efficiently used to monitor each customer and develop a warning signal for impending risk. When built and maintained properly, the scorecard utilizes customer payments—or lack thereof—and the pattern of payment mixed with other factors to understand whether risk is rising unnecessarily and whether an intervention is required. Combine this with balance or exposure behavior, and we can rapidly assess the difference between a customer who has become overly risky and the customer who is ready for additional or different products.

The ability to segment customers is a key component to doing this well. Understanding the specific nuances of each segment allows for quicker identification and development of strategies. So what is there to pay attention to here?

Speedy Refresh Rates   Much of the value of this approach is in the ability to identify patterns almost as they occur. This means the data supporting our models must be refreshed routinely. Some of this information can be refreshed as much as monthly. This may sound like an expensive proposition, particularly when it means obtaining public information or increased bureau data. Don't cheap out; even seemingly small differences in timing or amount of information can make an enormous difference.

In one case, we found that the use of an additional credit bureau, albeit very small, was intensely valuable. It had a slight variant on information and timing of information that allowed us to better differentiate customers sufficiently to save tens of millions of dollars per year—that is on an ongoing basis. This simple step was easily implementable within a few months time and the whole affair paid for itself within the course of the fiscal year.

Recalibration   The same is true of recalibration. Models need to be maintained and recalibrated routinely. This can be as important in the best of times and the worst. Much of the credit crisis could have been avoided if banks had been more vigilant about recalibration and the testing of their assumptions that supported the models. Models are a lot like cars. Cars require gas, a routine oil change, and regular tune-ups. Neglect your car, and it breaks down. Models are similar, so service them regularly. They must be supported with staff that has the bandwidth to manage this sort of routine maintenance. Most retail scorecards require quarterly reviews, and depending on market circumstances, may need frequent recalibration.

Test and Learn   This may seem obvious. But it's often the case that the analytical team has a wealth of information and knows what's going on, but the business doesn't have specific strategies, offerings, or interventions constructed to step in and provide the needed result. Fast response and test-and-learn approaches are critical components to honing these strategies. It's as important to be able to identify as it is to reach out to customers in the most efficient and effective method.

Collections and Payments

Here again, the same concepts apply. Once a customer has gone bad (that is, they've lapsed in their obligations or have defaulted) the question becomes: How do we get them to pay, and to do it before we lose a lot of money? There are some key aspects, best applied through, you guessed it, segmentation:

- **Collections scorecards, propensity to repay.** A key trick of the trade is to establish collections, or recovery, scorecards. These help us understand and categorize the likelihood that a customer will repay. We can construct these based on a variety of considerations: propensity to cure (that is, to pay without intervention) or the propensity to repay after varying points in time. This information helps us to understand which strategies are most appropriate with which customers, and how much intervention is necessary and with what degree of alacrity.
- **Cost to collect versus how much exposure on the table.** Some customers have more money outstanding than others. How much is it really worth to us to pursue repayment? Consider a credit card, for example. It's easy to imagine how a body of customers could have a very small payment outstanding—this could be a tiny residual amount from a larger payment, or perhaps someone moved and cancelled that card. So, at what point is it worth pursuing? If it costs us $20 to recover, and the outstanding amount is $15, then perhaps we wouldn't bother. The

surprising fact is that many institutions don't really have a good handle on any of this information.

The key here is to understand how much we're likely to get back for each segment (that old thing again), circumstance, and time delinquent. Then we need to marry that with the cost-basis required to collect. This may mean that the cost structure has to be almost as well-determined as the customer segment and circumstances. That's because these often will drive key factors associated with the cost. Clearly, the longer recovery takes, the more it will cost, both from the perspective of time-value of money and the specific activities being pursued.

As in all of these cases, the ability to manage the contact with the customer can be a major make-or-break factor. Speed to the customer and speed to entice the customer to pay you back can become the most important factor. Consider that if a customer is in the midst of a problem with your institution, it's likely that customer is in difficulty with others. So this becomes a sales process. It's about convincing a customer to pay your institution before all others. That is where many of the segmentation and contract-management capabilities we discussed can come in handy. Being able to identify relationship variables (customers who may be more vested with your institution) and the ability to appeal to them rapidly will define the ultimate success of the approach. That brings us to the last factor.

■ **Customer motivation.** This has been found to be a key factor in collections scenarios. So focus on the customers that have the most to lose by *not* paying. Are there customers who have broad relationships with your firm across many products? Does your institution have loyalty programs under which the customer may lose valuable points? Anything that may differentiate these customers from others can be used as an approach to prioritize and drive their payment strategy.

OPTIMIZATION

Although more of the applications we typically see fall into the categories we've discussed, there are other valuable applications of risk management and related analytics. These can often yield as big, if not better benefits than those already reviewed, but they may be more challenging. Most of these approaches affect a higher and broader scope of activities and decision-making, in some cases involving senior management. Many of these sorts of solutions happen at the portfolio level—they have sweeping impacts, which explain the need for senior-level support and also the reason for their great value.

Product Structuring

Products can be structured to specifically target, avoid, or manage risks. This isn't about buying or creating derivative products that hedge risks, although that is an option—and is one reason why they are created. This segment is about how you can think about structuring products that in turn help you manage risk at the portfolio level on several dimensions.

There are several things to consider on this front. Firstly, what sort of portfolio profile are you after? This may be from a broad risk versus return perspective, but also may be considered more specifically. What kind of duration profile are you looking for? How uniform is the portfolio in its structural profile? Are there economic circumstances that you are trying to manage? What is the outlook on interest rates? Inflation? Other factors? These questions can help decide what sorts of products you want to offer and which customers would they attract.

Here's the second factor to consider: What sort of customers are inherently attracted by your products? How might we alter the products to attract a different profile if that's desired?

The types of profiles that products lend to our balance sheet—and the types of risks they attract—must be considered in the dimensions discussed next.

No matter what type of financial institution we are, we can use the maturity and duration characteristics of products to enhance performance through better leverage of the balance sheet. Understanding the liability characteristics and behaviors will allow us to better define what types of assets we can use to match them, and if you're in insurance, vice versa. One of the most important aspects in doing this is not to be satisfied with the strict sense of contractual obligations. Go beyond that to understand actual behavior of these products.

For example, if we have deposits, a large portion of these may be considered overnight deposits. That means the customer has the right to withdraw them at any time without notice or penalty. But we know most of these deposits will stick around longer than overnight. In fact, some may stick around for many, many years. Exactly how many stick around may be driven by the market you're in, the profile of your customer base, the economic environment, reputation of your institution, and your rates relative to competitors. Chances are that the treasury, the asset liability management (A/LM) group and those who manage these products have a pretty good idea of what this means. If they don't, they can analyze and model the behavior and effects of all of these factors. Now use it.

You can match these liabilities with asset products that have similar characteristics. Liabilities that stick around for five years or more can be matched with asset products that have that type of profile—usually managed on a duration basis. This can be very useful—and an inexpensive way of funding. In some markets it can even become a critical market advantage.

One bank I knew in India used this technique to put out five- and seven-year small-business loans. This may not seem like such a big deal for many markets, but in India, it was a differentiating approach. There were no market instruments that allowed banks to easily fund and hedge out lending for that long. So, by understanding the behavior of the portfolio better, this bank was able to create products that were unmatched by competitors. You can imagine the market response!

What is duration? For some people, this term is not new but may be draped in cobwebs. Duration is a term commonly used in fixed-income management and refers to the period of time that a bond (or other fixed income products, like a loan) will take to be repaid. It is a measure of the bond (or loan's) sensitivity to interest rates and is a key determinant in its market price. For other products it is more useful in defining its likely time on the balance sheet—something less than its face value maturity. It takes into account prepayment and default characteristics and is an easy way of calculating how long cash flows will remain with the institution, and therefore, the profile of any cash flows used to offset or hedge.

The rule of thumb is that products with longer maturities are more susceptible to surprises than shorter-maturity products. This is simply common sense. During a longer horizon time, a product is likely to experience more economic changes, interest rate changes, and customer changes. Quite often, riskier customers are attracted to products with longer duration. This is especially true in the loan world where longer-dated products have smaller payments and a bit of a "mañana" effect. Both tend to attract customers who on average have fewer means, are riskier, and more likely to default.

Payment profile is affected by similar characteristics. In general, smaller payments and less frequent payments or delayed payments may attract riskier customers. This is especially true of consumer customers. Consider the interest-only mortgage products that became popular around 2005. These were especially successful with subprime customers.

Similarly, the degree to which embedded options are built into products can be both attractive to certain customers and something to consider as the product sits on the balance sheet. Many institutions overlook this factor and suffer for it. Consider the possibility for a customer to prepay or change its payments. If this exists, then it's important to understand it. Even if there are prepay penalties, many institutions suffer when prepay penalties may be waved or are not enough to manage out the cost of losing the hedge that the product has created for the balance sheet.

Finally, total balance is a factor. This seems like a small issue, but can become a bigger problem as balance structures get smaller. These tend to both attract risk and require a closer understanding of costs to ensure profitability.

The converse on these is true as well. Larger balances over shorter durations with fewer options tend to attract less risky customers—often more affluent customers, particularly in a consumer setting.

So on one hand, the use of product structures can be a great way to manage the balance sheet, create differential competitive advantage, and even manage portfolio risk through the types of customers that are attracted. However, it is equally important to understand the consequences of product structures as they prompt unintended consequences.

One European bank, reacting to impending interest-rate changes, got into trouble when it decided to construct more short-term products. Management rightly provided very attractive rates for shorter term personal loans and mortgages. These tended to attract more affluent customers who could manage larger payments. However, they also included in their list of promotional products more variable-rate products. These tended to attract riskier customers, initially drawn by lower interest rates. The bank hadn't considered the behavior of these products at the time because it was mostly concerned about its balance sheet. It fell into difficulty a couple of years later when interest rates rose and the variable-rate products created a combination of both unprecedented defaults on their portfolio and equally large prepayments. It wound up being a big loser in the long run.

Process Streamlining

Process streamlining is yet another way to use this information. The principles are simple: Identify and address risks early, and eliminate redundancies. It makes processes faster and more efficient by cutting losses before you get too far into a transaction-origination process.

What are the key results when a customer transaction declines, whether a consumer or corporate customer? Identify those and make sure the data to make the decision is available early on in the process and to those interfacing with the customer. Create simple and clear rules. Then, it's a matter of placing go/no-go gates at each key step of the process.

Lending is a really great example of this approach. If a customer walks in the door and is below a threshold credit rating, we know we're not going to make a loan regardless of what's going on. Find that out fast, and be done with it. If we know the customer's credit rating is adequate but not superb, then what key factors would make a difference? We've described step one and step two. Just move this information to the front of the process, and give the front line some very clear guidance.

I worked with one bank where we did just this. We restructured the entire credit process so we had credit grading as a first step, provided check lists of key information to obtain from the customer, and developed very simple and clear approval limits by credit type, industry, balance, and collateral. We worked with the loan officers so that they learned how to make trade-offs between balance and collateral to reduce risk and make better loans faster. This approach resulted in considerably faster throughput. It nearly halved the time for loan origination from the previous process, increased pull through (number of loans actually booked versus applications) because customers earlier in the process received clear indication of their likelihood of approval, improved the risk profile, and raised overall risk-adjusted profitability by 15%.

Portfolio Management and Strategic Asset Allocation

Going back to our introduction to risk and reward at the beginning of this book, managing the portfolio on the basis of risk and return is a clear objective. It's surprising, then, that few financial institutions do that in a literal sense. What I mean is, if we think about each product's or asset class's risk profile and return profile, it's no different than evaluating the efficient frontier curve we discussed earlier. We should find that, if products are priced efficiently, they should show an ascending return profile for their underlying risks. We can also use this approach to evaluate the total risk versus return profile that this array of products provides us, then compare our institution to others on the same basis.

There are three levels on which we can think about this:

1. **The total institution level.** How does the risk versus return profile of our institution compare to our competitors? How does our overall institution stack up against the market efficient frontier?
2. **The business-line or product-line level.** How does the array of products stack up? What is our internal efficient frontier? Which product lines may be a drag on the consolidated portfolio? Are they all lining up against their appropriate return relative to risk? Are we over- or under-concentrated in any area?
3. **Within portfolios.** Are we overly concentrated in any one name or type of profile, such as industry, geography, or the like? What sectors can provide improved diversification? Are there any specific sectors that may be a drag on the portfolio? That is they're not generating sufficient returns for the risk that they generate?

Let's look at an example. By plotting observed variations in risk/reward along a continuum, it is possible to construct an "efficient frontier" of

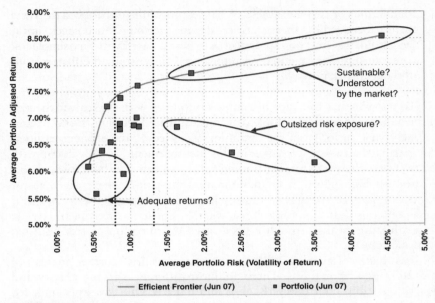

FIGURE 8.4 Efficient Frontier of U.S. Banking Institutions

risk-adjusted returns, providing a benchmark by which individual results can be evaluated. Figure 8.4, for example, shows how the retail loan portfolios of 17 major U.S. banking companies stacked up in mid-2007.

Three major types of issues can be identified from this type of analysis:

1. **Adequacy of returns.** In some cases, institutions were underwriting solidly overall but realizing only minimal comparative yields. This has a number of implications, including a slim margin cushion in the event of market turbulence and probable misallocations of capital into business lines where margin was sacrificed for growth.
2. **Outsized risk exposure.** Among other institutions, portfolios were exhibiting outsized volatility in the face of average to below-average returns. One of the institutions in this group later succumbed to a federally assisted merger; another has yet to emerge from an extraordinarily long and deep trough in performance and trading value.
3. **Sustainability of returns.** At least through mid-year 2007, some institutions appeared to be successfully stretching out along the risk continuum to capture superior returns. But banking history is loaded with examples of high-flying portfolios and institutions that subsequently lost altitude, many quite suddenly. It is well worthwhile to verify the

foundations of current success. What sectors of the portfolio are driving this performance? Is there a critical dependence on a few business lines? Do "strengths" rest on rapid growth in new areas? Even if a deeper look is reassuring, does the market understand the sustainable foundations of the high-risk portfolio?

To test whether this type of analysis resonates with the investor's view of the banking industry, we looked at how estimated retail portfolio returns for each bank varied from the optimum suggested by the efficient frontier. Comparing the two-year change in this measurement (2007 – 2009) with the two-year change in market trading value, we saw a 43% statistical correlation—a high figure in financial-market statistics, where the investor frame of reference changes constantly in a sea of emerging information. It seems obvious that many investors, whether consciously or instinctively, are evaluating banks through a peer-based examination of risk-adjusted portfolio returns.

Two banks offer starkly different examples to drive further analysis of mid-2007 retail portfolios. There are clear differences in the gravity and type of questions confronting Bank A and Bank B. One case appears laced with distress; the other seems more a matter of paying attention to outliers. Both profiles are based on data that was publicly available in 2007.

Bank A   For starters, Bank A was taking far more risk to achieve comparable levels of return with Bank B. To achieve a roughly 6% return in home-equity lending, for example, Bank A was incurring more than seven times the volatility in that line of business than Bank B. Looking strictly inside Bank A's retail portfolio, there was an overall pattern of declining returns relative to risk—the opposite from the norm.

Faced with an overall underwriting challenge, Bank A should have been looking at asset concentrations: places where growth should be stopped; places where risk-defenses should be strengthened; and places where pricing could be strengthened. Among banks in the study group, Bank A had one of the highest portfolio concentrations of home-equity loans—22%—with the highest comparative volatility in this asset category and the next-to-lowest yield. It also had a high concentration of residential mortgage loans—61%—with above-average volatility and below-average yield.

Bank B   While Bank B could take comfort in an overall cohesive risk/return profile, it still had extreme results in certain asset categories, warranting executive management attention. In particular, the credit card portfolio, while extraordinarily stable, seemed to be going nowhere in generating returns.

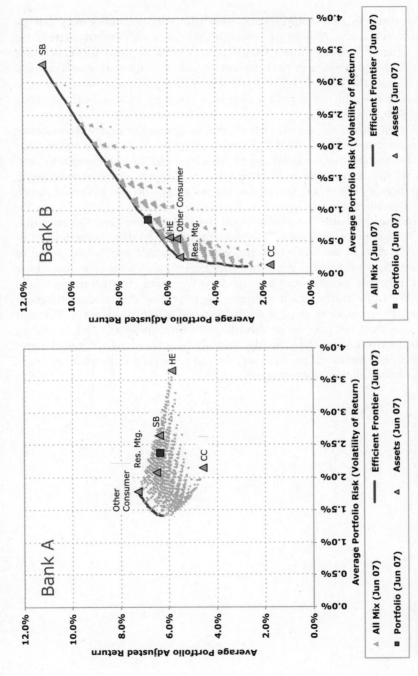

FIGURE 8.5 Efficient Frontier of Individual Banking Institutions

Meanwhile, the small-business portfolio was operating way out on the risk spectrum, raising questions about sustainability of current results; whether to continue expanding in that area; and ultimately the outlook for borrowers in that market sector. At mid-year 2007, in fact, Bank B had the highest retail portfolio concentration of small-business loans—22%—compared with a simple average of 15% within the study group (see Figure 8.5).

Within portfolios, we may use several analyses. The first and simplest is the *concentration ratio*. This is a simple index, usually dollar based, that describes the relative contribution of any one name, sector, geography, etc. to the total. It's as simple as dividing the consolidated exposure to the group in question by the total exposure of the overall portfolio. It's quick, easy, and makes the point.

Another measure is our old friend the Unexpected Loss Contribution (ULC). This gives us a more specific idea of the relative contribution of any given class to the total portfolio, while taking into account the effect of its diversification benefit. With this information, we can take a closer look at not only risk management but also how we might enhance the portfolio itself. We can identify which segments are providing diversification benefit and which are adding to concentrations and begin to target a different mix—one that will take better advantage of the capital at hand. If pricing equations are constructed properly, they also can take into account the preferred capital treatment for such sectors and price on a somewhat preferential basis until the portfolio is rebalanced.

CHAPTER 9

Basel II and Beyond

EXECUTIVE SUMMARY

In this final chapter, we look at Basel II—and beyond. We align the concepts we've discussed in the eight previous chapters and match them up against the regulatory framework. We also look at how the next evolutionary stages of risk management will add more capabilities and create more opportunities for generating business value. And we discuss how European regulatory reforms such as Solvency II, which is aimed at the insurance industry, will affect financial institutions all over the world. We also visit the notion of "too big to fail" and discuss the role of risk management at non-bank institutions that operate outside of the reach of regulators.

BASEL II: WHAT'S IT ALL ABOUT?

In 1988, the Basel Committee on Banking Supervision (BCBS) started the ball rolling with the first Basel capital accord. Its purpose was simple: to assure a level of agreement on minimum capital standards for banking among major international financial players. At the time, there was growing concern that certain large markets were developing sufficient global reach to destabilize the entire world economy if anything went wrong (think about the power of the yen during that period). The Basel Accord was a direct response to that concern. Although the focus was originally on G-10 countries, the Accord rapidly expanded its reach as more than 100 countries signed up voluntarily to comply with the committee's recommendations. Today, about 25 countries sit on the committee, and 120 countries follow its guidelines on some level.

Fewer countries are expected to follow Basel II, with only 43 expressing initial interest. The Accord, however, still is only specifically required of the original G-10, which actually is 13: Belgium, Canada, France, Germany, Italy, Japan, Luxembourg, the Netherlands, Spain, Sweden, Switzerland, the United Kingdom, and the United States. At that, only banks that are internationally active must be strictly included.

The BCBS often is referred to as the BIS, the Bank for International Settlements. The BIS, in fact, is an entirely separate organization, but the BCBS meets at BIS headquarters in Basel, Switzerland—hence the name, Basel accord. The BCBS has no authority to set binding regulation; it mainly serves as a forum to find policy solutions and promulgate standards.

How does that actually work? The BCBS and the banking community at large establish a view toward next-generation standards for safety and soundness. These standards typically are well vetted in both the regulatory and banking communities. Once they are published, however, it is up to local regulators in each country to put them into effect. Because of a wide variation in national requirements for adopting new banking standards and rules, the ultimate adoption of standards can take on a very wide variety of formats and timing. Some regulators take them up in their entirety. When there are options, some choose only the most advanced approaches; others adopt only the most basic approaches. Some may only require them for internationally active banks in their countries. Countries such as the United States often require some time and effort to marry the approaches into an already highly developed web of regulations—some already more stringent than BCBS recommendations.

So when it comes to managing international comparisons, although one of the BCBS goals is a level of uniformity across the international banking system, it is local regulators who often create many differences. These may carry a wide range of implications worth becoming aware of—particularly if your institution manages cross-border operations. In some markets local players may gain an advantage from lower effective capital standards, differing definitions of capital, or lower implementation costs resulting from simpler standards or longer implementation periods. In other markets, local regulators may have the most advanced requirements, yet with little capital relief, push for faster implementation. Still other markets may take hybrid approaches. So in the end, BCBS guidelines in the last decade—Basel II and its add-ons—seem to have resulted in less global uniformity, not more.

Nevertheless, the changes have launched a global movement toward more analytical approaches to risk management and closer scrutiny within institutions of some key factors that ensure safety and soundness. This has progressed with each revision of Basel I, then Basel II, and now the impending Basel III (see Figure 9.1).

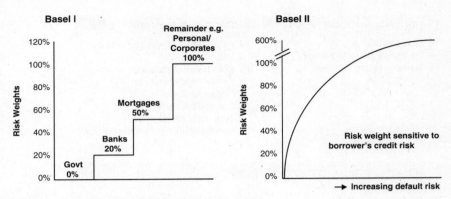

FIGURE 9.1   Basel I Versus Basel II Credit Impact

Basel I was a simplistic focus on credit risk and capital associated with that risk. It assigned simple risk weights based on credit exposure. Risk weights were differentiated solely by the class of lending—unsecured versus residential real estate secured versus commercial lending. The weights were simple and gross. But they were based on highly generalized estimates of the sorts of capital required to support portfolios—estimates based on experience of large portfolio lenders across several major countries. For this reason, they were directionally sound but little else. They did a lousy job of reflecting highly different risk profiles in a number of countries and among certain types of lending and customer profiles. Nevertheless, it was a start and largely served the purpose at hand—to get banks to build capital bases held to support their core risks.

Also, the concept of capital adequacy was simply defined. It is typically based on two tiers of capital, each with definitions and thresholds. These are established relative to the risk-weighted assets (adjusted exposure). Much of this general framework has remained unchanged since adopted in 1988. Only recently have more specificity and new definitions been issued for the types and amount of capital—particularly high quality, Tier 1, capital—and for liquidity and leverage-ratio proposals that further constrict freedom on quality of capital relative to risk-weighted assets (see Figure 9.2).

The following are the capital adequacy ratios:

$$\text{Total Capital Ratio} = \frac{\text{(Tier 1 Capital)} + \text{(Tier 2 Capital)} - \text{(Deductions From Capital)}}{\text{Risk-Weighted Assets}} > 8\%$$

$$\text{Tier 1 Ratio} = \frac{\text{(Tier 1 Capital)} - \text{(Deductions from Capital)}}{\text{Risk-Weighted Assets}} > 4.0\%$$

Over time, Basel I expanded to market risk and ultimately embraced the concept of "internal models." This allowed banks to put forward their own

Tier 1 (Core) Capital (> 50%)	Tier 2 (Supplemental) Capital
♦ Common stock ♦ Perpetual preferred stock ♦ Some minority interest	♦ Allowance for loan and lease losses ♦ Some perpetual preferred stock ♦ Hybrid capital investments ♦ Perpetual debt ♦ Convertible debt ♦ Term subordinated debt ♦ Intermediate term preferred stock

Deductions
♦ Goodwill ♦ Certain intangibles ♦ Certain investments in subsidiaries ♦ Reciprocal holdings of capital instruments

FIGURE 9.2 Regulatory Capital Defined

internal models as the means to determine capital. It was a huge step forward because it recognized more advanced institutions and their developments in risk management and allowed regulators to place some faith in the quality of these models. The internal-model recommendations did not prescribe the fine details of the models, only guidelines for key factors around which models would be built and capital would be measured.

In effect, this step forward started a new wave of banking regulation that recognized and encouraged internal models. It meant more-advanced banks could use relatively easier models—although "easier" is a relative term. The models are far more sophisticated than the regulators' measures and require more sophisticated and better-trained staff to manage and maintain them. Once in place, however, it's more of a hit-a-button thing, not the inefficient regulatory methods of calculation. Banks that already had adopted models for their own internal management benefitted from both faster calculation for regulators *and* from their capabilities to monitor other performance measures.

In most cases, these methods reduced capital because they took greater advantage of diversification benefits. So it effectively became a carrot-and-stick approach: Adopt more sophisticated measures and reduce capital; don't adopt them and live with higher capital or more labor-intensive calculations with fewer other uses. Enter Basel II.

Basel II came about in response to many banks' complaints that their own risk measures and approaches had well surpassed Basel I's and that they should be recognized ahead of Basel I's coarser approaches. This was particularly true in credit risk, where Basel I had not provided alternative methods. One of the best outcomes of Basel II was the ability to merge a number of concepts in risk management into an agreed platform:

- **Basel for Insurance.** Much of this played out a bit differently in insurance, although it appears it may end up in a similar place but at a slower pace. The insurance industry has no single central body, such as the BCBS, nor is there even a consistency around regulation at the broadest level in many countries. There's also much greater variation and less agreement regarding specific risk-management approaches.
- **Solvency II.** Solvency II grew from a set of proposals by the Committee of European Insurance and Occupational Pensions Supervisors (CEIOPS). Unlike The Basel Accord, Solvency is specifically focused on the European Union (EU). Like Basel, however, it's been adopted by many countries outside the EU, albeit with less rigor than its banking cousin.

  Similarly, international standards for insurance can vary widely— more so than in banking. In some countries, insurance is strictly regulated much like banking. In other countries, insurers are self-regulated through industry bodies. To make matters worse, insurance never has attracted the same level of regulatory scrutiny as banking, so it suffers from a very wide range of standards globally. In relatively recent years, the Solvency accord has functioned much like the Basel Accord has in banking. But fewer countries outside Europe have adopted it.

  Like Basel I, Solvency I started as a very simple framework. It relies on the concept of a solvency margin, the amount of regulatory capital an insurer is required to hold. Like Basel II, this margin was set up based on simple guidelines for general insurance and life insurance. As with like Basel, this approach decreased as insurers developed more sophisticated risk-management capabilities. Often called "Basel II for insurers," Solvency II attempts to account for a wider range of developments in insurance, risk management, finance, and governance techniques. It will consider the use of internal models for the setting of both a minimum capital requirement (MCR) and a solvency capital requirement (SCR).

THE REGULATOR VIEWPOINT

Despite the complexities of multiple regulations across different industries and countries, much of what goes on at BCBS, CEIOPS, and with local regulators is fairly easy to understand when you consider that regulators' general goals are broadly consistent worldwide. It's safe to say that much of what regulators concern themselves with falls into two broad categories. Firstly, they promote systemic stability, primarily nationally and secondarily globally, particularly when financial institutions under their watch can wreak havoc on the rest of the world. Secondly, regulators have a mission to protect depositors (or policy holders in the case of insurance). This is of interest to all regulators but particularly those who oversee markets that have no deposit insurance. Once you get the feel for how any issue impacts either of these two overarching objectives, you've got a bead how a regulator might act.

EXAMPLE

I worked with a bank to help it support a change in regulations. The bank had been providing what on the surface seemed a highly valuable product in the local market—five- and seven-year business loans. In most markets this isn't a big deal. But in this country, there was no funding for this sort of lending, and the product didn't exist except through this one bank. It had discovered this capability through keen understanding of their liabilities' behavior and used these "innovative products" to create a liability hedge. This sounded like a brilliant use of risk-management capabilities that reaped great income for the bank by providing what was effectively a national service. But when the bank wanted to change the specific nature of its license, it faced regulations for liquidity ratios that effectively forbid these five- and seven-year loans. You might think there would be a way to develop a waiver or change the rules to accommodate this application. But the regulator felt it could destabilize the economy. It endangered the ability to back liabilities, in the regulator's view, and therefore flew in the face of depositor protection. It was surmised at the time that, had the country instituted a form of deposit insurance, these loans would not have been an issue.

Deposit insurance and bank support are two concepts that frequently replay in the regulatory framework of any jurisdiction. Each provides a myriad of pros and cons and theoretical debate. On the pro side, if a bank fails, deposit insurance provides depositors some level of protection. This in turn, reduces the inherent tendency for a bank's instability to trigger a run on the bank. Deposit insurance is a stability backstop that promotes confidence in the financial stability of the banking sector. On the con side, it generates issues about coverage limits, fees from depository institutions and how to manage them, and the overall burden for the government to administer and manage the system. Some countries have even run into trouble when deposit insurance funds were misappropriated for other budgetary requirements, leaving no protection when needed.

Policy on financial-institution support takes on a similar set of arguments. When should banks be supported? Should they be supported at all? When can they be allowed to fail and are some too big to allow to fail? These are questions that intertwine with some of the issues surrounding deposit insurance. At the end of the day, regulators simply don't even want to *be* in a situation where these questions become real. Thus, their inherent conservatism. From their perspective, if they do their job right, even in the face of economic turmoil, most of these issues will become mute. This may be wishful thinking, but it helps to get inside the mind of the regulator for at least a moment.

There are a few more rules of thumb about regulators. They will always take the conservative route—especially with larger institutions more likely to destabilize a local market and those with international reach. This line of logic allows them to take simpler strokes that are more applicable across multiple institutions without worrying about systemic distress.

Another core tenet of regulation is ensuring against regulatory arbitrage—an increasingly tougher mandate. As regulations become more complex, international jurisdictions become more varied and banks merge with insurance companies and roll out new products, there is always some little loophole that can be found. This is why many regulators have moved from a strictly prescriptive approach to a principles-based approach. In addition, many of the new regulations place clear responsibility on boards to ensure that their organizations not only uphold the letter of the standard but the spirit of the standard as well.

Another objective becoming more challenging for regulators is to ensure competitive equality—both within any one country and internationally. The near explosion of regulations—particularly as a result of the global credit crisis—coupled with variances in regulatory frameworks under Basel II, anti money laundering (AML), and other accords, have created an increasingly complex field in which banks, particularly international banks, must maneuver. In some ways, this is the flip side of the arbitrage coin. The complexity fosters the potential for arbitrage but at the same time creates what feels more like an inability to compete at all.

I worked with a large international investment bank that was concerned about developing consistent treatment of and adherence to regulations throughout the Asian region. Top management quickly determined that if they adhered to homeland requirements and those of every other nation where they operated, they literally would not be able to conduct business. Moreover, in complying with one country's regulation, they were in some cases breaking another country's regulation. It was a losing battle. In the end, the best approach was to find and adhere to as much common ground as possible and accept that they would wind up paying occasional fines. It was a necessary cost of doing business.

A related concept is "home/host." Each regulator is both a "home" regulator of its local financial institutions and a "host" regulator of international institutions doing business within its borders. Regulators must manage requirements for their home constituency, typically their first priority, but also develop rules to ensure the safety and soundness of business conducted in their jurisdiction by foreign institutions. In some cases, this may be as simple as ensuring that the home regulator in the foreign institution's base country is sufficiently qualified and has sufficiently sound standards that it is "recognized" by the host regulator as an equal. In other cases, it may mean a level of regulation over and above what a foreign institution's regulator would require—particularly where depositors or policyholders interests are at stake or where foreign home regulations would stand to disadvantage local institutions.

As we'd imagine, a multitude of differing interpretations have arisen from standards that recognize internal models. These, in turn, have resulted in a complex minefield through which international banks and regulators must tiptoe. National interests often become embroiled in these discussions.

I became involved in a home-host regulatory standoff in a Basel II accreditation negotiation. Two major regulators ultimately had their respective reputations at stake; neither was willing to budge but neither wanted to take on the other directly for fear of international embarrassment. The bank ultimately was the loser, having to adopt far more rigorous standards and implement them at a faster pace than otherwise would have been required.

Keeping all of this in mind, the following points sum it all up. Regulators are inherently mindful of:

- Ensuring overall safety and soundness of the financial sector
- Promoting confidence in the stability of the financial sector
- Ensuring harmony across jurisdictions
- Reducing the risk that banks and insurers won't be able to support their obligations
- Reducing losses of depositors and policyholders if an institution is unable to fully meet its obligations

They do this through capital-based requirements that are determined through a heavy overlay of conservatism.

Considering everything we have just discussed, you'd almost start to feel sorry for the regulators. But take into account that their natural conservatism gives them at least a few outs. Most of the regulations we've focused on here involve capital and the quality of capital. So, in the end, the regulator's viewpoint is that it's a simple equation. Whatever they do, they just need to make sure they've required enough capital to support risks within the overall system and within each major institution under their watch. From this perspective, it's a fairly easy task and a simple set of levers. Basel II was once seen as a way in which many banking systems would release capital in massive amounts. In the end, few regulators have allowed this to happen. In some cases, regulatory capital has even gone up in net. Although the level of capital implied by Basel II's advanced methods may imply lowering levels, they actually have been bolstered in many jurisdictions by regulatory minimums and requirements for additional capital for operational risk and in some cases interest-rate risk. In many cases, the process was seemingly arbitrary. Capital levels increased until regulators were satisfied that it "felt" right. Capital is a relatively simple and transparent endgame, and it's the regulator's ultimate cushion. Ascribing to the "more is better" theory, regulators will do what they can to make sure there's enough capital.

Another key principle of the regulation is to ensure that financial institutions don't adopt internal models simply as a means of lowering capital. The principle behind the regulation is for financial institutions to use their advanced-risk models in their standard operations, not just for risk. For this reason, there is a standard called the *use test* that requires banks to demonstrate they use the models beyond strictly regulatory applications—generally for performance management, pricing, capital allocation, and other functions.

In this process, regulators are finding a new appreciation for the applications of risk-management approaches and for the cultural change required for an organization to embrace them. The moral is: Don't let the regulator get even a hint that the implementation of new models is strictly for regulation. They want to believe it's a choice the bank would have made in any case.

Despite this, the new wave of regulations has put regulators in an unenviable position. Most of their new requirements rely on increasing the use of economic risk models—financial institutions' internal models. So to enforce their own rules, regulators have had to become experts in this area. That is *all* areas of risk where internal models may be applied. This need for expertise quickly escalated from a point where regulators hadn't needed to know these approaches at all. Many regulators now are challenged not only to set policy but follow through with sufficient reviews. Further complicating matters, increased regulation has created enormous demand for examiners with financial-modeling capabilities, and in some markets, regulators are challenged to keep good talent. So it becomes clearer why some jurisdictions are reluctant to take on new risk-based standards—now or for a very long time.

BASEL II BASICS

Let's start with a few fundamentals. Basel II leverages off the concept of internal models. That is, banks are allowed to use their own internal models to support the measurement of risk and capital—with numerous regulatory guidelines on their construction, limits, and other features. This concept was introduced under Basel I with the option to use internal models for traded-market risk. Basel II expanded this approach, allowing banks to use internal models for credit risk, traded-market risk, and operational risk. Another fundamental tenet of Basel II is the carrot-and-stick approach. Regulators wanted to encourage banks to adopt more advanced capabilities for risk-measurement. A major fault of Basel I was that it had not sufficiently encouraged the improvements in risk measurement, and Basel's management did not pick up the more sophisticated risk-measurement abilities that many banks were adopting on their own. Basel II attempts to right that wrong. The "carrot" is that banks that adopt more advanced measures of risk will be rewarded with capital reductions, typically because of greater accuracies in risk measures and the ability to account for diversification benefit. The "stick" is that banks that use more basic measurement must manage within a regulatory overlay of calculations that are less useful for day-to-day management and don't fully account for risk. In most cases, the bluntness and layer of conservatism in these calculations results in higher capital charges.

High-Level Overview

Unlike the old Basel I Accord, the new Accord has three levels of implementation and three components of implementation. Basel II is organized into what is called the "three pillars." Pillar I describes prescriptive approaches for calculating core risk-weighted assets—or minimum capital—for each of three risk categories: credit risk, traded-market risk, and operational risk. Some jurisdictions, most notably Australia, have added non-traded market risk (interest rate risk) to this framework. Pillar II—dubbed "Supervisory Review of Capital Adequacy"—describes requirements for local supervisors and a set of overarching capabilities each bank is expected to demonstrate. It is a more highly judgmental framework. Pillar III, Market Discipline, is a set of detailed external reporting criteria for public disclosure.

Figure 9.3 summarizes the three pillars.

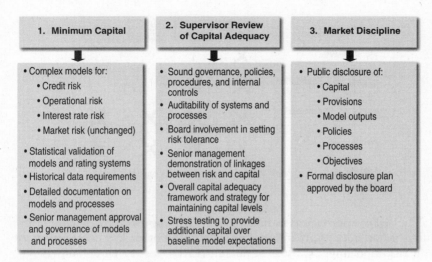

1. Minimum Capital	2. Supervisor Review of Capital Adequacy	3. Market Discipline

• Complex models for:
  • Credit risk
  • Operational risk
  • Interest rate risk
  • Market risk (unchanged)
 	
• Statistical validation of models and rating systems
• Historical data requirements
• Detailed documentation on models and processes
• Senior management approval and governance of models and processes
	• Sound governance, policies, procedures, and internal controls
	• Auditability of systems and processes
	• Board involvement in setting risk tolerance
	• Senior management demonstration of linkages between risk and capital
	• Overall capital adequacy framework and strategy for maintaining capital levels
	• Stress testing to provide additional capital over baseline model expectations
		• Public disclosure of:
		  • Capital
		  • Provisions
		  • Model outputs
		  • Policies
		  • Processes
		  • Objectives
		• Formal disclosure plan approved by the board

FIGURE 9.3 The Three Pillars of Basel II

Pillar I   In Pillar I, the accord spells out guidelines for the use of complex models for each of the core risk classes. These are further described on different levels of accreditation and vary by risk class.

For *credit risk*, there are two approaches: the standardized, foundation internal ratings based (FIRB) approach; and the advanced internal ratings based (AIRB) approach. The standardized approach has many similarities to the Basel I risk-weighted asset approach, but is more granular and more complex. It takes into account distinctive treatment for a wider range of asset categories, including further distinction around, banks, sovereigns, and multi-lateral development banks, plus non-performing loans, commercial real estate loans and securitization, and distinguishes public credit ratings (Standard & Poor's and Moody's, for example) on many asset categories. It also allows risk weightings to rise above 100% to 150%, considers treatment for off balance sheet items, and makes some effort to recognize collateral, although limited in practice.

The FIRB approach introduces the use of internal models for measuring probability of default (PD). This is the same sort of PD that we discussed earlier in the section on measurement. This step allows banks to use a wide spectrum of granular credit ratings generated from their own systems, but the level of complexity of the regulation itself is higher. Banks pursuing FIRB requirements are subject to a host of requirements for the set up and validation of the rating systems, as well as additional management controls.

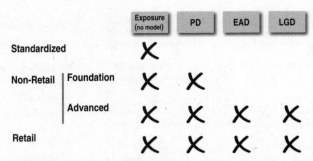

FIGURE 9.4 Internal Model Requirements for IRB Methods

The AIRB approach expands on the FIRB approach by extending the ability of banks to apply internal models to the other key components of credit risk modeling: exposure at default (EAD), loss given default (LGD), and maturity, although the maturity value is an equation provided, rather than a model per se. The approach is basically the same as FIRB, but where regulators provide specific values for these factors in FIRB, AIRB uses banks' own values. One wrinkle is that a bank pursuing either of the two IRB methods must use the AIRB method for retail exposures because FIRB has no retail (see Figure 9.4).

For *market risk*, the accord has only been modified. The framework broadly remains the same as in the 1996 market risk amendment, where the ability to use internal models for value at risk (VAR) was introduced. So there remain two levels of accreditation: standardized and internal models approach (IMA).

Operational risk was newly introduced under Basel II. It was one of the most controversial areas when proposed and was revised significantly over the course of the commentary period. This is because operational risk as a discipline is the least developed of all of the risk disciplines used in capital measurement. It's also quite particular to each bank. Ask 10 banks how they manage operational risk, and you're likely to get 10 startlingly different answers. This area was also one of the toughest for the committee to get their arms around, because no matter what they seemed to do, each level of accreditation advancement seemed to yield higher—or at least more variable—capital outcomes.

Operational risk is organized into three levels of accreditation, similar to credit risk. With operational risk, however, only the third level, the most advanced, involves the use of the banks' own models. The first two levels, basic and standardized, are constructed on increasing complexity of risk-weighting charges for gross income. The advanced measurement approach

(AMA) method, allows banks to use their own internal models to measure operational risk.

In practice, very few banks have adopted this approach, except in jurisdictions where regulators have not given the banks a choice. This method was viewed as challenging and time-consuming to adopt for an investment that clearly was not worth the return. Many banks reported that the adoption of the AMA approach would end up increasing their capital charge for operational risk, rather than lowering it. For banks that were underdeveloped in the pursuit of operational risk models, this was a killer not further debated because of more pressing issues on the accord's agenda. Many have chosen to compile operational risk aside of regulatory scrutiny until they are ready to tackle accreditation or until the regulation is amended.

Pillar II This laid out a different set of challenges for banks. It is far less prescriptive than other parts of the accord, so on initial launch it was heavily dependent on interpretation by local regulators. For this reason, it has been the last to be fully taken on by many institutions and local regulatory authorities alike.

Although it was initially positioned as the section "for regulators," it is a thinly veiled way of addressing all the issues that do not fall under the prescriptive minimum-capital guidelines of Pillar I, including other risks outside the main three.

This section of the accord is broadly split into four segments: the first addresses four principles of sound risk management; the second addresses specific issues regarding the measurement and management of risks not explicitly addressed in Pillar I; the third addresses certain regulatory management issues (this is the only part that is actually addressed specifically to local regulators); and the fourth defines details for the management of securitization.

In the first segment, the four principles set out a structure whereby a specific set of expectations are further delineated. These broadly call for several capabilities that go beyond simple minimum-capital levels and vary broadly across jurisdictions. Specifically, they imply that banks should develop clear statements of risk appetite and have management and measurement capabilities that go well beyond the core-risks detailed in Pillar I. They include interest rate risk, liquidity risk, and other risks beyond the core three. In addition, measurement and capital associated with those risks should be considered beyond the regulatory minimum and benched against risk appetite. In many jurisdictions, this has been interpreted as a requirement for economic capital models that are managed against target confidence intervals. This is where the internal capital adequacy assessment process (ICAAP) has been introduced and mandated in many locales.

In addition to the four principles, Pillar II describes additional consideration of specific issues. Notable ones to pay attention to include: stress testing for credit risk; credit risk concentrations; and counterparty credit risk, particularly in its approach to trading risk.

One other niggling detail of Pillar II is that it references a host of other guidelines outside of the immediate accord directives. Some of these include "sound practices" guidance the BCBS has issued before and after the publication of Basel II. This guidance is expected to be adopted as well. Much of it implies that banks should implement their own internal standards for stress testing, economic capital measurement, monitoring, and governance beyond those prescribed by the accord and possibly by their local regulators. Some regulators have used these as a license to reach interpretations beyond those items codified in local regulations. So the simple lesson is "beware" and "be aware."

Finally, the last component of Pillar II is a call for closer evaluation of securitization transactions. This addresses the regulators' right to add more capital for securitization where they believe Pillar I has not adequately addressed the economic substance of a transaction. In many jurisdictions, this has translated to regulatory approval of specific transactions as a standard step of a securitization process.

Pillar III Market disclosure calls for banks to provide a specific set of disclosures that can be published broadly to the market. They include both quantitative and qualitative disclosures of how banks have addressed specific components of their internal risk models as well as the quantitative outcome of those models. This segment caused great consternation in many banking systems. It suggests banks would have to disclose the nature of their exposures to the market at large—including their competitors. Their positions could in some cases be broken down to reveal their strategies and portfolio profile. As a result, in many cases this information is not disclosed to the market in its full form. Many jurisdictions publish summary information and only utilize the detailed reporting initially proposed within the regulatory process.

Key Requirements

The accord sets up key requirements and expectations for each risk class. It may seem like the responsibility of regulatory-compliance teams and risk analytics to sort through all of these. But one of the first requirements the accord set out is that senior management and boards should understand these requirements and understand the state of the models and processes used to fulfill the requirements—at a fairly detailed level.

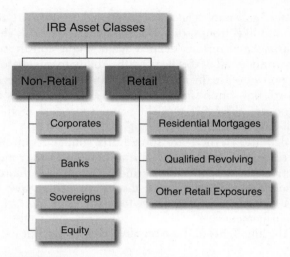

FIGURE 9.5 Credit IRB Asset Classes

Notable Requirements for Credit Risk

Credit risk is broken down into sub-categories based on definitions and treatments of asset classes. One of the first steps in understanding and implementing Basel II for credit risk is to categorize assets and the measurement models that support them so they align with the Basel II asset classes. A mapping is pretty much always required, since the Basel II asset classes probably won't fit the bank's natural asset class structure—at least not in its entirety (see Figure 9.5).

In addition to the four non-retail asset classes and the three retail asset classes defined in Figure 9.5, there are subclasses. In corporate lending, small- and medium-sized entities are distinguished, as is specialized lending, which is further broken down into five subclasses: project finance; object finance; commodities finance; income-producing real estate; and high-volatility commercial real estate. In some jurisdictions, local regulators have chosen to collapse these definitions in various ways or to consolidate their treatment back into standard corporate lending.

One wrinkle in the treatment of exposures involves small business exposures. They may be treated under corporate exposures as mentioned earlier, but if they meet certain conditions, they may be treated as retail exposures, the specific conditions are set by local regulators, but they generally involve a threshold on the size of a loan at about 1 million Euros. They are managed much like other retail exposures and through similar processes, but the loans must be managed as a pool. The loans are pooled for their risk modeling and management into like groups, or segments, with similar risk characteristics. Some regulators have further defined what might constitute a pool. In general, we care about all of this because the ability to qualify for retail treatment on this portfolio usually means banks can reduce their regulatory capital on the portfolio—often significantly. This, of course, has driven many banks to innovate their PD modeling and scorecard methodologies to support small-business loan PD modeling.

Beyond definitions, there are some fairly similar requirements on the whole. The requirements largely fall into categories that include: rating system design; operations; governance and oversight; use of internal ratings; risk quantification; validation; and disclosure. There also are specific requirements, particular to credit risk, for data and expectations of board and senior management.

Some of the highlights to these requirements are as follows.

Data   One thing that stops banks in their tracks is requirements for data. Banks must use five years of data for PD estimates, seven years of data for LGD and EAD estimates for corporate, and five years for retail. In most cases, it's not the use of the data that's the big issue—finding the data is the problem. Many banks don't have reasonable systems that go back sufficiently far and in the right data-field format to support this need.

Some banks have resorted to starting with what they have, then rolling in to Basel accreditation as sufficient data becomes available; others were graced with a regulator that established long implementation dates or transition periods during which relaxed data standards were allowed. For some banks, armies of data-entry people or retired bankers were used to key in data from files.

Banks also must be able to justify how they select and sample data, conduct well-documented suitability checks and data cleansing, and use all relevant material and available data in their estimations.

So, we're back to where we started much earlier in this book: Our old friend data comes back to raise its ugly head.

Rating Systems Requirements   Rating systems must include borrower-related factors and transaction-specific factors separately, and they must be tied to PD and LGD estimates. This means the bank has to generate borrower ratings and facility ratings.

The accord goes on to specify the quality of these systems—they must have a sufficient number of grades to adequately distinguish risk in a granular fashion and exposures should be distributed across the full grading scale.

Banks also must assure the consistency of the ratings from borrower to borrower. This means the rating systems either need to be constructed so that they are very black and white or that people conducting ratings must be very well trained to ensure consistency of their ratings from one borrower to the next and over time. Another wrinkle is that all borrowers and guarantors are expected to be covered by the rating systems. This can be a tough task because there often is insufficient information on a borrower or transaction—sometimes for good reason—leaving them unrated. The ratings also must be refreshed at least annually. So account officers must review each file at least that often and fully update inputs to the rating system and any assessment they make.

Finally, the rating system described in the accord, or one sufficiently similar, must be in use for at least three years before the bank can be accredited.

Risk Quantification The accord describes how banks should convert ratings to a quantification of risk. It mentions three broad types of modeling approaches and suggests banks can use any of them, as long as they choose a primary method. Other methods may be used as a point of comparison to external credit ratings and to public information where available. For many banks, this is no particular drama. But for some asset classes—or in some countries where public information is thinner and risk modeling therefore has been slower to adopt—these requirements often have led to much debate and large hurdles.

Other dimensions discussed in the guidelines include the default definition as well as the treatment of default and recoveries over time. The default definition required is 90 days delinquent. Although this was common for many banks before Basel II, others used alternate definitions to allow that the delinquents might resume payments on their own. Although this might sound like a small issue, altering this definition means major changes to a bank's operations, customer-treatment strategies, and to any risk models in place. These likely would need to be rebuilt. So this little definitional difference alone sparks a wave of activity, even for well run, fairly advanced institutions.

Similarly, although less traumatic, PD, EAD, and LGD models are expected to be built using long-run averages. Specifically, estimates should be constructed to include the average over an entire business cycle. In many jurisdictions, this requirement has been strictly interpreted and banks have had to find a range of creative approaches to ensure their estimates truly reflect a full business cycle. The issue here is multi-faceted: Business cycles often are hard to define—when exactly are we at the bottom or top of a business cycle? For some locations, business cycles may be quite distinct, but in others, say Australia, countries have enjoyed very long sustained growth with only the mildest downturns. It's difficult to find the stop and start points of a cycle, even looking retrospectively. To make matters worse, seven years of data may seem like a lot, but a full business cycle's worth could be an enormous amount that simply doesn't exist anywhere. So this task often becomes a true challenge of economic ingenuity.

Another by-product of this problem is that in some locales, regulators can't discern the right amount of conservatism for this sort of adjustment. There's been much debate over the right levels, and in some cases this has resulted in regulatory overlays to ensure the end result is sufficiently conservative and yields a level of capital that makes regulators comfortable. At the onset of the regulation, finding the final capital position often felt like trying to hit a moving target between banks and regulators.

This gives rise to the question of pro-cyclicality. To what extent does this long-term capital estimate serve to change bank behavior in the face of a collapse? Risks mount more aggressively in advance of a collapse. And once a collapse occurs—or is about to—how much regulatory capital and reserves can be released to support obligations, and how fast? If regulators are slow to allow its release, that could further a bank's downfall. The concept behind all this is that if individual capital assessments are sufficiently high, banks will move to find riskier and riskier assets—those with proportionally higher yields. The particularly attractive ones fall outside of the span of the regulation (there are always loopholes) or those not adequately covered within the regulation (where there are caps or misestimates). This would foil the entire premise of Basel II. It would lead to more banks chasing riskier assets to keep up with the returns competitors were getting. Ultimately a full stampede toward high-risk activities would collapse institutions and drive a major banking crisis.

Although there is much truth to the scenario—and let's face it, it does have the earmarks of many banking crises—it doesn't consider the role of prudent management and regulatory supervision. There are plenty of overlays within the accord to assure this sort of high-risk behavior is at least minimized. The issue of ramping capital against the interests of bank support, however, is one of the most salient points to this argument. The Spanish system has led the way tackling this issue, and it has been picked up to some degree in Basel III.

Overall, many of the requirements call for conservatism by both banks and regulators. For this reason, we'll find that many jurisdictions have adopted various floors and adjustments to measures to ensure sufficient capital. Again, this presents a challenge to ensure comparable rules internationally. In addition, the accord emphasizes the need to ensure supporting operations and policies are robust and in place. It emphasizes the need for rigorous analysis, monitoring, and consistency of processes and policies. In many institutions, this and the overall need for more routine and more rigorous modeling have resulted in severe shortages of analytical support. In many countries, good economic and financial modelers have become a highly sought after commodity.

Notable Requirements for Market Risk Very few actual changes occurred to the market-risk approaches that already existed under amendments to Basel I. The amendments, however, led the charge toward the use of internal-models approaches. Market risk is constructed in a less prescriptive framework, accounting for narrower degrees of variance in market-risk management than some other areas—particularly credit risk.

To be complete, let's see what some of the specific market-risk requirements look like. As a starting point, the market-risk methods focus strictly on traded-market risk. Non-traded market risk (interest rate risk associated with the mismatch position) is managed by a set of Basel guidelines, although several regulators have taken up their own approaches based on market-risk models.

Much like the other risk classes, there are two methodologies for market risk: standardized and internal models. The standardized method applies regulatory risk weightings based on different types of price sensitivities, somewhat like the standardized methods for credit risk. The internal models method allows banks to use their own VAR models for risk calculation. Unlike credit risk, however, relatively little is specified about these models. Banks are allowed to use any of the methods we've described in this book, as long as they can cover all the material risks. Also, the models must be able to capture optionality within the portfolio. Realistically, this means that either historical simulation or Monte Carlo methods must be used—and regulators more often prefer historical simulation.

The models have a few notable requirements. They should apply a minimum 10-day holding period. This is meant to simulate the risk associated with a market shock where an instrument cannot be traded for at least 10 days. Longer holding periods are encouraged where specific instruments are concerned. In addition, they should use a 99% confidence interval, multiplied up by a minimum of three times. The models must be back-tested for accuracy (tested against actual loss history) and differences between actual results and predicted results are counted against a scale which further increases the capital. For most regulators, a scale starting at 3× VAR at 99% to 4× VAR at 99% is used. If the bank exceeds the error limit at that amount, it must cease using the internal model method until the model can be re-accredited.

Notable Requirements for Operational Risk Operational risk has proven to be the most challenging to both banks and regulators, at least for those that have had to walk the AMA path. The definition of operational risk is a key starting point because it has varied across institutions. Under Basel II, it includes losses due to inadequate or failed internal processes, people, systems, or external events. The definition includes legal risk and is further described by these categories of operational risk:

- Internal fraud
- External fraud
- Employment practices and workplace safety
- Clients, products, and business practices
- Damage to physical assets
- Business disruption and system failures
- Execution, delivery, and process management

However, it excludes strategic and reputational risk, although these are picked up within Pillar II.

Under AMA, four components are specified: internal data; external data; scenario analysis; and business, environmental, and internal control factors (often referred to as BEICFs). The internal-data requirement specifies that a minimum of five years of data is captured and utilized in the modeling. Within that database, all material activities and exposures must be captured. The data-capture approach must include a method for capturing market and credit-related losses, and finally, the data must be mapped to regulatory categories. This has generally resulted in banks developing loss databases with clear minimum-materiality guidelines and ways for users to link losses directly to the regulatory categories of loss and to potentially more-granular categories of loss chosen by individual banks or their regulators. As a result, most banks have had to build loss-capture databases that are specific to the guidelines under Basel II.

The requirements for external data suggest it should be used in some form. The accord is not specific in any way about how it is to be used. Part of the application, however, must include a formal assessment of the relevance of the external-loss data. In addition, a systematic process for determining its use and incorporating the data must be developed and well documented.

Requirements for the use of scenario analysis are equally unspecific. It may be used in any number of ways but must be used in conjunction with external data to model the effects of high-severity events. It also specifies that expert assessments (generally from business managers) must be used to develop scenarios associated with severe loss. Scenarios also must take into consideration the impact of correlation assumptions, particularly in the case of contagion. In addition, the scenarios must be compared to the institution's actual loss experience to ensure they are sufficiently severe and provide adequate coverage of the possibilities.

Here again, BEICFs are not specified. Many banks interpret this requirement to mean they must use some form of rating method for risks. This usually plays out in the use of scorecards, the development and monitoring of key risk indicators, and/or self-assessment techniques that may include the mapping of capabilities and risks across the company. This requirement must be subjected to an independent review and must be validated through comparison to actual internal loss and relevant data.

Other requirements include ensuring that adequate staff is deployed to the management of operational risks, that routine reporting of operational risks is established all the way to board level, and that the bank can demonstrate actions are taken on these reports. Models also must be validated much as other risk models must. Two additional requirements particularly have created a bit of consternation for banks: Measurement systems must be integrated into day-to-day business; and capital must be allocated in a way that creates incentives for businesses to improve. For many institutions, these can be extremely difficult tasks.

Operational risk measures can be very amorphous and more difficult to link to specific risks than even credit or market risk. So it's very difficult for businesses to incorporate these measures in a day-to-day way. Moreover, operational risk allocations often can become relatively small compared to other risks, particularly as they make their way down to sub-business units and transactions. This, in turn, creates very little incentive for businesses to reduce operational risk in any meaningful way. In fact, the cost of doing so may be higher than the capital requirement. This is compounded by the fact that AMA measures of capital often can be higher than standardized or basic calculations, and there is little incentive for banks to jump full force into operational risk, at least at an accredited level, unless it is a mandate.

Notable Requirements for Pillar II Much of Pillar II revolves around its first segment and four key principles, particularly the first principle. The first principle is where most of the action happens for banks and where much attention has been focused in recent regulatory strengthening. Principles 2–4 simply reiterate the requirements of Principle 1, but with respect to the requirements of supervisors to ensure that Principle 1 is in place, that conservatism is expected (banks should operate above minimum capital ratios), and underscoring the right of regulators to step in and/or require increased capital in the event that they are unsatisfied with what they find.

Principle 1 sets up many of the concepts that we have previously discussed in this book regarding risk appetite, the use of ICAAP, and the integration of risk into the capital planning and strategic planning processes. It specifically says that banks should have a process for assessing their overall capital adequacy in relation to their risk profile and a strategy for maintaining their capital levels. They should feature:

- Well-founded internal capital targets
- Consistency with overall risk profile and operating environment
- Taking into account business cycle
- Rigorous, forward looking stress testing
- Adequate capital to support its risks

The five main features of a rigorous capital adequacy process are as follows:

1. Board and senior management oversight
2. Sound capital assessment
3. Comprehensive assessment of risks
4. Monitoring and reporting
5. Internal control review

These are further specified as follows:

- **Board and senior management oversight.** This specifies that boards and senior management should understand the nature and level of risk being taken by the bank and set the bank's tolerance (appetite) for risk and should understand how the risk relates to adequate capital levels. It also specifies that they should establish a view toward risk processes so that they can ensure that the formality and sophistication of the risk-management processes are appropriate in light of the risk profile and business plan and ensure the establishment of a framework for assessing the various risks. They also must develop a system for relating risk to the bank's capital level. Finally, they must ensure compliance with this framework and internal policies, adopt strong internal controls and written policies and procedures, and ensure that management effectively communicates policies and procedures.
- **Sound capital assessment.** This specifies the need for policies and procedures to evaluate all material risk that a process is in place that relates capital to the level of risk, and that there is a process that states capital-adequacy goals with respect to risk, taking into account the bank's strategic focus and business plan. This activity is generally interpreted to be the risk-appetite statement discussed previously. Also specified is a process of internal controls, review, and audit.

- **Comprehensive assessment of risk.** A process must be established to estimate all material risks. This recognizes that the industry will need to evolve capabilities and that, in some cases, methods may be very basic. This must include:
  - Credit concentrations
  - Liquidity risk
  - Securitization
  - Credit derivatives
  - Reputation and strategic risks
- **Monitoring and reporting.** There must be routine reporting to the board and senior management to:
  - Evaluate the level and trend of risks and their impact on capital
  - Evaluate key assumptions
  - Determine that the bank holds sufficient capital
  - Assess future capital levels and make adjustments to strategic plans
- **Internal control review.** This verifies that internal controls are adequate and that there are periodic reviews of risk-management processes. These need to ensure the appropriateness of the capital-assessment process, that large exposures and concentrations are identified, that data inputs are accurate and complete. These also must assess the reasonableness and validity of scenarios as well as routine reviews of stress testing, including an analysis of assumptions.

The overall requirements place a strong emphasis on capital planning and its linkage to the strategic plan, stating that capital planning should be viewed as a crucial element in strategic planning and that banks should analyze their current and future capital requirements in relation to their strategic objectives. The requirements also recommend that the strategic plan should include an outline of the bank's capital needs, anticipated capital expenditures, desirable capital level, and external capital sources.

All of these requirements in their entirety have yielded the processes we described earlier where a formalized risk appetite statement and ICAAP is put in place. We discussed this in Chapter 6. A number of regulators have mandated the submission of details of this process and a routine verification of its efficacy as well as the regular review of risk appetite by the board.

The other principles are less descriptive for banks. But they do assert expectations to the regulators, and warn banks that regulators will review the ICAAP (so this presumes that one is put in place), that regulators will expect banks to operate above minimum capital levels, and that a buffer, at minimum, is recommended. In the event that banks fail to do so, regulators may step in, at least until sufficient levels of capital are restored.

SPECIAL CHALLENGES AND REQUIREMENTS

1. Use Test

The use test has proven to be one of the most elusive items in the accord. In fact, it's arguable whether it is actually in the Accord at all, at least in the way it has played out. The Accord says:

> *Internal ratings and default and loss estimates must play an essential role in the credit approval, risk management, internal capital allocations, and corporate governance functions of banks using the IRB approach. Ratings systems and estimates designed and implemented exclusively for the purpose of qualifying for the IRB approach and used only to provide IRB inputs are not acceptable.*

It goes on to say that banks must have been using rating systems that are at least similar for about three years before accreditation. There are somewhat similar statements about other risk classes, although credit has the most applicability and reach overall.

How it has played out is that many regulators have become more specific in their expectation of the application of rating systems and other risk measures—particularly in the case of credit but often in other areas. Many regulators have mandated or provided a list of ways in which banks may demonstrate their use, in some cases expecting the specific application of the full list. In other cases, the expectation is that at least a reasonable representation of the list will be implemented. The expected list of applications typically includes reserves, performance measures, capital allocation, origination approvals, credit line management, and even pricing.

For some institutions this can become a major investment. We have spent a fair bit of time in this book describing the benefits of risk measures and their uses—all true and very exciting, particularly when it comes to the lifts and savings potential that these unlock. However, as a component of a regulatory mandate, these could take on an enormous investment and implementation complexity. In addition, they present change-management challenges, particularly given that regulatory implementation horizons are often limited.

Another complication of the use test is that beyond credit risk and market risk—where the applications are fairly clear—operational risk represents untrodden territory for many. Operational risk capital is often included in performance and pricing equations, but beyond that, it is less integrated into the fiber of the business. Many organizations struggle to bring it forward in a demonstrable way sufficient to support the regulatory expectations.

Timing also presents a challenge. Use for a minimum of three years has caused a number of institutions to delay final accreditation, or at least enter into back room negotiations for their role in timing.

2. Validation

Validation also has taken on a life of its own. Here again, the accord is relatively unspecific about many of the details. However, not to fear, the BCBS and other regulators have put forward working papers on the subject. These describe processes and statistical tests that must be included in a bank's validation framework. In addition, because of the reach of regulatory models into "uses" described earlier, many institutions have struggled to find a way to draw the line between models, calculators, and other methods that should be included. In some cases, the validation teams have created what is tantamount to a cottage industry to validate every aspect of what goes on in a bank. This may be on the extreme, but it's not far off. Numerous models and calculators that are not remotely related to Basel have been swept in (possibly not a bad thing on the whole, but certainly adding a level of cost to banks that was unintended by all).

There are a few simple things to keep track of when it comes to validation. First, consider, what is a model and what is a calculator? Models are meant to mimic or predict economic events. They generally involve the development of statistics that rely on using past information and scenarios in order to anticipate new events. They can be back-tested in most cases. Calculators are pretty much what they sound like. They may be a series of relatively simple equations generally meant to "sum up" or aggregate information.

A good example of the difference is a PD model and a pricing-floor "model." The PD model is a true model. It has been developed through statistical analysis of how borrowers have behaved in the past to ascertain how they are likely to behave in the future. It is predictive and can be back-tested. A pricing floor model is, in fact, a calculator. It may likely take inputs from many other models, but it ultimately sums up their economic impact to understand the minimum price that can be applied to a given price for the product, transaction, and customer characteristics. It is not back-testable in and of itself. This is not to be confused with elasticity models for price, described earlier, that are, in fact, models that predict customer behavior when presented with a price (i.e., volume).

Models can be subjected to a range of statistical analyses to ensure their reliability on many dimensions. Calculators can be reviewed to ensure their calculations and coding are accurate, but they cannot undergo the same level of statistical view as a model because they don't bear those characteristics.

As far as the accord requirements are concerned, validation is much as we described earlier in this book. In fact, much of that overview has come as a result of work I've done to implement improved validation frameworks for institutions seeking Basel II accreditation. However, one item that is notable among the required regulatory framework is the independent validation unit. The unit must be independent of both the business lines (as is the case of most risk activities and personnel) and must be independent of those tasked with building and managing the models. This last part often presents the most difficulty because many institutions do not have sufficient staff to serve both purposes—modeling and validating. Also, in many markets, good modelers are few and far between, so it's not an option to just hire more people.

Numerous creative responses to this problem have cropped up. Some have generated validation teams that are assembled on a short-term basis when a validation review is required. These individuals are drawn from other risk teams, perhaps unrelated risk areas. So, for example, a market risk team may be used to review a credit-risk model. Other solutions have drawn from a heavier reliance on internal audit teams, although less supportive of the review of the detailed statistical analysis. Finally, many institutions still augment the process with outside assistance from firms that specialize in modeling of varying sorts.

3. Stress Testing

The Accord requires numerous applications of stress testing and stressed scenarios. These must be both embedded in the assumptions as the underlying models are being developed and must be constructed post hoc as part of a routine stress-testing program developed by the institution to evaluate capital. The individual core risk factors must be stress-tested, and some cases, stressed estimates must be applied for regulatory capital purposes. They must use LGD estimates calibrated to recovery behavior during an economic downturn. In addition, each of the modeled elements of risk must be stress tested. The overall capital number and economic capital estimates must be stress tested as well. A bank's minimum capital standards must be tested and reinforced on this basis.

In recent times, as a result of the credit crisis, stress testing has taken on an even more elevated form with regulators stepping in to more closely evaluate the approach to stress-testing and to mandate specific stress tests for their banks. Banks themselves have evolved their stress-testing abilities to develop both general stresses on economic factors within their models. They have also used them to consider a higher order of scenarios that establish world economic and competitive scenarios and how they would affect the economic inputs of the models. In addition, the outcomes of stress test-ing are being more discretely rolled back into estimates of capital as a direct augmentation to the capital position, rather than as a "check."

4. Pillar II: Economic Capital and "Other Risks"

Pillar II has specified that banks should conduct a comprehensive assess-ment of risks that takes into consideration *all* risks. In addition, it also guides banks to ensure minimum capital is devised to ensure that all mate-rial risks are accounted for. Although the accord is not specific regarding the adoption of economic capital models, it mentions the application and use of economic models in numerous references. This implies that these are expected as part of a bank's risk framework. In many jurisdictions, regula-tors have made these an effective pre-requisite for accreditation.

In addition, economic capital models must include a broader considera-tion of risk, which should include "other risks." In general, "other risks" include risk categories that have not been explicitly addressed by Basel in Pillar I and in the core references in Pillar II. In general, it includes a list of strategic risk, business risk, liquidity, reputation, and the like.

Also included are risks that have not been directly modeled for the pur-poses of Basel II, such as interest-rate risk in the banking book. The general point is that banks must identify all of their risks and discern whether they can be built into their economic-capital framework or if they may be con-sidered under some other risk-management framework. For example, repu-tation risk may not be explicitly included in economic capital measures but could be managed through close scrutiny of issues and their affects on share price, external stakeholders, and others. All in all, this is another amor-phous area of the accord, and yet, one very important when it comes to a bank's management and investment in risk as well as when considering regulatory reach.

5. Expectations for Boards and Senior Management

One of the very new aspects of the accord is the degree to which it empha-sizes involvement of boards and senior management. The expectation is that these groups do not simply support and delegate to their risk-management teams, paying little more than passing interest and lip service. The expect-ation reaches far to rectify this sort of behavior by setting up expectations that boards and senior management become involved. Guidelines call for a relatively intimate knowledge of systems and models and it's expected that these become board-level discussions. Many organizations have responded by putting in mandatory training sessions, sometimes with their own internal accreditation, for board and senior management. In addition, many boards have taken on a separate board-level risk committee, distinct from the audit committee, and have elevated more risk issues to full board discussion.

Specifically, boards are expected to ensure that capital targets are consistent with the institution's overall risk profile. It's also expected that risk tolerances and risk appetite are clearly articulated and that they are applied to models, limits, and approvals. Boards also must ensure that economic capital is used in capital planning and assessing investments. They also must ensure there are frameworks for consistent risk-based capital adequacy. This means that processes must be in place suitable to the risks the bank takes, that they are applied at every tier of the banking group and subject to independent review.

In addition, the accord strives to ensure there is transparency of activities that contribute to corporate risk and expects the boards to ensure management reports risks, capital needs, and the adequacy of models. Also, boards are expected to monitor adherence to policies, including the explicit use and escalation of exception reports.

Finally, the board must ensure that there are systems for identifying, measuring, mitigating, and monitoring all types of risks. Specifically, models must be in place, operating properly, and being routinely validated. Sensitivity and stress testing must be conducted. Measures must be based in economic capital, and there must be routine assessment of systems, measures, and approaches.

Boards also must approve systems and processes (including approval of all material aspects of the rating and estimation processes), and have a good understanding of the design and operation of rating systems. Also, they must ensure the existence of independent credit-risk-control units responsible for the design/selection, implementation, validation, and performance of the internal rating systems. These units must be independent from the personnel and management functions responsible for originating exposures. They also must ensure the role of internal and external audit. This includes internal audit review of the bank's rating systems and its operations on at least an annual basis and indicates that some regulators also may require external audit of the bank's rating-assignment process and estimation of loss characteristics.

Boards and senior managements must show active involvement through a number of other ways. They must ensure there are appropriate resources for risk management and that these resources have sufficient seniority and integrity. They must also ensure that the risk-management team has the authority to reduce positions and portfolios as necessary and that they have independent reporting lines so as not to compromise their decisions. In addition boards must actively review the results of validation and stress testing and must be aware of the condition of models at all times. This, of course, presumes that they understand the models and the outcomes of statistical validation tests.

Each of the risk classes and a number of specific risk management issues are accompanied by a set of principles or guidelines associated with "sound standards." These further delineate board and senior management obligations carved out for their respective subjects. The trends of the documents are consistent with each other and clear. They emphasize boards' and senior managements' understanding of the risk classes, approval of policies and processes and a framework for how each risk is to be managed. Boards must sponsor routine reviews of the approaches and measures and ensure that internal audit makes regular reviews.

In addition, boards must be responsible for ensuring that the bank is adequately capitalized for each risk and that conservative measures are put in place toward that aim. The guidelines also call for active involvement by boards. Finally, the guidelines all call for boards and senior managements to ensure that all entities and subsidiaries are covered within the framework of risk management put forth for each risk and that all processes, systems, products, and transactions are included, and also that all levels of staff have at least a basic understanding of their requirements for managing risks.

IS IT WORTH IT?

The obvious question is always whether it is really worth using the standardized method or the internal-models methods. The internal benefits of better monitoring and management of risks and the ability to understand economic capital in a way that ensures the bank is pricing for risks and performing in line with shareholder expectations is often more than enough. Beyond this, the pure capital benefits of moving to internal models methods are fairly startling.

Let's take a look at a few examples.

Corporate credit risk is a good example to choose as it has seen possibly the most startling impacts, going from a single risk-weighting to recognition of multiple risk ratings. Table 9.1 is not specific or definitive; it is strictly illustrative, albeit a good indication of the general range to expect. Basel I had used a very simple approach that assigned a 100% risk rating to all corporate credits. Under FIRB and AIRB, there may be many more levels of granularity and specific risk weights will depend on banks' models and regulatory allowances.

We can see here that, taking an exactly similar deal structure, the difference in risk ratings alone can drive enormous differences in outcome. For example, a plain-vanilla corporate deal compared between two companies (one A+ and the other BB−) would yield: for the A+, 19.65% risk-weighted

TABLE 9.1   Corporate Credit Risk: Basel I versus Basel II

		Basel II		
	Basel I	Standardized	FIRB	AIRB
AA or above	100%	20%	14%–24%	5%–16%
A	100%	50%	24%–28%	8%–18.5%
BBB+ to BB−	100%	100%	38%–120%	12.5%–80%
Below BB−	100%	150%	100%–226%	33%–150%
Unrated	100%	100%	NA	NA

asset (RWA) under FIRB and 10.92% RWA under AIRB compared to 114.9% for BB− under both FIRB and AIRB.

For an AA− rated bank, these two transactions likely would attract a capital charge for the A+ transaction of 1.57% and .87% under FIRB and AIRB respectively and for the BB- transaction, 9.19%. Remember that the Basel I treatment would have assigned 8% capital to both transactions. Further compare this to economic capital of 1.09% and 8.85% for A+ and BB− transactions respectively, and we find that the IRB treatments have very much brought regulatory capital charges closer to economic charges—although there is still quite a bit left in differences.

We can rapidly see that banks with larger concentrations of lower-credit-rating customers—not uncommon when dealing with middle market or in countries with lower sovereign rating—might actually end up with higher capital levels in some cases than a bank that had a preponderance of high-credit-quality customers. So, particularly for larger, international banks, it's important to understand these differences and to recognize that there can be winners and losers.

Retail credit has had similar changes, albeit perhaps less dramatic. Most retail credit will have similar impacts as corporate, although tending to the lower end of the range because of considerations for increased diversification. Although, residential mortgage has always applied a lower risk rating, at 50% (or 4% capital), risk weightings have dropped to arrange closer to 30% to 42.5% risk-weighted assets, which translates to about 2.4% to 3.4% capital compared to an AA− bank with economic capital of roughly 2.85% for the same transaction. Clearly banks with large residential mortgage holdings will make out well.

For *market risk*, the difference is similarly startling. Consider a simple portfolio of three currencies: 100M British pound, 100M Euro, and 100M Japanese Yen. Assuming each of these converts to a current dollar exposure of $245 million, $167 million, and $120 million respectively, the standardized market-risk approach yields a portfolio capital requirement of $22.96 million. The internal-models approach would yield a capital requirement of roughly $0.20 million. This is a startling difference and comes in part from the allowance for diversification within the internal-models approach as well as for the use of actual market-rate variances, versus a regulatory overlay.

In the case of *operational risk*, the problem is a little different, although the concept is the same. Recall that the regulation allows for three types of accreditation—basic, standardized, and AMA—effectively the internal-models approach for operational risk. In this case, the first two approaches utilize regulatory dictates for capital allocations based on gross income. Any bank can qualify for the Basic approach. Banks that adopt many of the qualitative standards of Basel II can adopt the standardized approach, and banks that have sufficient internal models can adopt the AMA approach. The main quantitative difference between basic and standardized is that a distinction is made between retail banking activities, commercial banking activities, and corporate-finance-related activities. For these, a separate capital allocation is provided distinctive of each line of business by these specialties. These distinctions also tend to influence the likely outcome of the internal models. However, because these models are based on economic assumptions and actual loss experience, this outcome can be highly varied. All of this tends to play out as follows.

Three identical banks—each with $100 billion in average gross income but specializing as pure play institutions in each of the three different activities—would experience an outcome roughly as shown in Table 9.2.

Of course, this example is a little extreme; most banks would be a bit of a mix of at least two of these activities, if not all three. Clearly, a bank that was a pure play specialist (or one that had significant concentrations) in commercial banking might have incentive to strictly pursue the Basic approach. Conversely, only a retail banking organization would have incentive to move to AMA—and this would assume that the complication and direct cost of implementation doesn't outweigh the benefit. As you might imagine, fewer institutions globally have chosen voluntarily to adopt the AMA method. Most of those who did have done so at regulatory dictate.

TABLE 9.2 Operational Risk Weighted Assets: Basic, Standardized, and AMA

	Basic (bn)	Standardized (bn)	AMA (bn)
Retail	$15	$12	$7
Commercial	$15	$15	$16.75
Corporate Finance and Sales and Trading	$15	$18	$27.33

One of the big issues in Basel II is AMA's real impact on capital. One of the ideas behind the adoption of internal models methods was the carrot—a clear way to encourage banks to adopt more advanced approaches was the ability to release capital along the way. It's a nice side-benefit that helps make the process work. For operational risk, the fledgling methodologies are more obscure to estimate simply, so it's anybody's guess what a bank's internal model will yield. The upshot is that for most banks, capital actually goes up with the implementation of AMA and internal models, not down. This presents a structural problem that regulators haven't quite sorted out. Clearly, this falls into the category of "watch this space." Before the credit crises, operational risk was amongst the top bets for next-stage reform. It's likely to happen, but timing is now the bigger question.

KEY DIFFERENCES FROM ECONOMIC APPROACHES

Many institutions make the fundamental mistake of thinking that moving to Basel II is no different than adopting economic capital. For a number of executives, it has been a rude shock to discover there are a number of meaningful differences, some of which their local regulators may differentiate and demand—or possibly worse, they'll have to explain to their boards. Some of the fundamental technical differences can be surprising. It was certainly a surprise to many in the risk community when Basel II was first launched with so many notable and manageable differences. The key differences are as follows:

- **The credit loss distribution.** The core method of synthesizing individual credit transaction PD, EAD, and LGD measures into an estimate of RWA and capital is constructed around a normal distribution. Recall the section on credit-loss modeling and how the distribution that we demonstrated was skewed. Many loss distributions are traditionally skewed, particularly in credit, but also in other risk categories. The assumption of a normal distribution for credit loss typically underestimates credit loss, often by as much as threefold.
- **Credit class correlations.** The correlations associated with the degree to which transactions in each credit class are correlated is another critical factor within risk models. These can be challenging to estimate. However, those in Basel II vary in their degree of accuracy. Some tend to stray from observed estimations by startling amounts. This effect tends to both overestimate and under estimate risk, depending on a bank's mix of asset classes and where in the world the bank is located.

- **Static credit correlations.** Correlations in Basel II are assumed to be static. In reality, the changing business environment has enormous effect on correlations, particularly over time as the business cycle ebbs and flows. Correlations tend to rise as economic conditions worsen. None of this is picked up within the static estimates of Basel II.
- **Default correlation.** Basel II is benchmarked to a 99.9% default correlation coefficient, or a BBB rating. We saw previously the effects of correlation coefficient on how capital is determined. Most banks utilize between 99.93% and 99.97%, a practical difference of ~1.25 – 2.5 times the amount of capital implied by Basel II.
- **Maturity and optionality.** They're addressed only marginally in the accord—again, both over and under-estimating risk.

Overall, between these and a number of other variances, combined with regulatory floors, it's almost impossible to be sure what the tight relationship between Basel II and economic capital is. Some banks create scaling factors—up and down—for the differences, but there are no hard rules. The best way to think about this is that the ideas have moved closer, and many of the underlying components are largely aligned on the risk classes that are addressed directly in Pillar I, particularly for credit and traded market risk. However, there are still enough differences that Basel II is by no means a direct substitution for banks own good credit models.

BEYOND BASEL II: BASEL III AND REGULATORY REFORM

Basel III is not exactly what it sounds like. In fact, many people still don't call it that. But the BCBS is now using that term on its website and in many of its documents. Basel III is not a wholesale rewrite of Basel II, nor even barely a revision. It's more like an addition or appendix to Basel II. For this reason, it is likely to evolve for quite some time. Few of the core items already described under Basel II are changing notably, but a few more items are likely to change as BCBS continues to evolve the guidance. Unlike the first Basel Accord, it's best to think about the more recent activities of the BCBS as evolutionary.

Surprisingly to some, this approach is not specifically due to the credit crises or any other event. It has been in the cards for years. BCBS no sooner finished its final release of Basel II and they were at it again, discussing new items. In fact, it's not really so clear that they weren't working on some of those items before Basel II was even finalized.

In this category but not yet included in Basel III are interest-rate risk in the banking book and operational risk. I've mentioned several times that operational risk leaves something to be desired. For those who follow the BCBS and regulatory discussions with the keen interest of baseball or soccer fans, it's probably more akin to a five-day cricket match. You might recall that operational risk has taken many turns during its regulatory inception. We've noted in this book that it's the least developed of the risk classes featured in Basel II. So in short, this was no surprise. Interest-rate risk in the banking book is another not-surprising choice for new development. It's one of the major risks prevalent in virtually any financial institution and typically accounts for anywhere between 15% and 20% of total institutional risk. It also is closely linked to liquidity risk in both organizational management and measurement approaches.

Nevertheless, liquidity and the subject of capital quality have stolen the limelight as the two issues drawing the most attention at BCBS. These were perhaps the two biggest issues falling out of the global credit crisis and, thus, have captured regulatory attention everywhere. It's likely that these points would not have been addressed for some time otherwise, but regulators can be surprisingly expedient and have seized the opportunity.

Liquidity

Liquidity risk always has been an elusive subject in the regulatory world. Some jurisdictions have long required liquidity ratios, leverage ratios, or other limits or structural boundaries in order to support liquidity and balance sheet strength. Other regulators have been notably silent on the subject. Roughly 45 countries have previously utilized some form of leverage ratio or liquid asset ratio, or both. But relatively few European countries previously have adopted any of these approaches. This may be, in part, what lead to the crisis, particularly from the European side. In the United Kingdom, for example, pre-crisis, loan-to-deposit ratios were uniformly over 100% at an average of 145%. One notable failed institution reached ratios well over 300%. U.S. averages, although well heated, tended to run somewhat below 120%, in part due to regulatory limitations.

Needless to say, this became a core focus of the new regulation. One might ask, "Why haven't more countries adopted something before?" The answer is that it's pretty hard to gain attention on the subject unless there's a specific crisis. Liquidity is often considered a risk that only becomes important during a crisis. I've been in banks when the subject of managing liquidity comes up, and the discussion at the management committee level could be summarized like this: "We only need to worry about liquidity if there is a crisis, and in a crisis everyone will be having similar problems. The government will have to step in." Clearly, this is a bit naïve. Financial institutions can run into liquidity issues through other means—depositors lose faith and generate a run, bond holders decide to exercise their right to call. Regulators, likewise, have frequently felt that it was a battle not to be waged when there were more important issues on the table. Now is the time!

Where liquidity is concerned, two key changes have been made:

1. **Leverage ratio.** The leverage ratio is the ratio of Tier 1 capital divided by risk adjusted assets. The suggested minimum is 3%. Basel's definition of assets includes off-balance-sheet assets as well. There are several nice attributes of a leverage ratio: it is a simple approach; it's broadly a counter-cyclical approach that moves opposite to business cycles by taking into consideration the expansion of the balance sheet and increase in liquidity sources during boom periods and the decrease of these during periods of contraction. It is also more difficult to create regulatory arbitrage. Whether leverage ratio is considered specifically as a liquidity-management tool or not is less important. It does tend to constrain excessive balance sheet expansion and indirectly picks up the liquidity effects of this.

2. **Liquidity coverage ratio.** The liquidity coverage ratio (LCR) is a 30-day liquidity coverage ratio. Basically, this is the stock of high-quality liquid assets divided by net cash outflows over a 30-day period. This must be greater than 100%. In addition, this ratio must be constructed using a shock scenario, which includes:
   - A three-notch downgrade in the institution's public credit rating
   - A run-off of a proportion of retail deposits
   - A loss of unsecured wholesale funding capacity and reductions in sources of secured funding
   - Loss of secured, short-term financing
   - Increases in market volatilities that impact the quality of collateral or future exposure of derivatives positions
   - Unscheduled draws on all of the institution's committed but unused credit and liquidity facilities
   - The institution's need to fund balance-sheet growth arising from non-contractual obligations

Basically, the idea here is to try to mimic the recent credit crisis. In addition, a net stable funding ratio is required. This is the available amount of stable funding divided by the required amount of stable funding. It must be greater than 100%. Stable funding is defined as the total amount of capital, preferred stock with a maturity equal or greater than one year, liabilities with effective maturities of one year or greater, and the portion of non-maturity deposits and/or term deposits with maturities of less than one year that would be expected to stay with the institution for an extended period of time, even during a stress event.

Capital Quality

The definition of capital is a main focus. Here, the main objective of the BCBS is to both simplify definitions and ensure that capital is of the highest quality. This, in turn, works to ensure that sufficient capital is available during times of stress. The main requirement is associated with Tier 1 capital being emphasized as common shares and retailed earnings. This, in turn, ensures that higher levels of high quality capital are utilized when applied as such to the rest of the capital standards.

Forward-Looking Provisioning

Another aim of Basel III is to reduce or minimize the tendency for risk measures to be pro-cyclical. We've discussed this several times, and it is a key theme of Basel III. Specifically, the BCBS has recommended a series of measures to promote the build-up of capital buffers in good times that can be drawn upon in periods of stress. In addition, the more forward-looking provisioning, based on expected losses, also is established. It captures actual losses more transparently and is less pro-cyclical than the current "incurred loss" provisioning model.

In the case of capital, two buffers are included: The first is a capital-conservation buffer; the second a counter-cyclical buffer. The capital-conservation buffer simply makes more explicit a buffer above the minimum capital requirement that can be draw down upon in times of stress before a bank reaches the regulatory minimum. This is already a fairly common practice in many banks, and jurisdictions. The counter-cyclical buffer extends the amount of the capital-conservation buffer during periods of excessive credit growth. That sets aside additional capital buffer that can be drawn upon during a contraction.

Finally, the BCBS is promoting the use of expected loss as a means of provisioning, rather than incurred loss. In addition, some of the disincentives to fully account for provisioning in the capital framework have been removed. Overall, the idea is to make provisions more aligned with economic practices and to further reduce pro-cyclicality. Although all of this makes sound economic sense, the practical matters behind it may take a long while to sort out. The approach will require a change in accounting standards as well as regulatory agreement on how to manage the capital-conservation buffer—likely to become a politically charged event.

Securitization

Finally, the treatment of securitization exposures has been much expanded in Basel III from its previous forms. Further requirements include higher risk weights for re-securitization exposures, increased credit analysis of externally rated securitization exposures, and an increased emphasis on capturing additional exposures to securitization, the volatility of securitization, and other forms of embedded counterparty risk.

Interest-Rate Risk

Although interest-rate risk in the banking book remains outside the explicit focus of Basel III, it may not be too far off. Some regulators already have put in place various initiatives to make more explicit the monitoring of interest-rate risk in the banking book and its measurement. In Australia, for example, regulators already have adopted an explicit inclusion of interest-rate risk in the banking book to the Basel II framework with interest rate risk in the banking book (IRRBB) included as one of the Pillar I risks. This approach features an internal-models approach based on VAR, much like the traded market risk approach although, tailored for the specific nature of IRRBB.

Operational Risk

Possibly farther off but still on the agenda is the treatment of operational risk. This one has arguably become the elephant in the corner, as seemingly everyone is aware of the shortcomings of the current approach and the importance of operational risk in the banking sector. You may recall it is featured in virtually every crisis and bank failure and can be a major source of contagion. The inability for both industry and regulators to adequately get their arms around this risk is clear and looming. Given the number of variances in the proposals initially put forward during the making of Basel II, it is likely that regulators ultimately will return to this item and review it with an eye toward industry evolution. It is expected to draw from lessons learned under the adoptions of the AMA approach. It would do so with an aim to take on further advances and to better align both Basic and Standardized methods with repeatable measures of risk that scale capital in a positive manner in line with both risks and sophistication of measurement and management ability.

Rating Agencies

Yet untapped is the thinking about rating-agency reform. Another elephant in the corner, the "certification" of rating agencies and formal third-party review of their ratings and approaches is only beginning to find its way onto the regulatory agenda.

As it applies to Basel II, rating-agency assessments are mentioned in numerous places in the accord. There is much direct and indirect reliance on external rating-agency assessments. Many financial institutions rely on these assessments for ratings of PD, to support modeling efforts of PD indirectly, and to assess specific structured transactions and pools within structured deals.

In recent times, some of rating-agency practices have been questioned, particularly as they are applied to structured transactions. But the broader reliance is huge.

Many of the Basel III reforms appear to be finding a way to limit reliance on rating agencies, but the reality is that this reliance won't go away easily. They do perform an important function. However, their incentives and independence may be questionable in many cases, particularly in the securitization rating, and their practices may vary widely, particularly geographically. Big swings in the quality of assessments can be found within the same rating agency from one location to another, and often their ability to provide detailed risk assessments is remarkably limited and tainted by economic realities of time and resources.

In the early days of Basel II development, numerous questions were raised regarding the implications of such a regulation on the rating agencies. These questions have not been answered, and have only grown. It is yet an open question in the world of risk management, and one to pay attention to. It is hard to imagine that regulators will ignore the importance of their role and the need to ensure their independence and efficacy.

SOLVENCY II

Solvency II has been likened to the Basel II of insurance. Indeed, it has many similarities. Unlike Basel II, it is an initiative sponsored by and for the European Union, although a number of other countries follow its outcome and choose to adopt aspects of the directive. Nevertheless, for this reason, it has far fewer teeth than Basel II and, given the wide variation of regulation in the insurance industry, will not be adopted as completely or as broadly as Basel II.

The reason for Solvency II is mainly to unify insurance standards in Europe toward a single market while constructing a level of consumer protection. The original Solvency I requirements are fairly light, much like Basel I, with a simple measure of minimum capital. Many countries have concluded that these requirements were not sufficient and, as a result, implemented their own regulations, which lead to distinct market variances across the European Union. Solvency II is meant to unify these standards toward the functioning of a single market.

Much like Basel II, Solvency II is based on economic principles for the measurement of risk in assets and liabilities. It adopts consistent, risk-based principles and capital requirements. The stated purpose for the Solvency capital requirement is as follows:

- To reduce the risk that an insurer would be unable to meet claims
- To reduce the losses suffered by policyholders in the event that a firm is unable to meet all claims fully
- To provide regulators early warning so they can intervene promptly if capital falls below the required level
- To promote confidence in the financial stability of the insurance sector

Also like Basel II, the Solvency II framework is built around three pillars with the same broad framework of measurement, governance, and reporting:

- **Pillar 1.** Consists of the quantitative requirements (for example, the amount of capital an insurer should hold).
- **Pillar 2.** Sets out requirements for the governance and risk management of insurers, as well as for the effective supervision of insurers.
- **Pillar 3.** Focuses on disclosure and transparency requirements.

Solvency II is being created in accordance with the Lamfalussy four-level process. One might ask, "What exactly is a Lamfalussy process?" It sounds like a sophisticated way of making whipped cream. Lamfalussy was the head of the EU advisory committee that developed an approach to the implementation of financial services regulation. The four-level process includes:

- **Level 1: Framework principles.** These involve developing essential framework principles, including implementing powers for detailed measures at Level 2.
- **Level 2: Implementing measures.** These involve developing more detailed implementation measures (prepared by the Commission following advice from CEIOPS) that are needed to make operational the Level 1 framework legislation.
- **Level 3: Guidance.** CEIOPS works on joint interpretation recommendations, consistent guidelines, and common standards. CEIOPS also conducts peer reviews and compares regulatory practice to ensure consistent implementation and application.
- **Level 4: Enforcement.** More vigorous enforcement action by the Commission is underpinned by enhanced cooperation between member states, regulators, and the private sector.

5

230 BASEL II AND BEYOND

At any rate, the process is constructed to ensure that member states have adequate voice and the ability to fully explore the implications and implementation issues of a piece of legislation across the European Union and to garner member state support for its implementation and enforcement. Unlike Basel, there is no need to ensure a broader international process, as the framework technically does not apply beyond the European Union.

More specifically, Solvency II is constructed around two capital measures: the solvency capital requirement (SCR), and the minimum capital requirement (MCR). For the SCR, firms can either use the standard formula or the company's own internal model, if approved by the regulator. Much like Basel II, the key issue in adopting the internal models method is that the model must meet exacting statistical standards, including data quality, calibration, validation, and documentation requirements. It also must demonstrate that the model is an integral part of the business and meet the use test.

The MCR is used as a backstop and is provided as a regulatory calculation. Falling below the MCR will meet with immediate regulatory intervention. One of the most significant changes of Solvency II is the recognition of risk mitigation techniques, including the use of derivatives and securitization, as long as they are appropriately managed for their inherent risks.

For insurers adopting their own internal risk measures, a VAR approach is to be adopted with a one-year time horizon and a 99.5% confidence interval. This point is interestingly unlike Basel II, which adopted a 99.9% confidence interval. Thinking back to earlier chapters, recall that this sort of a difference equates to a much lower proportional capital requirement than is required for a like bank.

Risk categories explicitly included are:

- Non-life underwriting risk
- Life underwriting risk
- Special health underwriting risk
- Market risk
- Counterparty default risk

Also called out is operational risk, which may to an extent, be included within the models for other risks.

Similar to Basel II, capital definitions are provided and are linked to the company's own funds. These are divided into three tiers (Basel II refers to two tiers, although some jurisdictions have adopted a three-tier model), depending on a range of criteria including its availability, permanence, and efficacy in absorbing potential losses. There also are limitations on the amount of Tier 2 and Tier 3 capital that can count towards the SCR. MCR can only be supported by Tier 1 and Tier 2 capital.

IMPACTS ON FINANCIAL INSTITUTIONS AND FINANCIAL MARKETS

Although these regulations are meant to provide uniformity and an even market playing field, the unhappy reality is that there are great variances between regulatory interpretations and requirements. Many markets have not yet fully adopted Basel II, many will never adopt Solvency II. Those that are, have very much taken their own form of the regulation. Basel II has demonstrated an enormous degree of variance with some regulators adopting only the standardized approaches, some adopting only the advanced approaches and others allowing the full range of choice. In addition, there are huge degrees of interpretation available for all of these approaches.

I've worked at length on Basel II implementations in four countries, consulted on regulatory issues on Basel II implementation, been at the table with regulators, and supported specific implementation issues in another three countries. I can safely say that all of these countries have taken different approaches to many items. There is staggering variance in the degree of rigor around validating models, application of data, coverage of assets, use test, years in use, and, my old favorite, the interpretation of the definition of capital. In addition, a number of regulators have added minimum floors on internal estimates that have also served to raise capital in varying ways.

The bottom line, is that for those institutions that are active internationally, the playing field may be even more varied than under Basel I. So who are the winners and losers in all of this and how do we know what we're dealing with? We'll probably never know for sure, but there are some rules of thumb: In general, those banks from home jurisdictions that offered the range of implementation options (that is, standardized, FIRB, AIRB) and that have asset-class-coverage materiality forgiveness, generally have an advantage.

Going back to the example we used earlier in this chapter of two assets, one an A+ rated asset and one a BB– rated asset, it actually may make more sense for the BB– rated asset to adopt a standardized approach. For banks that have large exposures to poorly rated assets, this may be the winning strategy—if their regulators allow it.

On average, for those who are capable of adopting internal models, the AIRB approach, assuming limited local regulatory overlay, largely supports the sorts of improvements worth implementing. For primarily retail institutions, the benefits are large and very much in line with the systems and capabilities that are likely to be resident in order to be competitive in most markets.

For those that manage with highly structured deals, more market, and more institutional banking in their portfolio—particularly in developing markets rated BB and below—the benefits may be more mixed. These portfolios often are more difficult to implement and achieve a strong validating model—and less likely to yield the level of benefits that may warrant the investment. This, though, is highly dependent on the regulator and its relative acceptance of model validation results. This is one reason why some developing countries have been more interested in adopting standardized approaches, but this may challenge international banks that also do business in those countries and have regulators that demand higher levels of implementation (that is, AIRB).

NON-BANK FINANCIAL INSTITUTIONS

Another frequent question is the treatment for non-bank financial institutions (NBFIs). The financial crisis has done a pretty good job of eliminating many of them particularly those in the U.S. and UK markets. But there are a still a few around, and it's likely more will pop up. Many of the regulations globally have specifically targeted depository institutions, but it is certainly a growing movement to apply these same sorts of regulations to the NBFIs. Some regulators already adopt capital regulations of various forms for the NBFIs. Given the recent experience with NBFI failures, it would not be surprising if a regulatory framework were rapidly adopted in many locations. This is also frequently the case for foreign entrants that may be depository institutions in other locales but may not be in foreign markets.

Not surprisingly, many NBFIs are aware of this likelihood, and some have even prepared—at least the better ones have done so. Many also put out strong lobby efforts to prevent these changes. At this point there are still a number of players who can manage more or less outside of the cost of regulatory overlay. Only time will tell to understand the specific timing and outcome, but what is likely is that things will change.

TOO BIG TO FAIL

"Too big to fail" (TBTF) is a concept that comes up at every crisis. The TBTF institution is one that is so large that the government will not allow it to go under. TBTF institutions often experience ancillary benefits. Credit markets and rating agencies often recognize these institutions as lower risk and a more attractive investment. This often allows TBTF institutions to become even larger.

Outside of financial crises, there is always a debate about whether this really exists and whether any government would really allow a big institution to fail the next time. Clearly, we've learned recently that TBTF is alive and well. In fact, the opposite appears to be the case: We saw big banks getting bigger at low cost. The likes of Wells Fargo and PNC, for example, managed to take over failed or failing banks with the help of the regulator. So, not only were these too big to fail, they were aided in their quest to get bigger. Many other institutions received capital support in large bail-out amounts with relatively little penalty.

Of course, this is, at least in theory, an unsatisfactory arrangement, particularly if you are a smaller competitor. It encourages the TBTF institutions to take on more reckless behavior or become lax in their adoption of risk measures, monitoring, and governance. More importantly, it often drives the development of a more cavalier credit culture—or lack of one—which we have seen and regularly discussed here. That is probably the biggest risk of all.

There are certainly a number of variations on the issue of "what to do." Some suggest that these banks should be allowed to fail. Some suggest that these banks should be broken up—possibly at a time when the system is more stable. Regulations are surely meant to prevent these problems. Overall, there looms the question of whether these new regulations truly will do the job. Will we be brushing off the living will more frequently in the future?

Afterword

As we prepare this book for print, the regulatory environment continues to evolve, generating new activities across the world—and with those new activities come new uncertainties. In the United States, responses to the credit crisis have precipitated a wave of regulatory change. Equally, in preparation for Basel III, we are seeing sweeping changes and new proposals in many countries, particularly in the United Kingdom, where the banking system has been hard hit by the economic downturn. Even in Australia, where the local economy and financial system, has been far less affected by the weakened condition of the U.S. and European economies, regulators have taken the opportunity to address a range of concerns, some of which are unique to that country's relatively isolated and highly interwoven financial system.

At the same time, we are experiencing the new emergence of China and the strengthening of the broader Asian economies. With that, new questions are raised regarding regional stability, the stability of China and its financial system, and the potential emergence of new systemically important financial intermediaries (SIFIs) that may fall outside of the realm of Basel in the same way that many of the U.S. banks managed to stand outside of Basel during the Basel II reforms.

All of this begs the question as to whether the new reforms will indeed work well in practice or whether they will create an unrealistic burden on the financial industry, which, in turn, will likely trickle down to affect consumers—and not so positively.

Many of the reforms seem promising: Basel III addresses a number of age-old issues, particularly associated with the quality of capital and liquidity. As obvious as these may seem, particularly in the wake of the global financial crisis (and every other financial crisis of the past two decades), it has taken this big event to capture the attention of both financial institutions and policy-makers.

Even in the United States, where the complexity of law-making and regulation often baffles the rest of the world, the recent Dodd Frank Act seems to address many questions that have plagued the system for years. The new legislation addresses much of Basel III, and even goes beyond, including the inclusion of language addressing issues such as "too big to fail," executive compensation, limitations on exotic instruments and proprietary trading, new requirements for credit rating agencies, living wills, and extensions of reforms beyond banks to other financial institutions, including hedge funds. Indeed, the new law encompasses many of the issues that we have discussed during the course of this book.

Of course, there are always two sides to these sorts of things. Although there are some markets that have responded favorably, most notably, Canada, where the market was buoyant over the changes, there have been an equal number of criticisms. It is all too likely that the changes will stunt economic growth, just at a time when at least some countries are struggling to kick-start. Banks have claimed that the increased capital requirements will reduce profitability, and for some institutions, the changes will certainly eliminate entire departments that currently conduct prop-trading, private equity, or others that deal in exotic instruments or complex, high risk deal structures.

This in turn is likely to lead to further unemployment, or worse, a disintermediation into hedge funds and other types of risky unregulated fund structures, particularly those located in jurisdictions that are still unnerved by such entities. After all, there will always be investors willing to pursue higher returns and if they can't do so through the mainstream financial services industry, they will seek alternatives.

Overall, some groups have estimated that growth in much of the developed world will stall by about three percentage points between now and 2015 and others warn that roughly 9.7 million jobs will be lost. Others foresee capital flight to riskier investments coupled with blockades of capital restrictions that further drive investors to riskier, less well regulated, jurisdictions. This, in turn, could lead to destabilization of a new sort at some time in the future.

Realistically, the truth most likely falls somewhere in between. Already, many banks and financial institutions throughout the world have increased capital levels to the point where systemic averages have raised an additional two percent of capital, more or less in line with Basel III estimates. More than likely this is due to the long period of static growth and lack of investment opportunities, rather than smart forward planning, at least in many cases. Nevertheless, at least some of the changes have already been absorbed into the system—well ahead of schedule and with less trauma than many of the pundits would have us believe. This capital won't be further deployed toward new growth, perhaps extending the recession beyond when we would have naturally experienced recovery.

Nevertheless, it's hard to believe that improved measures of liquidity along with higher quality capital and more forward-looking provisions won't go a long way toward creating at least a certain level of improved stability. Will consumers bear the price of the new regulation? Probably, but estimates suggest that when spread across large economies, this effect will barely add up to a few cents on a loan transaction.

Will disintermediation into riskier investment vehicles occur? Probably. But even if those institutions fail and investors lose out, it will likely be a smaller, more focused incident that would affect a far fewer number of institutions and investors who can better afford it, on average. The real risks are more likely hidden in the next "hot item," the next trend or location that attracts higher returns.

These are the areas where the system is inherently weak, investors are less aware, and policymakers haven't thought through the implications. Could it be the emergence of China and the likely gyrations that even a hiccup in that economy could cause in world markets? If I knew, then I'd be able to join the ranks of those prescient modelers and economists who don't really need to work anymore.

About the Author

Annetta Cortez is an international expert in risk management and capital management at Novantas LLC, the leading provider of management consultancy and information services to the financial services industries. Before joining Novantas, she led her own firm, ACT Consulting, advising many of the major banks in Australia, Asia, the United Kingdom, and the United States. Formerly a Principal at Oliver Wyman LLC, Cortez also was a senior partner at the KPMG Barents Group, where she initially led the international practice for risk and performance management, and later led the Asia-Pacific practices in enterprise solutions and financial institutions. She has delivered numerous engagements in all areas of risk management and capital management, serving large corporations, financial institutions, governments and regulatory authorities throughout the world. She is the author of *Idiot's Guide to Risk Management* (Penguin Group, 2010).